HUNTING GROUNDS

A Scottish Football Safari

For you, Dad

HUNTING GROUNDS

A Scottish Football Safari

Gary Sutherland

Foreword by Stuart Cosgrove

BIRLINN

First published in Great Britain in 2007 by Birlinn Ltd.
Second edition published in 2008
This edition published in 2012

West Newington House
10 Newington Road
Edinburgh
EH9 1QS

www.birlinn.co.uk

ISBN 13: 978 1 78027 096 8
ebook ISBN: 978 0 85790 118 7

British Library Cataloguing-in-Publication Data
A catalogue record for this book is available on request from the British Library

Layout by Creative Link, North Berwick

Printed and bound by Cox & Wyman, Reading

CONTENTS

FOREWORD

'Have Fun in Methil.' Those are the first tantalising instructions in Gary Sutherland's ambitious and witty journey in search of hope and glory. Who could resist the offer to experience the heightened entertainment of East Fife?

Scottish football is an asylum and patients wander towards it every Saturday, muttering to themselves in various deranged states of insanity. I cannot look at the tortured faces in Hogarth's famous painting 'Bedlam', without thinking of Morton fans.

To suffer defeat and to be denied trophies are the childhood traumas that lie buried beneath our memories and anxieties. There are those that gravitate towards success hoping it will save them, they are the fans that follow 'big teams' hunting the glory of fame and greatness. But viewed clinically, this is little more than a Napoleonic complex, and proves that imperious grandeur is the most distressing illness of all.

Gary Sutherland spends more time with the charming eccentrics of the lower leagues, people, who do not conceal their deficiencies and could not even if they tried. I count myself among their number. As a fan of St Johnstone, I have always been 'at-risk,' a psychologically-troubled child, vulnerable to breakdown, and trying throughout life to stave off full-blown mental illness. To help me, I hoard memorabilia, collect worthless trivia and pursue bizarre and often paranoid theories about my club's uniqueness.

Did you know, for instance, that Pontius Pilate was a St Johnstone fan? The guy who sent Christ to his crucifixion was born in the small Perthshire village of Fortingall, where his father was stationed as a

Roman centurion. When it comes to celebrity-fans, few teams can match Pontius Pilate. Hearts have Ronnie Corbett but it's not even in the same millennium, never mind the same league. I like to imagine that Pontius didn't gloat and gave the Saviour a good send-off. 'Sorry to sentence you to death Jesus, but here's a DVD of Roddy Grant's goals for your Last Supper.'

I share Gary Sutherland's belief that you can pursue enlightenment in the most mundane places – Glebe Park, the pie-hut at Montrose, and the historic Portaloo that once disinfected urine with considerable dignity at Dumbarton's Boghead stadium.

Boghead, even the name bristles, with filth.

By embarking on this journey you will soon discover that it is in lower-league Scottish football where history is really made. Queen of the South are the only team whose name appears in the Bible. Raith Rovers are the only team who have been shipwrecked on their way to a pre-season friendly. And Alloa Athletic fans show a deft understanding of fascism when they claim that Adolf Hitler got them relegated.

These shards of uniqueness should be cherished. Hundreds of players have won a Champions' League medal, but only Livingston have had the sheer bravado to go into administration when their shirt-sponsor was *Intelligent Finance*.

So go with Gary, meet the muttering masses, drink from the stained glass of Saturday, and relish the unexpected eccentricity that you meet on the way. Have Fun in Methil.

SJFC, close season, 2007/8

INTRODUCTION

42 grounds in the space of eight months. Dozens of pies and more pints than I probably needed. Countless trains and numerous buses. Many miles walked and one ditch fallen into. Howling wind, torrential rain, snow, sleet and that other phenomenon which I'll call 'sleesh', which is a bit like sleet only wetter, though not quite rain, and unique to Scotland.

To be honest, I don't know how I managed it. I had 15 grounds under my belt by the end of September and 33 before January was out. That's ridiculous. I'm not sure I could repeat the feat and I suppose I don't have to. But would I do it again? Don't be daft. I had my Scottish football safari and lived to tell the tale.

It was a time of Jose Quitongo. A time when St Mirren played at Love Street and Gretna were busy living the dream. A time when the very notion of Rangers facing the threat of liquidation would've seemed preposterous.

I don't remember there being so much doom and gloom around Scottish football back then in the 2006-07 season. I mean, it wasn't all magical. Some of it was dismal but it wasn't this grim.

Hey-ho.

Casting my mind back now, a wet Tuesday night in Coatbridge sticks out, though not because it was terrible. Whereas the pie at Somerset Park truly was terrible. But I smile at the memory of bringing an Italian postman to a Dumbarton game and watching East Stirlingshire run rampant at Firs Park.

East Stirlingshire no longer play at Firs Park. They play at Ochilview, the home of Stenhousemuir. And guess what? You can now take the train to Alloa!

Not long after I completed my Scottish football safari, Gretna stopped living their dream and Annan arrived on the scene. I've gone to Galabank for this new edition and also made a return to Methil to see East Fife in action, something I'd been meaning to do. Talk about bonus chapters, eh?

Five years ago, my original ground-hunting expedition reached its conclusion on the edge of the world on a particularly gusty afternoon at Gayfield. I was almost swept away that day in Arbroath.

If you're reading this, it's likely that you spend your Saturday afternoon, and perhaps the occasional midweek evening, at a football ground, whether it be at Glebe Park or Borough Briggs or Firhill or wherever it is your team shines or otherwise. And if not, then I recommend you get out there and catch some games. Because Scottish football needs you. You just don't need to be trying to cram 42 grounds into a single season like I did.

But explore away. Go to Methil, if you like.

Gary Sutherland, May 2012.

KICK-OFF

'Listen, dear, I'm going to be late tonight.'

'Where are you off to?'

'I'm journeying to the centre of the earth.'

'Oh. Where's that then?'

'Methil.'

'Have fun now.'

'I will. Bye.'

Have fun in Methil. Ha. What does my wife think is in Methil? Disneyland? I'll tell you what's in Methil. East Fife are in Methil. And Methil is in east Fife. A paradox that does not concern me, because only the football matters. Or, more accurately, the grounds. All forty-two of them. That's how many there are in Scotland. That's how many I'm checking out, in one season. Before I check out.

Welcome to my …

(a) season of misadventure (b) magical mystery tour (c) odd odyssey.

Or all of the above.

People do strange things. Even football supporters. For instance, collecting grounds as if they are bagging munros or tigers. Not all football supporters gather grounds. It's more a minority pursuit. The vast majority make do with the one team, turning up at the same place every other week, perhaps travelling to away games, depending upon the extent of their passion. I am joining the tiny minority. My intention is to bring this peculiar habit out into the open, so that there can be a better understanding. (Because it's not normal.) You never know, perhaps in describing my personal descent into madness, I will sow the seed of obsession in others, and they might follow. Or maybe they won't. Still, there are lessons to be learned from this tale. Like the difference between Fir Park and Firs Park (aside from the obvious fact that one is singular and the other is plural). And being able to tell your Balmoor from your arse and your Borough Briggs from your elbow.

I am a ground-hunter.

Admitting you have a problem, they say, is the first step on the road to recovery.

The Scottish football season is a long, hard season. That season is winter. Everywhere you go you always take the weather with you. Snow, sleet, hail, rain, a hundred different strengths of wind, ranging from windy to really windy. Look! The sun! And there it goes, behind a cloud. Never to be seen again.

If nothing else, I am well equipped. My wife can confirm that. Coat. Check. Hat. Check. Gloves. Check. Scarf. Check. Balaclava. Check. Silver long johns. Check. Climbing boots. Check. Crampons. Check. Flask of soup. Check. Kendal Mint Cake. Check. Compass. Check. Satellite Phone. Check. Distress Flare. Check.

Am I ready? Ready as I'll ever be for this mostly solo expedition to the North Pole (Elgin), South Pole (Berwick-Upon-Tweed), Back of Beyond (Forfar) and, as previously hinted at, the perilous Journey To The Centre Of The Earth (Methil).

If all roads led to Hampden, this would be a piece of cake. I would get on the Cathcart Circle at Glasgow Central and get off at Mount Florida. Simple. I live and work (sort of) in Glasgow. But not all roads do lead to Hampden, or all railroads for that matter. There is another matter. I cannot drive. Not because I have had one too many. I just can't drive. I have never tried and I never plan to. And my wife won't drive me. And neither are any of my friends willing to ferry me about. (Call yourselves friends?)

Ground-hunting without a car does make it more challenging but I like a challenge. Show me a challenge and I'll show up and take it on (within reason). Relying on the vagaries of public transport to get you to the

Scottish football church on time would just be too much for some folk. However, I don't have a problem with public transport. In fact, I quite like it. Particularly trains. They struggle to run at times but so do a lot of Scottish footballers. Anyway, why would you want to be in a car, stuck in weekend traffic due to 'essential' roadworks, when you could be enjoying the freedom of the train and the convenience of a table upon which to sit your can - or indeed crate - of beer?

I could rail against the shortcomings of the rail service in Scotland. Platform alterations, delayed departures, outlandish fares, signal failure. The default Scottish response to being stuck-on-the-track is hacked-off passengers muttering 'this is ridiculous' and tutting a lot. Tut enough and the train might start up again. What we, the Scots, do is stoicism, with an air of disgruntlement. That is our failsafe coping mechanism. We're good at it.

We are also good at drinking on trains. Especially on Saturdays when battalions of broad-shouldered blokes in T-shirts (whatever the weather) clamber aboard with clinking bags. Tssst. The grand opening of the first can before the journey gets under way. Yes, it's nine o' clock in the morning, but so what? You'll have had your breakfast. Time. To. Drink. And by the second can you're shouting. And by the third can you're singing your team's songs. And by the fourth can you're swearing and staggering with your swollen bladder down the aisle in search of a toilet (which will be out-of-order). Your drunken antics are annoying the heck out of your fellow passengers, but you are oblivious to them. Everything is a blur. Probably the match will be too.

Naturally, there will be none of that nonsense from me. Well, maybe a wee bit. We'll see. I need my wits about me. Otherwise I might end up stranded in Alloa. Then I won't know what to do. Probably set off the distress flare and chew on some mint cake while awaiting the arrival of the rescue helicopter. 'Winch me up and get me the Clackmannanshire out of here.'

I'm not blind to this. I've seen Scottish football. But not all of it. I have some notion of what I am letting myself in for. I know that the fancy-pants player in the white boots will have trouble trapping the ball. That the completion of a pass merits a round of applause (especially a square pass). That winning a corner kick is the next best thing to scoring a goal. That there will be extended bouts of head tennis in the middle of the park. That the ball will be booted out of the ground. That with hoof there is hope. That showboating leads to sinking. That hatchet-men like to hatchet. That supporters heckle and curse and bawl and spew. That there is fat chance of quality amid slim pickings. That it will probably be more eye-watering than mouth-watering. That this business is the results business. ('We are not here to entertain.') That wonders will never cease. While the wind and the rain never let up. That the floodlights will come on at half-past three.

Oh God. What have I done? What am I doing? Football can be a cruel game but this is bordering on self-abuse. Football flagellation. It is probably illegal.

Hey, it might all work out. Maybe I will have F.U.N. on my tour de ground force. Once I have seen all that there is to see, from Aberdeen to Stranraer, and reached Level 42 along with Nirvana, I might want to do it all over again. In reverse.

Scottish Premier League, Scottish First Division, Scottish Second Division, Scottish Third Division, Scottish Cup, CIS Insurance Cup, Challenge Cup ... Cowdenbeath, Stirling Albion, Queen of the South, St Johnstone, Airdrie United, Kilmarnock, Clyde ... Somerset Park, Stair Park, Easter Road, New Douglas Park, Cappielow, Almondvale, Tannadice ... wherever I lay my hat is my home. But I have to wrap this all up in one season. (I'm being hard on myself. Plus there's a certain satisfaction in it. If I make it.)

There aren't forty-two weeks in the Scottish football season. I will have my work cut out. I'll be fitting in a few Sundays ... and Tuesdays ... and Wednesdays. This will take over my life and I will have to be extra-nice to my wife, but hopefully it won't be grounds for divorce. I'm not overly bothered about the order of grounds that I visit. I'll be making it up as I go along. I work best that way. But it's not fiction. My one desire is to make the last ground Arbroath's. I'm not sure why. There is something about Gayfield. The idea of concluding my mission on the edge of the world. And who knows, maybe Gayfield will throw up a surprise ending. We will just have to wait and see.

I'll be sitting with the home fans. In all cases, even head-cases. I'll be away from home, but I won't be an away supporter. If I'm at Recreation Park, I'm with Alloa. If I'm at Dens Park, I'm with Dundee. If I'm in Methil, I'm sure to be having a whale of a time.

I have a season ticket to Scottish football. Here I go, into the great wide open, on safari. I'll survive. I mean … it's not like it's Mission Impossible or anything.

EPISODE 1

MISSION POSSIBLE 1

(THE POLISH MENACE)

OBJECTIVE:
*To go to Celtic Park
and watch Celtic.*

SCENARIO: Celtic, the defending Scottish champions, are playing Kilmarnock in the Scottish Premier League.

DATE: Saturday, July 29, 2006. A significant day. One overflowing with optimism. The first day of the Scottish football season. Oh, it's going to be good this year. Haud me back.

LOCATION, LOCATION, LOCATION: Celtic are located in the east end of Glasgow. Parkhead precinct to be precise.

CULTURAL NOTES: In the east end of Glasgow - the Celtic end of Glasgow - there is plenty to see besides football. For instance. There is the People's Palace on Glasgow Green, and near that is the people's market, The Barras, where you can buy fags and socks, amongst other stuff, and, if you fancy a music gig instead of a football gig, there is the people's concert venue, the unbeatable Barrowland.

CELTIC PROFILE

KICKED OFF: Three fat ladies ... 1888. Hearing of Celtic's formation, Vincent van Gogh cuts off part of his left ear and gives it to a prostitute.

TRUE COLOURS: The Celtic colours are unmistakable. Red, white and royal ... I mean green and white. Hoops.

BADGE OF HONOUR: The four-leaf clover on Celtic's badge is symbolic of the club's Irish roots. We asked all 42 clubs if we could use their badges in this book for illustration purposes. Celtic said no. So we're not displaying any badges. Thanks Celtic.

NAME CALLING: Not content with one nickname, Celtic have several. First of all, there is the Hoops. Then there is the Bhoys. And there is also the Tic, which sounds parasitical.

MORTAL ENEMY: Amazing But True. Celtic are not that keen on Rangers. Yawn. And the feeling is reciprocated. The Old Firm. Where would Scottish football be without them?

AREN'T WE BRILLIANT?: Celtic's greatest achievement was in becoming the first British club to win the European Cup. Jock Stein masterminded the defeat of Inter Milan in the 1967 final in Portugal. And the Lisbon Lions were lionised. Heck, they deserved to be.

MISSION LOGISTICS

ALIGHT AT: Dalmarnock train station. Reasonably close to Celtic Park with trains running regularly from Glasgow Central lower level. You could catch a bus to Celtic Park from the city centre, with local services trundling along either London Road or Gallowgate. If you are fighting fit you can actually walk to Celtic Park from the city centre and there are Celtic fans who do just that. Allow yourself half-an-hour. Excluding pub-stops. There are an unfeasible number of pubs on the way to Celtic Park, so one thing is certain. You will never have a drouth. I start counting pubs on my walk to Celtic Park, but I decide to stop when I reach 100.

A Pint At: There are a gazillion Celtic-friendly pubs lining the path to Celtic Park. If you are looking for something traditional (sawdust on the floor etcetera) then one well-known Celtic pub on Gallowgate is Baird's Bar, where Kenny Dalglish once held a Celtic press conference, just for the hell of it.

MISSION DEBRIEFING

Field of Dreams: Celtic Park is the home of Celtic but it is also known as Parkhead and as Paradise in the minds of the Celtic fans. There is no doubt about it that Celtic Park is an outstanding amphitheatre. They don't throw Celtic fans to the lions or anything like that, but if they were to throw them to the Lisbon Lions, then they would not mind too much. The Celtic crowd is renowned for generating an incredible atmosphere, without the aid of a generator, on European nights. But on a run-of-the-mill-dull-as-ditchwater domestic day, with, say, Kilmarnock dropping by instead of, say, AC Milan, you could hear a pin drop. The front façade of the ground is quite ugly, architecturally, but it is what's inside that counts, isn't it? And Celtic Park shows up nicely given the correct conditions (i.e. testing opposition in a decent competition) when the up-for-it Celtic supporters do their scarves routine with 'You'll Never Walk Alone'. A sight-and-a-half to behold. Celtic Park is the biggest football ground in Scotland and is also one of the biggest in Britain. I happen to discover that the Celtic Park toilets are a hotbed of illicit smoking in a smoke-free nation. The steward is not a happy steward as he too makes the discovery when he walks in and finds legions of Celtic supporters contentedly puffing away. 'Anyone caught smoking in here,' shouts the steward, 'will be pissed on by Gordon Strachan.' At least I think that's what he said. Lordy.

Super Pies Me: The match-day catering vans which clog up the approach to Celtic Park, and will clog up your arteries if you're not careful, offer a wide range of culinary treats. Simply you are spoiled for choice. You can have chips and curry sauce. You could have chips and cheese. Chips and bolognaise. Chips and chips. It is difficult to decide. Once you get inside Celtic Park, they won't even sell you chips. Instead they serve 'fries' which come as part of the 'Captain's Deal' of burger, fries and coke, for just under a fiver, in a deal negotiated by Neil Lennon's agent. (Stephen McManus has since held out for an even better 'Captain's Deal'.) For a split-nanosecond I am tempted by the 'Rollover Hot Dog'. It is, allegedly, 'The Best Hot Dog In The World'. But I don't play the lottery and don't really fancy my chances with the Rollover. So, instead, I play it cagey and plump for the Celtic pie. I find the meat interior of the Celtic pie to be pinkish, a slight worry, but not sufficiently worrying to warrant me not scoffing it. It is also very, very salty. I have no option but to buy a bucket of coke and wash it all down and hope for the best. I feel quite sick.

GAME ON: Celtic 4-1 Kilmarnock

CELTIC GOALSCORERS: Zurawski 25, Jarosik 38, Nakamura 75, Zurawski 90.

KILMARNOCK GOALSCORER: Naismith 87.

CELTIC: Boruc, Wilson, Caldwell, McManus, Camara, Nakamura, Petrov, Jarosik (Sno 84), McGeady, Zurawski, Miller (Riordan 88).

KILMARNOCK: Smith, Fowler, Lilley, Greer, Hay, Naismith, Johnston, Wright, Di Giacomo (Leven 69), Invincibile, Nish (Wales 63).

HEAD COUNT: 54,620. Surely the biggest crowd of the season. For me at least. Unless there is unexpected unprecedented demand for the Angus derby at Links Park.

Report Card: Celebrating Celtic unfurl their championship flag and promptly set about flogging Kilmarnock. Maciej 'Magic' Zurawski magics up a magical finish after Kenny Miller robs David Lilley, but not at gun-point, as the defending champions get their title defence under way in the proper manner. New Bhoy Juri 'Jurassic' Jarosik feasts raptor-like on Celtic's second before Shunsuke Nakamura knocks in Celtic's third from a crafty free kick. Steven Naismith pulls one back for Kilmarnock and offers his side some hope (some hope!) before zippy Zurawksi decides to order a double and Celtic's fourth. Which upsets one Celtic fan who suddenly leaps from his seat to shout 'Polish bastard!' because Zurawski, the cretin, has only gone and ruined his coupon. Celtic ease to an easy opening day victory and canter on to have another league title wrapped up by, oh, October, since everyone else in the division is, well, rubbish.

Going For Gold: My piano teacher used to give me gold stars if I had practised. You may wonder why I am telling you this, but the system used by my piano teacher is the system I propose to use for the purpose of rating the matches I attend throughout the silly season. I never, ever, got ten gold stars in one sitting from my piano teacher but the perfect match will be awarded the perfect ten gold stars. Conversely, any game that scrapes the bottom of the barrel will be denied any gold stars. Logically, an average contest shall receive five gold stars. So there we are then. Now. Celtic versus Kilmarnock? Good value for goals and some neat passages of play from Celtic, but let's face it, as a 'contest' it is pretty one-sided, and the Celtic supporters don't seem terribly excited about it either. It may be that they are hard to please but it could be that there are simply too many foregone-conclusion fixtures like this for Celtic in the Premier League. Kilmarnock are one of the better teams in the top flight, but not today sadly. Over the piece, I believe this one merits a total of seven gold stars, which is the benchmark for the other forty-one games I am planning to fit into my packed social schedule between now and next summer. Jesus, that seems miles away. It is only July now.

Fanfare: The Celtic supporters seem strangely subdued. In fact, it would appear that the majority of them are half-asleep. Maybe they are blowing off their post-season cobwebs still. They haven't fully got into the swing of things yet. The Celtic season ticket holder whose seat I am occupying isn't here today - he fancied a game of golf instead. That's devotion for you. The idea of Kilmarnock does not arouse much excitement. Not even when it is flag-raising day and Celtic are cuffing Kilmarnock. The first Celtic chant clocks in at 73 minutes. It is a lacklustre chant of 'mothehoo, mothehoo'. Which roughly translated means 'c'mon the Hoops, c'mon the Hoops'. One thing you can say about these Celtic supporters, and you can't take it away from them ... they manage to out-sing those Kilmarnock supporters. Wherever they are.

Music To My Ears: The contented Celtic fans filter out of Celtic Park with Goldfrapp's 'Number One' on the sound system. You cannot really argue with that. Celtic currently are Number One.

Incidental Weather Report: It would not be Glasgow in July without a downpour. The Celtic fan in front of me picks up a discarded plastic bag and puts it on his head. An improvised hat. Nice look. Practical use thereof.

MISSION POSSIBLE 2

EPISODE

OBJECTIVE:
To go to Fir Park
and watch Motherwell.

(ATTACK OF THE PRSO)

SCENARIO: Motherwell are playing Rangers in the Scottish Premier League. Rangers have a new manager and his name is Pepe Le Pew. No it isn't. It is Paul Le Guen.

DATE: Sunday, July 30, 2006. The first Sunday of the new Scottish football season. The day after I witness Celtic take care of Kilmarnock. My wife is totally thrilled by my absence. No, really, she is.

LOCATION, LOCATION, LOCATION: The shire of Lanark. Or Lanarkshire, if you like.

CULTURAL NOTES: According to my dog-eared copy of *Scotland The Braw*, a singular guide book which is now sadly out of print, 'Motherwell has little to offer the visitor'. But if I were you, I would not want to be turning my nose up at the Motherwell Heritage Centre, where the industrial history of Motherwell is laid out before you. On top of such treats, if you make your way to the top of the glass tower, you will be afforded a stunning panorama of the surrounding area. Sounds like the perfect day out to me, but I'm easily pleased. I'm looking forward to my trip to Cowdenbeath.

MOTHERWELL PROFILE

KICKED OFF: 1886. Queen Victoria receives Burma as a birthday present.

TRUE COLOURS: Motherwell are the only Scottish football club to combine amber and claret. I mean, why would you?

NAME CALLING: The Steelmen. Because Motherwell was the steel town but the steelworks are gone now. The Well is acceptable shorthand for Motherwell. If your team happens to lose to Motherwell, which might not happen very often, someone might ask you 'is your mother well?' The important thing for you to remember is that this individual cares little about your mother and they are just taking a rise out of you. Motherwell were at one time known as the Dossers. Whether this was because they were a lazy bunch of arses, I'm not entirely sure.

BADGE OF HONOUR: The Motherwell badge tells you everything you need to know about Motherwell and then some. The crest incorporates a football (because Motherwell play football, sort of), some fir trees (because Motherwell play football, sort of, at Fir Park) and a depiction of the now-defunct Ravenscraig steelworks.

MORTAL ENEMY: Motherwell's enemies are football clubs from other Lanarkshire towns, like Hamilton and Airdrie. And Albion Rovers if you really want to stretch the regional rivalry.

AREN'T WE BRILLIANT?: Didn't Motherwell do well when they became Scottish Champions? In season 1931/32. Much later, in 1991 in fact, Motherwell were involved in a gripping Scottish Cup final with Dundee United at Hampden, and emerged victorious in a 4-3 thriller choreographed by Michael Jackson.

MISSION LOGISTICS

ALIGHT AT: From Motherwell Central train station it is about a fifteen minute walk to Fir Park through the people-heavy pedestrianised shopping precinct. Top tip. Airbles train station is closer to Fir Park. It leads to a similarly scenic stroll but minus the commercialism of the shopping precinct. Trains to both Motherwell Central and Airbles can be caught, with a large rod, from the lower level of Glasgow Central and journey time is approximately half-an-hour.

A Pint At: The Fir Park Social Club is bang next to Fir Park would you believe. As an away fan – or neutral – you are sure to be made most welcome, provided you make a donation at the door. Say £20. I am faced with a lengthy queue at the bar because there are a lot of Rangers fans here today. Half-a-dozen of them are deep in discussion about their drinks order. 'Right. So that's twenty Miller, two spicy and coke, five vodka lemonade, three Bacardi Breezers and two Irn Bru?' Steady on the Irn Bru I'm thinking. A lot of Scottish football fans are as much devoted to drink as they are to their football team. With such a high alcohol intake, they surely can't be taking in much of the match. At the bar I call out the modest order of 'a pint of lager, please'. The smell of pakora wafts through the corridors of power of the Fir Park Social Club. They are happy to feed you here, as well as water you. Overall, the Fir Park Social Club is an agreeable beer haven, but if you are looking for an alternative then there is the Electric Bar next to Airbles station, where the atmosphere is electric.

MISSION DEBRIEFING

Field of Dreams: Fir Park is one of those higgledy-piggledy stadiums where the stands are all different sizes and seem to bear no relation to each other. But you get a great view of the game. At least from the East Stand which is full of Motherwell supporters and me. One thing that puzzles me about Fir Park is that I don't recall seeing any trees. Next to the club shop at Fir Park is the Davie Cooper Memorial Wall. All the bricks carry inscriptions from Motherwell fans praising the late wing legend and proclaiming their feelings about their club. Best Left Foot. Born To Be Well. Mon The Well. A Fan Through Thick And Thin. And, my personal favourite, Ah'll No Be Back Next Week.

Super Pies Me: The Motherwell pie is a pie of convenience. Convenience food, if you like. Basically, you can join the East Stand pie queue before half-time – thus significantly slashing the waiting-time – and, by simply rotating your head 90 degrees, you can continue to watch the match unfold as you await delivery of your baked goods. Now how handy is that? Unless, of course, the match happens to be shite, and you want to avoid watching it for a bit, in which case, I suggest you should just look straight ahead at the pie counter, or shut your eyes. The Motherwell pie is okay. But no better than that. I wouldn't have it again. And I don't have to. No one's going to make me go there again.

GAME ON: Motherwell 1-2 Rangers

MOTHERWELL GOALSCORER: O'Donnell 52.

RANGERS GOALSCORERS: Sionko 8, Prso 65.

MOTHERWELL: Smith, Kerr, Craigan, Quinn, Donnelly, Foran (Fitzpatrick 78), O'Donnell, McGarry (Clarkson 78), Paterson, McCormack (McDonald 61), Hamilton.

RANGERS: Letizi, Hutton, Svensson, Rodriguez, Smith, Sionko (Novo 80), Clement, Hemdani, Adam, Prso, Buffel (N'Diaye 90).

HEAD COUNT: 11,745.

Report Card: A wasteful Rangers side pass up hatfuls of chances but still manage to beat Motherwell. Libor Sionko nets on his Rangers debut, the highlight of his Rangers career. But, after a bad batch of botched bloopers from the bungling Thomas Buffel (the chief miscreant in the misfiring Rangers ranks) Phil O' Donnell levels for Motherwell to make them feel better for a bit. It looks as if the home side might just pinch themselves a point from this keenly-contested contest. Until, that is, big giant Dado Prso makes amends for a pony-tale of missed opportunities, the muckle Croatian cracking in a winning header at the near post near the end. New Rangers manager Paul Le Guen later expresses his Gallic relief at victory. This is just the beginning for Le Guen. And it's quite near the end too.

Going For Gold: You know, I have got loads of these gold stars. I keep them all in a box. Motherwell and Rangers together serve up a reasonable treat (albeit with some crap shooting from Rangers) and keep us all guessing almost until the end, like Rolf Harris used to do. ('Can you tell what it is yet?' I dunno, Rolf. A kangaroo?) I was about to award this fixture seven-and-a-half gold stars. But I fear that may be me being overly generous. I have a very ungenerous nature. So I will rein myself in, and put on my sensible beret, and dish out a level-headed seven gold stars. Which is the same as Celtic received. Which means neither of the Old Firm can complain about bias or agenda, which is what some of their fans tend to do when they think somebody's got it in for them. But that is enough Old Firm. There is more than the Old Firm in this all-encompassing book. There is Peterhead. And Raith Rovers. I could go on. I will go on.

Fanfare: Not much in the way of melody from the Motherwell supporters. Meanwhile, the Rangers fans sing songs they shouldn't be singing. The Rangers fans are quite close to the Motherwell fans and there is one dodgy moment when a rotund Ranger fan stands up and makes an obscene gesture in our direction. His gesture consists of him clutching his crotch. Nice. A Motherwell fan jumps from his seat and makes a measurement with his index finger and thumb. A small measurement. 'It's that size!' he shouts. This does not dissuade the Rangers fan who persists with his public show of vulgarity. He does not give a monkey's how small the Motherwell fans think it is. You get away with an awful lot at football grounds. If you tried in the streets, you would likely land yourself in a real spot of bother.

EPISODE

MISSION POSSIBLE 3

(REVENGE OF THE SAINTS)

OBJECTIVE:
*To go to Love Street
and watch St Mirren.*

SCENARIO: St Mirren are playing Motherwell in the Scottish Premier League. Motherwell again. I don't really want to be watching Motherwell for the second week running. I don't have anything against Motherwell. No grudges. It's just that, unless you're a Motherwell fan, you probably shouldn't be watching Motherwell every week. Or two weeks in a row. I guess these are the kind of hardships I have to deal with between now and the end of the season, or between now and whenever I eventually make it to match forty-two. Better to grin and bear it ... barely. At least my friend Alex is joining me for this one. Alex is a Buddie. He is a St Mirren fan. This is the only flaw I can think of in his otherwise faultless character.

DATE: Saturday, August 5, 2006. Amazing! August already. The season is flying by. Blink and I'll miss it. This will all be over in no time. Won't it?

LOCATION, LOCATION, LOCATION: Paisley is situated on the northern edge of the Gleniffer Braes on the banks of the River Cart. Basically, it's near Glasgow.

CULTURAL NOTES: The Paisley Pattern was actually designed in Paisley. You will notice that pretty much everybody in Paisley sports the Paisley Pattern. On ties, shirts and what-not. You can seek out the story of the recognisable swirling teardrop at Paisley's museum and art gallery. You might not want to do that. But the option is always there.

ST MIRREN PROFILE

KICKED OFF: 1877. Swan Lake debuts to rave reviews but there is a lukewarm reaction from Scottish football fans.

TRUE COLOURS: Black and white vertical stripes.

NAME CALLING: The Buddies refers to both the people of Paisley and their football team. (When I say 'both the people of Paisley' I don't mean that there are only two people in Paisley.) The Saints is another nickname of St Mirren, who are renowned for playing in a saintly manner. St Mirren players rarely receive yellow cards. Never mind red ones.

BADGE OF HONOUR: The St Mirren badge is a variation on the Paisley coat of arms which appears to involve a couple of stars and what looks like a bit of a chessboard.

MORTAL ENEMY: That would be Greenock Morton then. Paisley Panda, the confrontational and often controversial mascot of St Mirren, has long been known to rile the good folk of Greenock with his soap-brush brandishing and banjo-strumming. Except today when I look at him patting little St Mirren children on the head, I think: 'What a nice panda'.

AREN'T WE BRILLIANT?: St Mirren are so astonishingly useful they have won the Scottish Cup three times, most recently in 1987 when they defeated Dundee United in the final, the last time the Scottish Cup was won by an all-Scottish side. It has since been won by an all-Lithuanian side. St Mirren's list of honours also includes the Barlow Cup which was a short-lived cup competition, jointly-sponsored by Ken Barlow and Gary Barlow.

MISSION LOGISTICS

ALIGHT AT: How to get to Love Street ... well, you could fly to Glasgow airport. It's only half-a-mile from Love Street. Maybe you can take a taxi to the ground? Alternatively, trains run frequently from Glasgow Central to Paisley Gilmour Street from where it is a two-minute walk. If you require any clothes washed, you can pop them into Soapy Suds Laundrette on Love Street. While you are waiting on your wash cycle to finish you could drop into Davies Deli for a bite to eat. That is if you can't hang on until the half-time pie.

A Pint At: As you exit Paisley Gilmour Street station you will probably spot The Hole In The Wa' across the road. The Hole In The Wa' is a pub - with four walls - and I note that you can get a half-and-half for £1.70 and that their karaoke list has just been updated. The Wee Barrel, on Love Street, is well-placed for the football and this is where I've arranged to meet Alex, my Buddie. The pub has a most unappealing frontage and had Alex not recommended the Wee Barrel, I do not think I would have given it a second glance. I barely give it a first glance. But I make my way in and it is actually quite a good pub, all things considered. If you happen to be in Paisley in spring, you could do worse than make for Paisley Town Hall and the Paisley Real Ale Festival, which is the biggest beer festival in Scotland and has been on the go for over two decades. Belch. Probably better doing the beer festival after the football.

MISSION DEBRIEFING

Field of Dreams: The eponymous St Mirren Park is home to St Mirren but the fans and everyone else call it Love Street. Love Street is a true jumble of stands, old and new, the main stand pinched from somebody's Subbuteo set and the more new Reid Kerr College stand vaguely resembling one of these new supermarkets that keep popping up across the country. St Mirren, in fact, struck a deal with a supermarket, which dealt with the club's debt problem and they are soon moving into a new stadium not too far away. But, meantime, the North Stand is where the barmiest Buddies can be found grumbling or cheering, depending on what is happening on the park. The North Stand is reached via a steep ramp and it is a satisfying ascent. It is also a satisfying descent. They should build more of these ramps in Scottish football, you know.

Super Pies Me: Oh dear. There is either something lurking in my St Mirren pie that shouldn't be lurking. Or I am hallucinating. How should I put this? Hmm. This is difficult ... I know! Have you ever seen The Lost Boys? Well ... you know the scene in Kiefer Sutherland's cave where Michael and the vampires of Santa Carla are tucking into Chinese takeaways and Michael looks down into his carton of noodles and the noodles are worms? And Kiefer, the cool vampire, laughs at Michael and looks him right in the eye and says 'Noodles Michael ... they're only noodles.' Now, I am not suggesting for one moment that there is an actual worm in my St Mirren pie. But there is a minuscule rogue element amid the meat. It could be a bit of an eyelash - a cow's eyelash? - but then again it would seem to be moving.

GAME ON: St Mirren 2-0 Motherwell

ST MIRREN GOALSCORERS: Sutton 17, Quinn 51 o.g.

ST MIRREN: Smith, Broadfoot, McGowne, Potter, van Zanten, Lappin, Brady, Molloy, Murray, Sutton, Kean (Corcoran 75).

MOTHERWELL: Smith, Quinn, Craigan, Donnelly, Paterson, Kerr, McGarry, O'Donnell, Foran (McDonald 53), Hamilton, McCormack (Clarkson 59).

HEAD COUNT: 5,036.

Report Card: Dining in the Premier League restaurant again after five years' absence, St Mirren go to the top of the table (eh?) after their not-very-difficult win over an out-of-sorts Motherwell side. The First Division flag is hoisted on the tiniest flagpole before the game gets started and the home fans are lifted not by the police but by man-of-the-match John Sutton who is presented with an opportunity he simply cannot miss, being a striker and all that. Motherwell's Paul Quinn thoughtfully extends St Mirren's lead with a goal all of his own, or an own goal if you prefer, and the buoyant Buddies run down the remaining minutes on the clock to raise a revenue of three points. Buddies two, Well pooh.

Going For Gold: This is not the level of football that the words 'Premier League' would tend to suggest. Take nothing away from St Mirren, they have enjoyed a great start to the season. A St Mirren supporter, like my Buddie Alex, would gladly give out ten gold stars. But Alex does not have the box of gold stars. I have and I am now picking out five of them.

Fanfare: The St Mirren fans are in party mode. 'When the Saints go marching in' is their calling card (even if they are at home). While 'Que sera sera' demonstrates their aptitude for foreign languages. There's not much emerging from the Motherwell supporters. Not even a smattering of German.

Music To My Ears: The Thin White Duke is in command at Love Street. We are treated to both 'Heroes' and 'Starman' by David Bowie. So why don't they play 'The Laughing Gnome'? Or that one from Labyrinth? 'Dance Magic Dance' was it?

Mike Check: The Love Street MC issues a pre-match health and safety reminder to the crowd. 'Ladies and gentlemen, we would like to remind you that St Mirren Park is a no-smoking zone, apart from the home section of the North Bank.' Cue: an almighty roar from the North Bank as cigarettes are lit and raised aloft in celebration of the right to puff away, while the players puff about on the pitch. Scottish football. It's bad for your health.

MISSION POSSIBLE 4

(A NEW HOPE)

OBJECTIVE:
To go to Cliftonhill and watch Albion Rovers. Now we're talking.

SCENARIO: Albion Rovers are playing Stenhousemuir. Wait for it … in the CIS Insurance Cup first round! The word belter was invented for games such as this. Never mind all that Champions League nonsense.

DATE: Tuesday, August 8, 2006. Well what else is there to do on a Tuesday night? What? 'Anything but watch Albion Rovers?' Goodness me. You need to get out more often.

LOCATION, LOCATION, LOCATION: Albion Rovers can be discovered in Coatbridge which is in North Lanarkshire. Coatbridge is not 10 miles from Glasgow. Perhaps you are detecting a trend. At this early stage of my ground hunting, I have little inclination to venture too far from Glasgow. I will worry about Dingwall and Stranraer later. They're not my problem, even if later on they might become my problem. But, for now, let's press on. There is not a minute to lose, and we don't want to be losing any of this momentum we have gained.

CULTURAL NOTES: If you are planning on coming to Coatbridge, you should be aware of top local visitor attraction Summerlee Heritage Park. If you want heritage, then this is the place.

ALBION ROVERS PROFILE

KICKED OFF: 1882. Tchaikovsky's 1812 Overture debuts in Moscow and is soon ringing around the football grounds of Scotland.

TRUE COLOURS: Yellow and red (like Melchester Rovers) is a rather fetching combination.

BADGE OF HONOUR: Two swords crossing a rose, suggesting an element of romance mixed with a hint of danger.

NAME CALLING: The Wee Rovers. The great thing about Albion Rovers, I find, is that they never get ideas above their station. A lot of other clubs would do well to remember that. The Wee Rovers. Paragons of humility. And sometimes humiliated on the football field.

MORTAL ENEMY: Was Airdrieonians. Until they ceased to exist. I suppose Airdrie United are the same thing (aren't they?).

AREN'T WE BRILLIANT?: Albion Rovers were not so wee when they finished runners-up in the Scottish Cup in 1920. They mauled Rangers in the semi-finals and lost to Kilmarnock in the final. Idiots. Since then the Coatbridge collective have been decent enough to conquer the Second Division on a couple of occasions. Who knows what will happen in the future? Psychics.

MISSION LOGISTICS

ALIGHT AT: Make sure you get off the train at Coatdyke. Not Coatbridge Central. Not Coatbridge Sunnyside. And definitely not Coatbridge Darkside, which is where Anakin Skywalker got off, and look what happened to him. You can catch the train to Coatdyke from Glasgow Queen Street lower level. It takes about twenty minutes. From Coatdyke station it is about a ten-minute walk to Cliftonhill. The walk is not the most beautiful of walks, but then I am not anticipating beautiful, so I am therefore not disappointed.

A Pint At: Big Owen's Bar. Thai green curry and buffalo mozzarella are on the menu and I begin to wonder whether I am in Coatbridge or not. This is a handy, comfortable, warm, welcoming bar and they have all the newspapers - plus the *Daily Record*. There is even a beer garden out back for puffing pariahs.

MISSION DEBRIEFING

Field of Dreams: Cliftonhill feels ancient. Like the pyramids, but less so. Judging by all that splattered paint on the terracing, Jackson Pollock has been here. The main stand is a curious affair. Painted bright yellow and bright red - you cannot miss it from a distance - there is seating at the back and terracing up front. A lot of Albion Rovers fans (not that there are a lot of Albion Rovers fans but you know what I mean) like to stand at the front. And the away supporters have deposited themselves here too. Which makes for some interesting exchanges. The Stenhousemuir fans have a few things to say. Within the main stand, there is a bar furnished with garden furniture. But no booze. Coffee and juice. The dug-outs are on the far side of the pitch with the Albion Street Terrace. On the hill high above, a bloke in a white vest and tracky bottoms is practising karate kicks in the rain. He is oblivious to the match going on below because Mr Miyagi is inside his head telling him to wax on and wax off. Cliftonhill is otherworldly. Well worth the trip, even on a wet Tuesday night. You will not be disappointed. All right then, you might be disappointed.

Super Pies Me: A perfunctory Albion Rovers pie is procured from … the Snack Shack!

GAME ON: Albion Rovers 1-2 Stenhousemuir

ALBION ROVERS GOALSCORER: Chaplain 10.

STENHOUSEMUIR GOALSCORERS: Nichol 74 o.g., Baird 77.

ALBION ROVERS: Ewings, Nichol, Lennox (Chisholm 77), Lennon, Watson, Donnelly, Friel, Chaplain, Felvus, Bonnar, Sichi (Cleary 69).

STENHOUSEMUIR: McCulloch, Murie, Dillon, Henderson, Cowan, McBride, McLaughlin (Templeton 68), Murphy, Diack (Baird 73), Hutchison, McAlpine.

HEAD COUNT: 228. (And I'm one of them!)

Report Card: A resilient Stenhousemuir storm back to knock ten-man Albion Rovers out of the CIS Cup. Scott Chaplain's leap of faith puts Rovers in heaven early ('time up ref, blow the whistle,' cries a Rovers fan) but the wheels start falling off this mixed metaphor when Rovers' Scott Friel is sent off for an out-of-order-off-the-ball incident on the hour-mark. 'What did you do Scott?' asks an Albion Rovers supporter as Mr Innocent trudges off to an early bath. (I am assuming that they do have a bath at Cliftonhill.) 'Nothing,' shrugs Mr Martyr. Rovers' fortunes further deteriorate when Kevin Nicoll astutely heads the ball into his own net to bring a grateful Stenhousemuir level in this increasingly intriguing cup tie. Canny Stenny substitute John Baird then bashes in a late winner to leave Rovers reeling; not so much an Eightsome Reel, more of a Canadian Barn Dance. The travelling Stenhousemuir hordes are now as happy as Larry. Whoever he is. Rovers waste a great chance of a late leveller with two of their players lunging to head the same ball into the same net but somehow they both end up missing the ball and instead form a heap on the ground. Agony for Albion Rovers and Agadoo for Stenhousemuir. If there were any pineapples, they'd be pushing them off the trees right now.

Going For Gold: I am glad that I made such a super-human effort to be here tonight. A cracking cup-tie spiced with a sending-off and a sting in the tail. Seven gold stars is about the measure of it and that's without resorting to measuring tape. The football isn't top grade but then what did I expect?

Fanfare: You would draw a bigger attendance at an agoraphobics convention in a field. Despite the low turnout (the lowest turnout that I have ever known at a football match), there is some noise. With everyone housed under the one roof, Cliftonhill rocks. Kind of. The Stenhousemuir supporters are fairly boisterous and the Albion Rovers fans have their moments too. There aren't many songs, but there's enough slagging to be getting on with.

Music To My Ears: I am not convinced by the football on show, but the half-time show is superb. Cliftonhill turns into a disco, minus the disco lights, but we have the floodlights, as the Albion Rovers DJ spins his top tunes on the tunnel roof. 'All along the watchtower, princes kept the view, while all the women came and went, barefoot servants too …' We are also party to 'Town Called Malice' by The Jam and 'Echo Beach' by Martha and the Muffins. I can still hear the echo. This is music to warm your cockles and sore muscles on a cold night in Coatbridge. There are punters pogoing and punching the air. I swear.

Mike Check: 'Welcome,' booms the Cliftonhill MC, 'to the San Siro.' I think he is being a little bit disingenuous here. We are not in Milan. We are in the opposite of Milan. You really could not be much further from the San Siro. 'Ssshhkkkkkkwwwwkkkkkk … Hughie can you come and fix this Tannoy for me?' Once the technical difficulties are resolved, the Cliftonhill MC announces that his daughter has passed her Higher exams. 'Well done Emma, you are nearly as intelligent as your father … whoever he is.' At the end of the game, the kind of game you would never see in the San Siro, unless Albion Rovers got involved in a three-way ground-share with Milan and Inter, we are congratulated by the MC for bothering to turn up on such a sodden evening. But we have to do more. We are urged, as Albion Rovers foot soldiers, to go forth and to spread the word about the Wee Rovers. We are to enlist extra troops to this questionable cause. As the man says: 'Rovers fans! Don't forget. Silky soccer. Saturday. Three o' clock. Tell your friends!' Sometimes Scottish football needs talking up.

EPISODE **5**

MISSION POSSIBLE

(THE DEEP-FRIED PIE STRIKES BACK)

OBJECTIVE:
To go to Somerset
Park and watch Ayr
United.

SCENARIO: Ayr United are playing Berwick Rangers in the CIS Insurance Cup first round. I can't get enough of this CIS Insurance Cup. Like I could not get enough of those Blue Riband blues.

DATE: Wednesday, August 9, 2006. The night after my night in Coatbridge. Strange. My wife is not even beginning to act like she is missing me. But she is beginning to question my sanity. What is it she would rather have me do? Stay in and watch Ugly Betty?

LOCATION, LOCATION, LOCATION: Ayr is in Ayrshire, funnily enough. Ayr is not the largest town in Scotland. It is not even the second largest town in Scotland. But it is the largest town on the Firth of Clyde coast. Here endeth your geography lesson. Class dismissed. No, hold on: come back here.

CULTURAL NOTES: According to my indispensable *Scotland The Braw* guide, Ayr is 'seedy'. What is seedy about the Auld Brig? And the Auld Kirk? They're not seedy. Just auld.

AYR UNITED PROFILE

KICKED OFF: 1910. The first Zeppelin flight doesn't go down like a Led balloon.

TRUE COLOURS: Not everything in black and white makes sense.

BADGE OF HONOUR: Ayr United fly the flag for Scotland with their snazzy saltire.

NAME CALLING: The Honest Men. Ayr United's nickname was dishonestly taken from a line in the Robert Burns poem 'Tam o' Shanter'. 'For honest men and bonnie lassies.' Ayr plumped for Honest Men, because Bonnie Lassies would have left them open to ridicule.

MORTAL ENEMY: Kilmarnock. There is only one other team in Ayrshire to hate. And Ayr hate them real good.

AREN'T WE BRILLIANT?: Surprisingly, Ayr United have never won the Champions League. They have never won the Uefa Cup. They have never won the Scottish Premier League. They have never won the Scottish Cup. They did reach the League Cup final in 2002 but Rangers pooped on their party.

MISSION LOGISTICS

ALIGHT AT: Ayr is a pleasant enough fifty-minute train journey down the west coast from Glasgow Central. If you wish me to spell it out for you - you get off at Ayr station. The walk to the ground should take you around fifteen minutes although it takes me more than an hour to get to Somerset Park. This is because of the detour I take, which has the desired side-street-effect of me bumping into a couple of pubs along the way. I feel like I am on holiday. I think this is because I might have been in Ayr on a Caravanette holiday with the Sutherland family once when I was at a younger and more sensible age, not in the least interested in ground-hunting and just wanting to kick a football about with my brother Stewart instead. I think we went to Irvine as well because I remember the flumes. Unless the fumes from the Caravenette have clouded my memory.

A Pint At: The Black Bull is nowhere near Somerset Park, but somehow or other I end up there. Supposedly the Black Bull is Ayr's oldest pub. They have an impressive range of cocktails on offer anyway. The Black Bull Special consists of vodka, Aftershock and lemonade. The Robbie Burns involves vodka, white rum and orange. This was Burns' favourite, naturally. And I can't quite recall the ingredients of Sex On Ayr Beach, but I suspect a towel was involved. Leaving the Black Bull behind, the Horseshoe Bar may not be the oldest pub in Ayr but it is a damn sight closer to where Ayr United play football. You will be served the coldest pint in the known universe. And a dog ate my crisps. Without even asking first. Some dogs have no manners.

MISSION DEBRIEFING

Field of Dreams: Depending on what kind of mood you are in, Somerset Park is either a complete dive or an anachronistic treat. My mood is changeable, much like the Ayrshire weather, so I find Somerset Park an anachronistic dive. The main stand is seated. But I have no intention of sitting there. I am making straight for the Cowshed where the most avid aficionados stand up for Ayr. There are some impressive acoustics in the Cowshed and the vocal Ayr fans put them to good use. The Cowshed is also the home of the Black & White Shop, which sells all manner of Ayr United merchandise, and is really the Black & White Shed. There is a weird monstrous corporate box-type structure opposite the main stand, which may or may not offer hospitality to the more well-heeled punters. I tell you, Somerset Park is The Ground Time Forgot. But I, for one, shall always remember it. You never forget your first dump. Well, okay, it's my second one. I've been to Cliftonhill.

Super Pies Me: The Ayr United pie can be easily summed up in two words. Deep fried. This, however, does not begin to convey the full, unimaginable horror of having to scoff the Ayr United deep-fried pie in the name of duty. I'll have a go though … [whispering] … the horror … the horror … I've seen the horror … horror has a face … it's the face of the Somerset Park pie … and I have that sinking feeling in my stomach [I have stopped whispering] as soon as I see the pie I have foolishly ordered being plunged into the deep fryer. Ten minutes later, and three hours still after that, the Ayr United pie is stabbing the inside of my stomach. Over and over and over again. I think of Alien. Make it go away. Please.

> **GAME ON**: Ayr United 2-0 Berwick Rangers
>
> **AYR UNITED GOALSCORERS**: Casey 18, Caddis 39 pen.
>
> **AYR UNITED**: McGeown, Forrest, Robertson, Lowing, McKinstry, Weaver, Casey (Logan 86), Dunn, Caddis (Strain 73), Vareille, Friels (Reid 83).
>
> **BERWICK RANGERS**: O'Connor, Notman, Campbell (Smith 81), Brittain, Horn, Fraser, Manson, Thomson, Haynes, McCallum (Greenhill 72), Paliczka (Noble 57).
>
> **HEAD COUNT**: 902. Not too far short of four figures.

Report Card: Ayr United trample all over Berwick Rangers with big boots and into the next round of the CIS Cup, courtesy of a well-drawn and well-executed battle-plan and key first-half interventions from Mark Casey and Ryan Caddis. Private Casey snipes from long distance and Private Caddis fires past the Berwick keeper from the penalty spot. Berwick are left in No Man's Land, while the enemy advances in the competition, ensuring that every Ayr fan exits Somerset Park, on a freezing cold night, with a warm glow. A bit like the glow you get from a bowl of Ready Brek.

Going For Gold: My expectations are low so I am therefore thankful for what we get. But I would be diagnosed as clinically insane and sectioned under the Mental Health Act if I was to award this earthy cup tie any more than six gold stars. So I will give it five. Just to be on the safe (and sane) side.

Fanfare: 'Ayr, Ayr, super Ayr, Ayr, Ayr, super Ayr, Ayr, Ayr' - you get the general idea. Sometimes this Ayr standard gets twisted and thrown back at Ayr, with the word 'super' replaced by something else which substantially alters the original meaning of the piece. But not tonight. There are not enough Berwick Rangers fans to corrupt it. The Ayr fans are eminently capable of combining rhythm and rhyme. 'We are Ayr, super Ayr, no-one likes us, we don't care.' While yet another Ayr aria begins 'We're black, we're white' but it is not the Michael Jackson song. It is a song about dynamite. The Ayr fans confess their deep love of Kilmarnock with 'Stand up if you hate Kilmarnock'. We are standing up! We are in the Cowshed. 'Let's all have a disco, let's all have a disco, na-na-na-na, na-na-na-na' sparks some bountiful bouncy, with the Ayr fans treading that fine line between dedicated and demented. You, the reader, must decide. '2-0 to the Honest Men' is self-explanatory. 'We are Ayr supporters, faithful through and through' should really be 'We are Ayr supporters, freezing through and through', unless the Honest Men are not feeling the cold like I am. I wonder if any of them are feeling their pies like I am. There is clamour in the Cowshed at everything. Somerset Park might be right dilapidated, might be a fair midden, but these Ayr United supporters seem to enjoy getting worked-up. And they are playing Berwick Rangers. In the CIS Insurance Cup. Imagine getting all hot and bothered about that! The Somerset Set sing loud and curse loud. There is no Ayr of calmness here, but there is a tremendous Ayr of energy. Apart from the pie, and the cold, I am enjoying the night.

Music To My Ears: The Somerset Park DJ plays 'Waiting For A Star To Fall' by Boy Meets Girl. And I am still waiting for my pie to digest. 'Pure' by the Lightning Seeds reminds me of earlier days, pre-deep-fried pie.

Incidental Weather Report: I cower in the Cowshed as black clouds dump black rain on Somerset Park. Suddenly the sun comes out and I cannot see a thing and I have to shield my eyes from the blinding light.

Seconds later, as rapidly as it appears, the sun disappears. Never to re-appear. Normality resumes. Dreich beyond belief. Be steadfast. Confront the Scottish weather while it does its worst. You've paid good money for this. Hang in there, man. Even if you can't feel your legs and your face has gone numb.

Incidental Digestion Report: That pie is still lodged there. I think I'll need surgery.

MISSION POSSIBLE 6

(RETURN OF JOSE QUITONGO)

OBJECTIVE:
To go to The Rock(!) and watch Dumbarton. This sounds brilliant. I might call up Sean Connery. And Nicholas Cage.

SCENARIO: Dumbarton are playing East Stirlingshire in the Scottish Third Division. I have brought my Italian friends Paolo and Roberta along for the ride. They have been fed such an unhealthy diet of Serie A crap that I think it is time for them to detox. And I believe Scottish football can help with the cleansing process. Dumbarton versus East Stirlingshire is a suitable form of treatment. A course of shock therapy. Paolo is a postman in Verona. The real life *Il Postino*. Paolo loves football, especially Hellas Verona, but there is part of me wondering if he might end up hating football after this and end up hating me too. I am taking a risk here. Maybe it's not the way you should be treating visitors to your country.

DATE: Saturday, August 12, 2006. A return to the Saturday schedule at least. The only day football should be played on. Those Tuesday and Wednesday nights were beginning to do my head in.

LOCATION, LOCATION, LOCATION: The royal burgh of Dumbarton. The ancient capital of Strathclyde. Where the rivers Leven and Clyde meet. As if you needed to know that.

CULTURAL NOTES: *Scotland The Braw* condemns Dumbarton for its 'brutal concrete sprawl'. And recommends that the town is 'best avoided'. But surely Dumbarton Castle is worth a visit? The location of Dumbarton Castle is magnificent. It sits atop a volcanic plug called Dumbarton Rock. Fancy a spot of rock climbing?

DUMBARTON PROFILE

KICKED OFF: 1872. The *Mary Celeste* is found off the coast of Portugal.

TRUE COLOURS: White, black and gold.

BADGE OF HONOUR: An elephant. Never forget that. They say Dumbarton Rock resembles an elephant. Looks more like a rock to me.

NAME CALLING: The Sons. Don't know who the father is though.

MORTAL ENEMY: It was Clydebank. But it is Clydebank no more. Now that Clydebank, the football team, is no more. I suppose, with an elephant on their badge, Dumbarton might be scared of mice. Still talking elephant bollocks, Dumbarton haven't had a mascot since Nellie the Elephant packed her trunk.

AREN'T WE BRILLIANT?: Dumbarton beat Blackburn Rovers 6-1 in 1883 and were promptly crowned British Champions. Incredible. More recently, as recently as 1891 in fact, Dumbarton claimed the first ever Scottish League title. Astonishing. They were forced to share it with Rangers, which is hardly fair, but then Dumbarton won the league title outright the following year. Which is great. Dumbarton have even won the Scottish Cup. Amazing. You know, Dumbarton aren't half as bad as I thought they were. They once tried to sign Johann Cruyff, but he was having none of it.

MISSION LOGISTICS

ALIGHT AT: Dumbarton East train station is on the Glasgow Queen Street to Helensburgh line. The journey time is approximately forty minutes. When you get off at Dumbarton East it is a fairly straightforward walk to the ground. See that rock? No? Just follow the signs for the castle then. The football ground is between the rock and a hard place.

A Pint At: I have trouble dragging Paolo from the Horseshoe Bar in Glasgow but we get to Dumbarton eventually. The bar lounge at the ground has abstract photographs of geese and watermills on the walls. But don't let that put you off. After the game, the teams stop by for sandwiches. I must say I am star-struck but I am far too shy to ask for an autograph from anyone. I ask Paolo if he will ask them on my behalf but Paolo is not sufficiently star-struck to comply with my request. There is a useful pub close to Dumbarton East station. It is called The Stag's Head. They have a stag's head on the wall. There is a beer garden too. A good spot for quenching your thirst and for soaking up the legendary Scottish sun.

MISSION DEBRIEFING

Field of Dreams: Dumbarton did have a ground called Boghead. A brilliant name for a football ground. Now Dumbarton have a modern stadium with a more fragrant but duller name: Strathclyde Homes Stadium. But the Dumbarton fans have come to the rescue and they call it The Rock. The location of The Rock is a spectacular one set at the foot of Dumbarton Elephant and Dumbarton Castle. The only problem is that when you sit in the main stand, the only place you can sit, because there are no other stands, the elephant and castle are behind you, so you can't even see them, but never mind. You can always watch the football, can't you?

Super Pies Me: The Dumbarton pie is … they've run out! Mercy me. This is a disaster. How can it be? I have waited so patiently in this half-time queue only to be told that there are 'no pies left'. How on earth can you run out of pies at a football match? When half-time isn't even over yet? And when the attendance is 623? This is scandalous. It simply should not happen. Ever. I console myself by rationalising that no pie is still better than the Ayr United pie. But the problem remains that there is a pie-shaped hole in my belly that needs filled. The hunger … the hunger … the anger … the anger …

> **GAME ON:** Dumbarton 2-0 East Stirlingshire
>
> **DUMBARTON GOALSCORERS:** Bagan 24, Quitongo 75.
>
> **DUMBARTON:** Grindlay, McCann (Dillon 46), Brittain, Canning, Craig, Bagan, Borris (Quitongo 64), Gentle, Boyle, Gemmell (Winter 22), McNaught.
>
> **EAST STIRLINGSHIRE:** Tiropoulous, Smith, Learmonth, Thywissen (Livingstone 85), Brand, Ure (McKenzie 53), Nixon (Malloy 74), Stewart, Adam, Ward, Tweedie.
>
> **HEAD COUNT:** 623.
>
> **PIE COUNT:** 0.

Report Card: Dumbarton remain unbeaten in the league - so hats, but not trousers, off to them – after seeing off an East Stirlingshire team who still give a decent account of themselves in defeat. The Sons of the Rock would seem to suffer an early setback when their striker John Gemmell is injured, but the stricken Gemmell's replacement David Bagan quickly gets on the score sheet with a confident long-ranger. Dumbarton substitute Jose Quitongo (Jose Quitongo?) seals the three points for The Sons when he cuts inside with ridiculous panache and pulverises the defence with a sumptuous finish, finer than marble. Long before Jose Mourinho, there was Jose Quitongo. Today he sports yellow tips on his dreadlocks. Perhaps as a tribute to Dumbarton, perhaps not. He gives a big grin and the home fans cry 'Jo-se! Jo-se!' Jose misses the chance of a glorious double when he makes an attempt to meet a cross but ends up sitting on the ball. Later he bends down in the centre circle to tie his lace and I reflect on the fact that nobody on this pitch (other than Quitongo himself) is fit to lace his boots. Paolo is impressed. 'Better than Totti' I tell him. Paolo shakes his head and tells me I have gone too far. An East Stirlingshire player takes a wild free kick that flies 17 miles over the Dumbarton crossbar. 'He's no Pirlo,' remarks Roberta and I can't really argue with her.

Going For Gold: Dumbarton versus East Stirlingshire is not the most wonderful match I have seen this millennium - the 2002 Champions League Final at Hampden was better - but thanks to an inspired cameo by Jose Quitongo the game merits six gold stars. However, I feel strongly that it would be negligence on my part not to deduct at least two stars due to the non-availability of pies at half-time. Therefore … four gold stars. And I am not being petty about the lack of pie. Or pious.

Fanfare: The Dumbarton fans are nuts. And I mean that in the nicest possible way. It is more a faction of the Dumbarton fans. A small and peculiar pocket of them. Adopting a novel approach to home entertainment. They entertain themselves at The Rock. And if anyone else within earshot finds it funny - then great. The live sketches performed by the Dumbarton Comedy Unit are mostly of a scatological basis. So, for example, you get the East Stirlingshire goalkeeper taking a goal kick and you get the Dumbarton Comedy Unit accompanying the goal kick with an extremely loud and elongated and off-putting shout of 'wwwoooooOOOOAAAAAAHHHHH… SHITE!' This from the bowels of the main stand. Then shedding some valuable light on their state of mind, the Dumbarton Comedy Unit strike up the self-revealing chorus of 'We're only here because we're mental'. They are a rowdy box of cracker-jacks, but remain amusing with their inventive interjections. To be honest, I don't think Paolo is picking up on much of it. Twice myself, I mishear a DCU chant. 'Shove yer salmon, shove yer salmon, shove yer salmon up yer arse, shove yer sa-aa-l-mon up yer arse.' No, that can't be right. I train my ears and listen more closely, and here they go again. 'Shove yer Stanley, shove yer Stanley, shove yer Stanley up yer arse, shove yer St-a-a-anley up yer arse.' Who is this Stanley? Or do they mean Stanley as in … no, they can't mean that. Wait, I have got it! 'Shove yer Stirling, shove yer Stirling, shove yer Stirling up yer arse, shove yer Sti-i-i-rling up yer arse.' But East Stirlingshire are from Falkirk. Not Stirling. Never mind. They're having fun with it. One of the best solo cries from a member of the DCU is intended to motivate the Dumbarton team - while simultaneously disparaging the visitors. 'C'mon Sons! Get intae this reekin' heap!' Reekin' heap? Love it. Go to Dumbarton. It is a reekin' heap of fun. Even when the game isn't. But if you want my advice, go on an early pie run, just in case.

EPISODE **7**

MISSION POSSIBLE

OBJECTIVE:
To go forth to Forthbank
and watch Stirling Albion.

SCENARIO: Stirling Albion are playing Stranraer in the Scottish Third Division. Think that I will stick with the lower leagues for a bit. I am stubborn that way.

DATE: Saturday, August 19, 2006.

LOCATION, LOCATION, LOCATION: Stirling straddles the River Forth in the Central Lowlands. In 2002, Stirling gained city status. Whoopy-ding.

CULTURAL NOTES: Stirling offers a gob-smacking smorgasbord of sightseeing possibilities. There is so much history to unravel that your head might explode. Stirling Castle is the thing you really want to see. You can't miss it. You can climb up the Abbey Craig to the William Wallace/Mel Gibson Monument. And you could even go and have a gander at Bannockburn where two armies once fought over a recipe for cakes.

STIRLING ALBION PROFILE

KICKED OFF: 1945. World War II ends. Stirling Albion begin.

TRUE COLOURS: Red and white. A sensible combination of colours.

BADGE OF HONOUR: The Stirling Albion club crest features the Wallace/Gibson Monument with the Ochil Hills in the backdrop. It's a very spiffy club crest. I like it.

NAME CALLING: Stirling Albion wish to be known as the Binos. But don't go rhyming it with biros and giros and rhinos. Because it is pronounced 'Beanos' like the comic. Or a bunch of the comics.

MORTAL ENEMY: Alloa Athletic are the nearest and queerest neighbours of Stirling Albion.

AREN'T WE BRILLIANT?: Stirling Albion thrashed Selkirk 20-0 in a Scottish Cup first round tie in season 1984/85. Selkirk were playing rugby.

MISSION LOGISTICS

ALIGHT AT: Whit a scunner! Getting to Stirling is a cinch. The trains are as regular as the bowel on a high-fibre diet. But the problem of finding Stirling Albion's ground is like something out of the Krypton Factor. An answer is not forthcoming. Initially, I tackle an unappealing underpass (of the piss-stained variety) and then wind up losing myself on an industrial estate. Which gets me really wound up. (Much later I discover that there is a Saturday bus service that runs direct to the stadium from Stirling bus station. If only I had known that when I set off from the train station. Which is next to the bus station.) Really, at this point in the crisis I should be looking for someone and asking them to point me in the direction of the football ground but how many people would you find, sir, wandering about an industrial estate on a Saturday afternoon? And how many of them would have knowledge of the whereabouts of the residence of a Scottish Second Division football team? I see a man in a forklift truck but he scowls at me. Possibly because I am standing in his way. He seems to be contemplating something. (Whether to run me over or not?) I sidestep to safety and somehow get my sorry arse off the industrial estate and back to the main road where, miraculously, I spot an oldster in a red and white scarf but he has other clothes on too. He is striding purposefully in a consistent direction. He must be a Stirling Albion fan! He should be going to the game! I follow him, and he speeds up a little, so I speed up a bit, and he speeds up a bit, and then I glimpse the Halfway House and I forget about the old man and getting to the ground safely. This is a diversion worth making. I'm thirsty.

A Pint At: You are taking your life in your hands by crossing the busy bend in the road to reach the Halfway House. But it is probably worth the risk because once you get in there, past all the flock wallpaper in the porch, the Halfway House has Elvis on the jukebox and toasties for a pound. At about a quarter-to-three, with kick-off fast approaching, a Stirling Albion supporter rises from his seat and announces he is off to the game, but his friend is having none of it. 'Take a drink.' 'No.' 'Go on.' 'No.' 'A quick drink.' 'No.' 'You want a vodka.' This is a statement and in no way a question. 'No.' 'Come on. One more for the road.' 'No.' 'House vodka hen,' the persistent friend calls to the barmaid regardless of his friend's wishes. See, there is always time for one more. Now. If you want a pub smack in the centre of Stirling, and not five minutes' walk from the station, how about the fittingly-named and nicely-fitted Albion Bar? It has candelabras, cornicing, battered leather seats, pumping dance music and various football teams' scarves pinned to the walls, including the scarf of the Blue Toon. There is also a Lion Rampant flag covering one window with William Wallace's freedom speech. A proper Stirling hostelry then. There is even a queer foreign chap who takes sips from other customers' pints when they happen to go to the toilet. One man comes back and stares at his drink. He seems puzzled. A sign above the bar reads 'prices subject to change, according to customer's attitude'. I try to be nice but receive no discount. When I leave the Albion Bar, I meet a Rottweiler in a denim jacket. Not dog-clothes denim jacket. I'm talking proper denim jacket. On a Rottweiler. In the street. Stirling seems a strange place.

MISSION DEBRIEFING

Field of Dreams: It's so pretty. Oh so pretty. Forthbank may languish on the outskirts of Stirling. It may be situated on the edge of an industrial estate, but this is a lovely, lovely football ground and it has such a calming effect on me after all the hassle involved in trying to find it. I marvel at the perfect neat line of trees behind the goals and gaze at the Ochil hills in the distance, flaunting their splendour. Some Scottish football grounds will compensate you with a decent view if you feel short-changed by indecent football. The game has not started yet but already I like Forthbank. A lot. You can wonder at the surroundings while wincing at the tomfoolery on the pitch. I wish I had taken a picnic. There are two tidy stands facing each other - and the West Stand is the bigger of them. The ground is well-kept and well-kempt. Stirling Albion used to play at Annfield. I have no idea if Annfield was much kop because I was never there, but Stirling Albion flitted to Forthbank in 1993 - and this is a small corner of football paradise. Hark! The twittering of the birds! It's so dreamy ...

Super Pies Me: The Stirling Albion pie proves more than satisfactory and, what's more, it is served on a paper plate. A paper plate is the height of sophistication in the football pie world. I'm loving it. I go for the pie before the match starts. This is partly to do with my Dumbarton trauma but also because I am famished. Then the game begins, and you know what? It's brilliant!

GAME ON: Stirling Albion 3-3 Stranraer

STIRLING ALBION GOALSCORERS: Shields 6, Tomana 34, Cashmore 88.

STRANRAER GOALSCORERS: Hamilton 10, McNally 16 o.g., Moore 46.

STIRLING ALBION: Hogarth (Christie 75), Nugent, Forsyth, McNally, Roycroft (Gibson 70), Fraser, Bell, Tomana, Cramb (Cashmore 80), Shields, O'Brien.

STRANRAER: Morrison, Snowdon, Sharp, Hamilton, Walker, Crilly, Lyle, Burns, Moore, Wright (McGroaty 46), McMullan (Ramsay 77).

HEAD COUNT: 638. Another bumper audience.

Report Card: Whit a game! (Despite kick-off being delayed because there aren't enough pegs to hold down the net.) Stirling surge in front to the perfect start with Dene Shields nodding the Binos ahead in these early stages only for David Hamilton to hammer in the equaliser for Stranraer. With barely a quarter-of-an-hour of the match gone Stranraer jump into the lead, when Stirling Albion's Mark McNally adeptly slices the ball into his own net. Not disheartened by this cruel setback, Stirling strike back ... Marek Tomana is top banana as he dribbles like a wizard and finishes like a ... like a ... finisher. This levels a gripping encounter at 2-2. Shortly after half-time - while I am still catching my breath - Michael Moore makes it 3-2 to Stranraer from an impossible angle. (Well, almost impossible.) The brave Binos barge back and rescue a draw as super sub Ian Cashmore cashes in for a precious point with two minutes remaining. Stirling even have a brilliant opportunity to steal the game but one of their players makes a hash of it in the six-yard box. 'All he had to do was knock it in,' sighs one Stirling Albion fan. 'With anything ... even his knob.' Still, a magnificent feast of football action. Phew!

Going For Gold: Had either team snatched a last-minute winner, I would have had no option but to decorate this fizzing joust with the maximum of ten gold stars. But, as it stands, a draw can never be viewed as perfect, so, though taking into account all of the drama that has passed before my disbelieving eyes, and the six goals hitting the back of the net, I believe that it would be proper to bestow nine gold stars on this smashing advert for Scottish football. If only more than 638 football supporters had been party to it, as there can't have been a better match in the country today. Well done Stirling Albion and well done Stranraer.

Fanfare: My sole criticism is that not even a late Stirling equaliser has the home support singing for their supper. Unless they happen to be singing quietly to themselves and the sporadic bird noise is drowning them out. There is one late and lame attempt at 'C'mon the Binos' but it is very much over before it gets started. Being at Forthbank is like being in a silent movie. About football. Stirling Albion do not stir the natives of Stirling much. Even if this was frenetic fare to quicken the blood.

Music To My Ears: El Presidente. Que?

Additional Travel Report: Making my way back to Stirling train station after the game, I decide to call up the automated train service to check the time of the next service back to Glasgow. I am surprised to find myself being interrogated by Stephen Hawking's sister.

'Where. Are. You. Travelling. From?'
'Stirling.'
'Where. Are. You. Travelling. To?'
'Glasgow.'
'What. Time. Do. You. Intend. To. Travel?'
'Five-thirty.'
'Was. That. Twelve. Thirty. Or. Ten. Thirty?'
'No.'
'Was. That. Ten. Thirteen?'
'No.'
'Please. Repeat. Time.'
'Five-thirty.'
'Searching. For. I'm. Sorry. We. Do. Not. Have. Times. For. This. Service. At. The. Moment. This. Could. Be. Due. To. Technical. Difficulties. Would. You. Like. Times. For. Other. Destinations?'
'No.'
'Thank. You. Goodbye.'
'NnnnnnoooOOOO!'

GET WITH THE PROGRAMME

In exchange for a couple of your hard-earned earth pounds the pimply teenager with the luminous satchel hands you a match programme. You open your pamphlet of pleasurable reading and the very first item to confront you is the Manager's Column. Brilliant shafts of football philosophy, beamed from the boundless brain of the boss onto the page. These deep-thinking reflections, such careful cogitations and wry observations from giants amongst men are always refracted through the cliché prism, which results in every single Manager's Column sounding EXACTLY THE SAME.

Filching inspiration from all the programmes I procured during an arduous season of toil (alas Cowdenbeath's white-hot publication *The Blue Brazilian* was 'sold oot' long before kick-off), I have concocted (in other words, cut-and-pasted) what is, in my own inflated opinion, the definitive Manager's Column.

Gaffer's Guff (Where's The Gaffer Tape When You Need It?)

Good afternoon.

Last week we were not at the races. We gave away daft goals. Individual errors proved costly and mistakes get punished. If you had offered me a draw beforehand, I would have taken it. I'd have bitten your hand off and chewed on it for a bit. Instead, we were beaten 6-0. We are not looking for excuses, but there is a fine margin between winning and losing.

It has been a rollercoaster season (you've probably puked) and we need to be more consistent, we need to be more ruthless in front of goal. It will not happen overnight. It won't happen in my lifetime, or yours.

There is a long way to go and a lot of points to be won. At least we've got some points on the board. Not many mind you.

We need to get another win under our belts. We have to get back to winning ways. A win here today could be the springboard for our season. We would hope to be knocking on the door. Who's there? It's time we mounted a serious challenge. Maybe we just need that wee bit of luck. That little rub of the green. I can't fault my players. I cannot ask any more of them. They're shite.

Today we face difficult opponents. It won't be easy and we won't be taking them lightly. This is a chance to test ourselves. It's about how the players react. We are looking for maximum points but we can't find them. I ask you, the fans (hello?), to be patient. I know we can count on your support. But don't count on us.

Hopefully, by 4.45pm today, we will be celebrating.

Enjoy the game.

Gaffer.

After the Manager's Column, you are ready to treadmill to the very heart of the matter. That's right. The Player Interview. But we will have none of that banal badgering and prosaic probing along the routine lines of 'looking forward to the game?' 'how's the knee?' 'will you be signing a new contract?' No, we are not remotely interested in any of that. We want the best gear. We wish to get-right-down-to-the-nitty-gritty. We, the paying punters, demand the sort of ferocious, forensic examination that puts footballers, and their tastes, mainly their lack of taste, firmly in the spotlight. We just don't want to hear them droning on and on and on about their groins and 100 per cent and bemoaning their hernias. We demand that the key issues are addressed. For instance, and these are all genuine ...

Dream Date?

Jessica Simpson or Jessica Alba.

Why not both? And why not throw in Jessica Rabbit while you're at it?

Last book you read?

I don't read books, but the last magazine I read was FHM.

One needn't expect footballers to be literate. I enjoy reading but I'm crap at football.

Here is another brave Scottish footballer baring his soul.

    Celebrity Babe?

    All of Girls Aloud …

What? All of them?

    … but my wife Joanne's the only woman for me.

Ah, textbook. He covered himself brilliantly there.

    Favourite magazine?

Again with the magazines!

    Zoo or Nuts.

Make up your mind. Aren't you forgetting your New Yorker subscription?

    Favourite film?

    Snatch.

Absolutely. People are always going on about Citizen Kane. But Snatch. Now, there's a film.

Sometimes the Player Interview mines so deep that the actual results are quite shocking.

    Who's your favourite children's TV character?

    I can't really think of any, but when I was young I used to dress up as the Pink Panther.

Oh. You'll be ribbed mercilessly for that. Especially by the joker in the dressing room. But you just remember that he's just bitter he never got to be Batman. He cross-dresses as Wonder Woman you know.

Once in a while the Scottish footballer shows wisdom beyond the perceived wisdom of the Scottish footballer. Observe this adroit subject, toying with his interrogator.

    Worst habit?

    Biting my nails.

    What would you change about yourself?

    My bad habit.

Good one!

But mostly Scottish footballers act like Scottish footballers and conform to stereotype.

Pre-match rituals?

I always go out second from the dressing room and shake hands with everyone before kick-off.

Superstitions?

None.

To be fair, that was a devious line of questioning.

One of the most alarming Player Interviews I encountered involved this offending item. It serves as a savage indictment of the sort of lardy lifestyles led by Scottish footballers.

Put the following in order of preference: Pizza Hut, Burger King, KFC, McDonalds.

McDonalds, Burger King, Pizza Hut, KFC.

Did you really have to answer that? Do you know how that looks? Don't you know you are implicating yourself?

Here is the same jigsaw, but with different pieces …

Put these in order of preference: Eastenders, Hollyoaks, River City, Coronation Street.

Hollyoaks, River City, Eastenders, Coronation Street.

I would have gone for River City myself.

You get a lot in match programmes these days. Much more than the Manager's Column and Player Interview. Keen contributors provide articles on a wide array of topics ranging from referees to sectarianism to referees to world football to referees to conspiracy theories to referees to the Tennents Sixes.

Some match programmes even contain articles about match programmes.

The Elgin City match programme is hilarious. It kicks off with a joke. A really long joke about two Mexicans in the desert. It has nothing to do with football. I forget the punch-line but I suppose if your team is toiling in the nether regions of the Third Division you could probably do with a laugh.

The award-winning Brechin City match programme *The Spire* is something to aspire to. One copy is autographed by Gareth Evans. The lucky punter who buys the signed copy is rewarded with a free bottle of whisky. How about that?

During a lull in a match, I find myself scrutinising the adverts in match programmes. You get a glimpse of the town through the ads for plumbers, butchers, opticians, glaziers, taxi-hire, weld-cladding, shot-blasting, ship repair, fishbox hire. A couple of those ads were placed in the Peterhead match programme (in case you hadn't guessed). The Queen of the South match programme is ablaze with pub adverts. You are never too far from a drink in Dumfries. I suppose that is why Burns liked Dumfries. My favourite pub promotion is not in Queen of the South's match programme. It is within the pages of the East Fife match day publication: 'Britain's No. 3 Toughest Bar. As seen on Sky One. Ask for Big Davy'. I'm there already.

Don't know about you, but I always feel sorry for a footballer without his own individual sponsor in the match programme. When all his team-mates have one of their own. What's the reason for this? Is he new? Are there not enough sponsors to go round? Is he rubbish? 'No. We don't want our world-famous confectionery associated with the likes of him. He calls himself a striker, but he can't shoot for toffee.'

Finally, it's back to the Queen of the South match programme, for this poser from trivia corner. Who said football is more important than life or death? (Yes, I know it was Bill Shankly. I was being rhetorical.)

Q: I watched an excellent programme on Border TV last Tuesday night about the tragic sinking of the Stranraer-Larne ferry *Princess Victoria* and, if my memory is correct, did Queen's not play Celtic that day?

Old-Timer, Dumfries.

A: Your memory is spot on auld yin, as in horrendous stormy weather Queen's beat Celtic 2-1.

MISSION POSSIBLE 8

SCENARIO: East Stirlingshire are playing Stenhousemuir in the Scottish Third Division. My postie pal Paolo enjoyed Dumbarton so much that he has despatched from Italy two more gentlemen of Verona who would like to sample Scottish football and revel in its glory. My travel companions today are Matteo and Denis. Matteo is a football correspondent for *Corriere della Sera*. So he knows his football. Matteo and Denis would really like to go to Celtic Park and watch Celtic but I convince them that we are far better off watching East Stirlingshire instead. Again, this is a risky strategy. I am the host and I cannot be seen to mistreat my guests. But the thing is, I have been to Celtic Park to watch Celtic. My cross-country-football-rail-and-road show must go on. Firs Park and East Stirlingshire it is. I have a gut-feeling this is going to be good. Bella calcio! Forza Shire! (The Shire being East Stirlingshire.)

DATE: Saturday, August 26, 2006. I read in the paper that Pluto is no longer a planet. It has been downgraded to a dwarf planet. A bunch of astronomers had a vote and Ainsley Harriott was in charge. The astronomers had to hold up either a red tomato or a green pepper. One astronomer held up a red pepper and caused chaos. Back to the football ...

LOCATION, LOCATION, LOCATION: Falkirk. Not a lot of people know that. Some people think East Stirlingshire are found in Stirling. These people are so wrong and should be flogged to within three or four inches of their lives. Now that you know that East Stirlingshire are based in Falkirk, maybe you could mention it down the pub tonight. It's the sort of thing that would impress friends. Or you might lose all of your friends. It could go either way.

CULTURAL NOTES: Okay! If you really must ... go and have a look at the Falkirk Wheel ... still 'turning the canals full circle'. I'd rather stare at a Wagon Wheel.

EAST STIRLINGSHIRE PROFILE

KICKED OFF: 1881. Fyodor Dostoevsky dies having never realised his wish of seeing East Stirlingshire play football.

TRUE COLOURS: A monochrome combination of white and black. Can white and black be monochrome? Or is monochrome the one colour? White, or black. Could somebody find out for me please?

BADGE OF HONOUR: A shield and a football. Were East Stirlingshire defenders equipped with shields, they might prevent more goals from being scored against them.

NAME CALLING: The Shire. It feels like you are in Middle Earth. All the curious creatures.

MORTAL ENEMY: The other club in Falkirk. Which would be Falkirk. Not that The Shire play Falkirk that often. Falkirk would have to drop down three divisions, because pigs will fly backwards before East Stirlingshire ever get one promotion, never mind three.

AREN'T WE BRILLIANT?: East Stirlingshire lay no claim to being brilliant. They are habitual bottom feeders, habitually propping up the Third Division, along with Elgin City. Some people think East Stirlingshire should be kicked out of the Scottish Football League set-up. I reckon they should stay where they are. And, after today, I will not be changing my mind. The fans are great. The team isn't great but the fans still support them, through thick and thin. The Shire were brilliant at one time. They won Division Two in 1932, fending off late challenges from Lothlorien and Minas Tirith. The epic tale of that heroic campaign has been told countless times and made into a book by Tolkien.

MISSION LOGISTICS

ALIGHT AT: Falkirk Grahamston train station is nearer to Firs Park than Falkirk High train station but the train from Glasgow Queen Street to Falkirk Grahamston takes fifty minutes while the one to Falkirk High only takes half-an-hour. I weigh up my options and go with the Falkirk Grahamston train. Of course, it is possible that you are approaching from the Edinburgh direction, but I wouldn't know about that. It is a ten-minute walk to Firs Park from Falkirk Grahamston. You head through the retail park and eventually walk down a terraced street to the 'Theatre of Dreams' which is so well hidden that you may walk right past it.

A Pint At: The Gordon's Bar and Lounge is close to the ground and I wade straight into the Tartan Special with Matteo and Denis following suit. They don't need much encouragement these Italian boys. They like their beer, and they are loving this slice of Scottish culture. Mind you, they have not seen any of the football yet. Meantime they are content to examine the photos of The Shire on the wall. I point out some of the players to them. 'There's Frodo ... there's Bilbo ...'

MISSION DEBRIEFING

Field of Dreams: When you pass through the turnstile at Firs Park the first thing to catch your eye is the condemned terracing roped off from use. Right away you get a feel for the place. This is the arse end of Scottish football. The main stand is a shoebox - size eight - that looks like it may never have seen better days. Opposite the shoebox is covered terracing, which is in use by the deranged - I mean passionate - Shire supporters, who like to hang about in the hope of a rare victory though they are inured by the regularity of defeat. Just behind one of the goals is a giant wall. It looks almost to be meeting the touchline, which is pretty strange really. Such is the proximity of the wall to the pitch that a powerful shot off-target has the potential to rebound to the centre circle. I believe this is possible. Were indoor-five-a-side rules applied in the Scottish Football League, then matches at Firs Park would prove quite interesting because you would always have the option of a one-two off the wall to flummox a defender. Behind the wall are Land of Leather, Currys and Allied Carpet. If only these shoppers could drop into Firs Park on a Saturday afternoon, the club might get a half-decent crowd. But that's not going to happen, is it?

Super Pies Me: The pie of The Shire is not a shining example of a pie. Just like The Shire are not a shining example of a football team. But it is a decent pie and I am not grumbling. Matteo and Denis refuse my challenge to a pie eating contest. They're Italian. They know better.

GAME ON: East Stirlingshire 5-0 Stenhousemuir

EAST STIRLINGSHIRE GOALSCORERS: Thywissen 16, McKenzie 58, 65, 70, Tweedie 90.

EAST STIRLINGSHIRE: Tiropoulous, Smith, Learmonth, Oates, Brand, Thywissen (Nixon 58), McKenzie, Stewart, Ure (Blair 60), Tweedie, Adam (Boyle 71).

STENHOUSEMUIR: McCulloch, Murie, McAlpine, Henderson, Cowan, McBride, Connelly (Templeton 76), Murphy (McLeish 58), Baird, Hutchison (McLaughlin 45), Diack.

HEAD COUNT: 363. (I counted them.)

Report Card: Whit a game! East Stirlingshire kick Stenhousemuir off the top of the table and send the world spinning from its axis while they are at it. Five goals the Shire stuff past their stunned neighbours. Five goals. With no reply. Marc McKenzie gobbles a hat-trick and it is all quite astonishing. Carl Thywissen (try saying that when you're pithed) heads in the opening goal for The Shire and man-of-the-match McKenzie smacks in the second before striking the third and then dinging a screamer from thirty yards for his treble. What a solo performance! Paul Tweedie adds some injury-time polish to an already unbelievable scoreline and it needn't be said, but I will say it anyway, that the home supporters go mental. 'Have you ever been to such a party?' screams an inhabitant of The Shire and I have to be honest with him - I haven't been to such a party. It truly is an unbelievable afternoon of football. There had been no hint of what was in store for Matteo, Denis and me, indeed anybody, when an early East Stirlingshire shot was sliced for a throw-in. This had Matteo and Denis shaking their heads, the pair of them wishing that they had ignored me and gone to Celtic Park instead. Matteo makes an early assessment (before the deluge of goals) of Scottish Third Division football. 'In Italy, we don't have anything this ... how you say ... shit.' But once those goals start crashing in from all angles, Matteo begins to relax and enjoy the match a little, while retaining his sense of perspective. 'Beautiful goal,' he murmurs, 'and the worst defending in the world.' By the end, when The Shire fans are hugging each other and celebrating one of their best results in decades, Matteo is speechless and Denis is smiling. I'm rubbing my eyes. It really did happen.

Going For Gold: Given that I have never seen anything like it and will never see anything like it, I am driven to reward this remarkable football match with eleven gold stars out of ten.

Fanfare: This is a once in a blue moon result for East Stirlingshire. Usually the team falls short of impressing their small band of supporters. And these long-suffering fans make do with amusing themselves. Whatever happens. Thus, their repertoire of terracing songs is considerable and considerably silly. 'Stand up, stand up for Jesus' does make them sound fairly unhinged. 'Just one Cornetto' is confirmation, if confirmation were needed, that not all is right in their heads. But they could be honouring the presence of Matteo and Denis, who look non-plussed. 'Self-assembly, self-assembly, self-assembly furniture' (to the tune of 'We'll support you ever more') is, without a Shire of a doubt, the most baffling song I have ever heard at a football match. While 'Silky, silky Shire' would usually be dismissed as the sound of a deluded bunch of Shire fans, but in their defence, their over-achieving team has just stuck five goals past the Stenhousemuir defence. Then we hear (to the tune of 'Go West') '5-0 … to the pub team'. The Stenhousemuir contingent, who were very rowdy at kick-off, have fallen rather silent. What amazes me is that they are still prepared to hang about and witness the embers of this ridiculous humiliation. The willpower of some football fans never ceases to amaze me.

Mike Check: Even half-time throws up its moments, with the man on the mike at Firs Park talking the talk. Boy, does he talk! There is, though, a seamless quality to his chatter, as he natters away smoothly and rapidly without pause for breath and crashes one topic into the next. It is as if he is reading from a script. Wait a minute, he is reading from a script! And he has written it and he is getting on his high horse and riding it and highlighting the sheer lunacy of The Shire having to play a home game on the same day as Falkirk play a home game. "It is a sorry state of affairs. Illogical. Complete madness. Shows a total disregard for floating neutrals. Ninth time it's happened. And, by the way, East Stirlingshire are the only team in Falkirk town centre." I really do not mind his patter. My only issue with the man on the mike at Firs Park is when he announces the half-time scores from around the country. 'Elgin Shitty 0 East Fife 0'. First, I think it is a slip of the tongue. Then he reminds the Firs Park audience that The Shire have a forthcoming fixture with Elgin Shitty. Elgin is my home team. My wife is from Elgin. I'm telling you, Elgin is a far better place than Falkirk! And, as for The Shire, well, they are just one letter away from being The Shite. But not today, I suppose. So I let it lie.

EPISODE **9**

MISSION POSSIBLE

OBJECTIVE:
To go to Ochilview and
watch Stenhousemuir.
That is a right good
Scottish sentence that.

SCENARIO: Stenhousemuir are playing Elgin City (not Elgin Shitty) in The Scottish Third Division. I wonder if Elgin can beat Stenhousemuir 5-0 like East Stirlingshire did? Don't be so bloody silly. I have extended an invitation today to Neville from the publishers for this one and Neville has eagerly accepted. He has been a Stenhousemuir fan all his life. He hasn't really. Just like I haven't been an Elgin City fan all my life.

DATE: Sunday, September 3, 2006.

LOCATION, LOCATION, LOCATION: The twin villages of Stenhousemuir and Larbert are within the district of Falkirk. I reveal this to those readers whose general knowledge is so riddled with gaps that they did not even know that.

CULTURAL NOTES: The name Stenhousemuir derives from a stone house that was built next to the Carron River in Roman times.

STENHOUSEMUIR PROFILE

KICKED OFF: 1884. The German paleo-botanist Heinrich R. Goppert expires.

TRUE COLOURS: Maroon and white. Like Hearts, but different all the same.

BADGE OF HONOUR: The Stenhousemuir club crest is pretty straightforward really. sfc in italics, yellow lettering on a maroon background. You don't always have to have shields and castles and boats and stuff on badges you know. Sometimes it pays to keep it simple. Though it doesn't pay very well.

NAME CALLING: The Warriors. Ooh, I'm scared.

MORTAL ENEMY: Rival warriors. Plus East Stirlingshire and Falkirk.

AREN'T WE BRILLIANT?: Stenhousemuir reached the semi-finals of the Scottish Cup in 1903 which is quite something isn't it? On November 7, 1951, Stenhousemuir created a piece of Scottish football history when they played Hibs in the first floodlit match in Scotland. Before that, clubs used a combination of torches and car headlights. I do like my facts to be illuminating. Here's another one. Stanley Matthews once played for Stenhousemuir. I'll rephrase that. Stanley Matthews played once for Stenhousemuir. It was a fund-raising friendly with Falkirk. The Wizard Of Dribble was trying to raise his one-way train fare out of Larbert.

MISSION LOGISTICS

ALIGHT AT: Larbert. Not Tarbert (which I don't think has a train station in any case). From Larbert station (trains run from Glasgow Queen Street as well as Grand Central Terminal in New York) it is about a fifteen-minute walk to Ochilview and a rather monotonous walk it is too. But you will soon perk up when you arrive at your sporting destination. Honest.

A Pint At: My top tip for a top tipple in Stenhousemuir is the bar inside the main stand at Ochilview. It is more of a mini bar really. Broom cupboard proportions, but don't worry, Gordon the Gopher isn't there. Neither is Philip Schofield for that matter. You could not swing a gopher in the Ochilview bar, never mind a cat, and it is essential, at all times, to tuck in your elbows. This makes dealing with a pint quite difficult but it is well worth the effort to breathe in and squeeze in to the Ochilview mini bar somehow. There are dozens of pennants decorating the walls. Chesterfield, Manchester United, Peterhead, Linfield, Keith (who's Keith?). The friendly barman offers a standard response to any order of a coke. 'Fat or thin?' I remark that this is a handy bar. 'Too handy,' smiles the barman. I do wonder if some of these customers ever manage to un-wedge themselves from the mini bar and go and watch the football. I think Neville likes it here. We are standing on each other's toes. But neither of us seems to mind. There is also a pub next to Larbert station but it is more of a maxi bar than a mini bar. They have giant rail timetables posted on the walls. If you are in danger of missing that last train back to Carnoustie you have that final reminder right in front of your eyes. There is a lot of chapping action going on. Nothing untoward. Just men playing dominoes.

MISSION DEBRIEFING

Field of Dreams: It stands to reason that you get a view of the Ochil hills from Ochilview and the ground itself is a riot of maroon. STENHOUSEMUIR FOOTBALL CLUB is in giant bold white lettering at the main entrance to confirm that you have come to the right place. The pitch is artificial and the dugouts are opposite the main stand. Next to one of the dugouts is a mound of gravel and behind the dugouts is a fun fair which looks frozen in time. The main stand is comfortable and feels reasonably busy. Some punters stand to the side of the stand and watch over the low wall while smoking a fag or whatever. There is not much atmosphere but it is quite pleasant. The best thing about Ochilview - besides the window on the Ochils - is undoubtedly the mini bar in the broom cupboard.

Super Pies Me: I usually opt for a mince pie but this time I decide to upgrade to a steak pie, if indeed a steak pie is an upgrade on a mince pie. Not everyone would agree, and I don't think I do either, but I don't want to start arguing with myself, because sometimes I am my own worst enemy. The Stenhousemuir pie is gloopy. Yes. That's the word. Which doesn't necessarily mean that the Stenhousemuir pie is any good. I want a Wham! bar now.

GAME ON: Stenhousemuir 2-0 Elgin City

STENHOUSEMUIR GOALSCORERS: Low 24 o.g., Templeton 38.

STENHOUSEMUIR: McCulloch, Murie, Dillon, Paul Tyrell, Cowan, Mark Tyrell, Templeton, Murphy, Baird, Hutchison (Diack), McLaughlin.

ELGIN CITY: Renton, Kaczan, Dempsie (Charlesworth), Low, Dickson, Hind, Campbell (Knight), Booth, Johnston (Easton), Mackay, Trialist.

HEAD COUNT: 430. Slightly higher than the previous week's attendance at East Stirlingshire. They really do turn out in force to support their football teams in this part of the world, don't they?

Report Card: Stenhousemuir regain some self-respect after their barmy battering at the unlikely hands of East Stirlingshire with this easy enough victory over an anaemic Elgin City side. Elgin's Stephen Lowe fiendishly heads beyond his own surprised keeper to gift Stenhousemuir the lead and young David Templeton wraps up three points with a pretty ribbon of a free-kick. Elgin simply are not at the races and need not have bothered turning up. In fact, I am not sure that they have turned up. A nice passage of play from the home side has one excited home fan proclaiming 'liquid football!'. Steady on. It is good to see Brian McLaughlin still playing though. He still has skill in his boots. He must have been playing Scottish league football for, what, forty years now? Looks like he's shrunk a bit too.

Going For Gold: Stenhousemuir are all smiles but this is awful Ochilview viewing from Elgin's point of view. It is not much of a contest. It isn't a contest. I will fish out five gold stars and leave the rest in my box under the bed. Damn. Now I've told you where I keep my box. I'll have to shift it now. I think I'll put it under the kitchen table for safe keeping.

Fanfare: The Stenhousemuir supporters were much more vocal on their away day outing at Coatbridge than they are here. I don't think there are any Elgin City fans at the game. I can't see any. Stenhousemuir defender Mark Cowan has his own song. As he thunders forward with the ball, the home fans start singing 'What's that coming over the hill? Is it Mark Cowan? Is it Mark Cowan?' He also has a good pet name: The Beast. 'C'mon The Beast!' is a regular cry. It is worth having the right nickname in football. If only for unsettling the opposition. My brother Stewart player-manages Hopeman FC, the Real Madrid of the Moray Welfare League. Hopeman have this handy player called Psycho. His real name is Alan but 'tackle him Psycho!' has much more of an effect than 'tackle him Alan!'

MISSION POSSIBLE 10

SCENARIO: Partick Thistle are playing St Johnstone in the Scottish First Division. I see in the paper that former Thistle player Martin Hardie is getting ready to Bury His Former Club. 'Saints pay my mortgage now,' he points out.

DATE: Saturday, September 9, 2006.

LOCATION, LOCATION, LOCATION: The Maryhill arrondissement of Glasgow. Towards the utopian west end of the city. Partick Thistle have not played in Partick since 1909.

CULTURAL NOTES: Since you are on the doorstep of the fabled west end of Glasgow you can skip down Byres Road, bohemian parade of estate agents, charity shops, coffee shops and estate agents. You can also pop into the Botanic Gardens for some plant action. And also you are not too far from Scotland's most visited tourist attraction, the Kelvingrove Museum and Art Gallery.

PARTICK THISTLE PROFILE

KICKED OFF: 1876. Alexander Graham Bell makes the first ever telephone call. He dials the wrong number.

TRUE COLOURS: Red, yellow and black, with plenty of stripe action.

BADGE OF HONOUR: A contemporary black thistle with a yellow and red background.

NAME CALLING: Partick Thistle are possibly the most romanticised club in Scotland, but they are, in their way, a refreshing alternative to the Old Firm, although one should not forget Queen's Park. It is not in the very least surprising that Thistle carry a number of nicknames. First and foremost they are the Jags, but they are also the Maryhill Magyars and the Harry Wraggs, which is Cockney rhyming slang for fags, and now Jags. Harry Wragg was a champion jockey, in case you're interested. You're not interested? Tough.

AREN'T WE BRILLIANT?: Partick Thistle won the Scottish Cup in 1921 and the League Cup in 1971. Stretching the numerical sequence, the Jags are due to win another cup in 2021, but which cup, I have no idea. Possibly a tea cup.

MISSION LOGISTICS

ALIGHT AT: Get on the Glasgow Subway to St George's Cross or Kelvinbridge. It is fifteen minutes' walk from either to Firhill. You could walk it from the city centre, if you don't mind the walk (allow half-an-hour) or you could indulge in the Glasgow taxi experience, but don't say I didn't warn you. You can also catch a bus up Maryhill Road. There are enough of them.

A Pint At: The Munn's Vault on Maryhill Road is about as close as you will get to Firhill for a pre-match pint and it is really close. There are pictures on the walls of The Messiah. That'd be John Lambie. The Munn's Vault has two lounges, so lots of room, even when it starts filling up on match days with two sets of supporters.

MISSION DEBRIEFING

Field of Dreams: Most Thistle fans at Firhill occupy the Jackie Husband Stand, a large single-tier structure with the canal behind it and a few folk fishing. For what I'm not sure. Bicycles and shopping trolleys, I would imagine. Facing the Jackie Husband is the main stand but there are not many faces over there. It would seem you need to be dressed up to get in there. Just a smattering of suits. The North End is allocated to away supporters, in this case St Johnstone supporters. Behind the North End there are towering student halls of residence. That's towering halls and not towering students. I have no idea how tall the students are. The South End is not currently in use. From up high in the Jackie Husband Stand you get a decent view of Glasgow, especially of Park Circus.

Super Pies Me: There is a pie that you really should try, if you're interested in pies, called the Partick pie, but alas it is not on sale at Firhill, so you will have to search for it elsewhere. Try a baker's in Partick. The trouble with the pie they sell at Firhill is that it has no discernible filling. It is stingy. Unlike the Thistle defence. There is more mince on the pitch than there is in my pie, by my reckoning.

GAME ON: Partick Thistle 1-5 St Johnstone

PARTICK THISTLE GOALSCORERS: Donnelly 77 pen.

ST JOHNSTONE GOALSCORERS: Scotland 1, 6, Milne 43, 64, Scotland 90.

PARTICK THISTLE: Arthur, Sives, Boyd, Keogh (Graham Gibson 58), James Gibson, Brady, Ferguson (Campbell 46), Billy Gibson, Donnelly, Young, Roberts (Strachan 66). Maybe one day Thistle will field an entire team of Gibsons.

ST JOHNSTONE: Halliwell, Mensing, McManus, James, Lawrie, Hardie (Stevenson 83), Sheerin, McLaren (Sheridan 74), Stanic, Milne (MacDonald 69), Scotland.

HEAD COUNT: 2,914.

Report Card: There is dog's abuse for Dick Campbell and a hat-trick for Jason Scotland as pitiful Partick slump to an embarrassing defeat. St Johnstone striker Scotland delivers the first blow for club, but not country, from the edge of the Thistle penalty box, as early as the second minute, but no later. A few minutes later Scotland lands yet another punch on the punch-drunk Partick defence. Steven Milne makes it 3-0 St Johnstone with a lob and then volleys home on the rebound for his second and the Perth side's fourth! Simon Donnelly converts a consolation for the home side from the penalty spot, before Scotland scoops his third, in injury-time, to complete his hat-trick. The Thistle fans are furious and no bloody wonder. Their team's defending is terrible and a perfect barometer of the Jags' misfortunes is the supporter sitting in front of me who has had the bright idea of bringing his wife along to the game and is having trouble dealing with it. As is she. 'A don't know whit's wrang wi them the day,' says the exasperated fan to his clearly bored wife. He tries to placate her by doing an early pie-and-bovril run. When he returns to his seat, he tots up the total cost, including food and beverage, of an afternoon at Firhill. 'Thirty-five quid to watch this shite.' A long silence ensues as they tackle their pies, before the man breaks the silence. 'Seven minutes to half-time.' The only response from his good lady is a barely audible sigh. Even the students with the free view from the high-rise flats over there have given up on the game and gone and done something less boring instead. Like study or have sex. When the fourth goal goes in, there is a small exodus from the Jackie Husband Stand. Wife to husband: 'How much time?' Husband: 'Twenty minutes.' Yet another outbreak of hush in glorious weather with gory football. This is the long goodbye because sometimes that is what football fans must do. Sit tight and suffer fright. Whether they like it or not.

Going For Gold: As far as Thistle are concerned, the art of defending is a lost art. St Johnstone fully exploit the home side's rearguard incompetence and for that they can collect their seven gold stars and go back to Perth happy in the knowledge of an easy job well done.

Canon And Ball: I have been thinking they should introduce canons to Scottish football grounds. Not cannons, but canons in the form of rounds, distinct from the rounds you buy in pubs. If the Thistle fans had a canon to practise it might have taken their minds off the thrashing their team was accepting from St Johnstone. At the very least, some loud canon participation would have alleviated some of the pain the Partick supporters were feeling. Football grounds offer the perfect environment for a canon because a canon has four parts and football grounds have four stands. I suppose a problem with Thistle is that they never fill four stands. And one of them they can't use anyway. Hamilton only have two stands. Clyde meanwhile fall a stand short of the complete canon, and even two of their existing stands are usually empty, which is a fat lot of good if you are trying to get a decent canon going. But with the right conditions the possibilities are endless. You could feasibly keep a canon going for ninety minutes. It would be like an oral version of the Mexican Wave, and, admittedly, a bit naff. But imagine all those canons cannoning around the grounds of Scotland? It would be brilliant. Wouldn't it? My suggestion for Thistle is that they should split the Jackie Husband Stand into four sections and start from one end, maybe the end nearest the city centre, and work along from there. The first-ever Partick Thistle canon is based on London's Burning.

Partick's losing, Partick's losing,
Fetch the valium, fetch the valium,
Shite, shite, shite, shite,
Pour a large one, pour a large one,
Partick's losing, Partick's losing …. [and repeat until it peters out]

Of course, this canon is multi-purpose. It can be used for Elgin, Airdrie, Brechin, Dundee …

Music To My Ears: The Verve's 'Bitter Sweet Symphony.' There is nothing sweet about a 5-1 defeat. Any sweetness belongs to St Johnstone.

Mike Check: The man on the mike at Firhill has an announcement to make. He issues an appeal to the crowd that serves to reinforce the stereotype of Partick Thistle supporters. 'If anyone here today is willing to accommodate a German postgraduate student next semester, could they please let us know.' You would not hear that at New Broomfield. The Jags fans look up momentarily and listen to the words of the MC and then bury their heads in their books again. The Thistle fan next to me is reading Goethe. You'd think he might find room for a German lodger, but maybe he doesn't have the space.

MISSION POSSIBLE

OBJECTIVE:
To go to The Falkirk Stadium and watch, eh, Falkirk.

SCENARIO: Falkirk are playing Aberdeen in the Scottish Premier League. Back among the big boys again. They had better be good. Gold stars are at stake.

DATE: Saturday, September 16, 2006.

LOCATION, LOCATION, LOCATION: Falkirk is situated in the Forth Valley, somewhere between Glasgow and Edinburgh. No one is entirely sure.

CULTURAL NOTES: There are remnants of the Antonine Wall around Falkirk. William Wallace was defeated in the Battle of Falkirk by King Edward I in 1298. Oh, and there's the Falkirk Wheel.

FALKIRK PROFILE

KICKED OFF: 1876. Which was a leap year.

TRUE COLOURS: Navy blue and navy white.

BADGE OF HONOUR: The Falkirk Steeple is on the Falkirk badge. The Falkirk Steeple is the symbol of the town and indeed it can be found in the town if you look up.

NAME CALLING: The Bairns. If you beat them, they cry. In fact, the nickname comes from the Falkirk burgh motto, which is 'Better meddle wi' the deil than the bairns o Falkirk.' So don't mess with them: Falkirk are worse than Beelzebub.

MORTAL ENEMY: East Stirlingshire are not really of an acceptable standard to be considered mortal enemies of Falkirk. So it will have to be Dunfermline then.

AREN'T WE BRILLIANT?: Falkirk have won the Scottish Cup twice. They have also won the Challenge Cup. And the you-can-do-it-if-you-B-&-Q-it-Cup.

MISSION LOGISTICS

ALIGHT AT: Falkirk Grahamston station. Wait a minute. I've been here before. I retrace my steps through the retail park, with a feeling of déjà vu, but then I have to take the pastoral Grangemouth Road, which is not without charm. Follow the flames and please mind yourself crossing that traffic-crazy road in front of the stadium. It is like a game of Frogger except that is you in danger of getting squashed.

A Pint At: Behind the Wall, behind Falkirk Grahamston station, is a good bet. There is loads of Falkirk FC memorabilia upstairs on the walls and a wide range of lagers and ales on tap. Over at the Falkirk stadium they have the Amarillo bar. With a sign on the stairs saying 'This Is The Way'. Good grief. I am not supposed to be in the Amarillo bar. I am not even meant to be in the main stand. I had to buy a ticket for a less groovy part of the ground because the main stand is sold out. But while I am skulking about in front of the front door, Walter Smith walks in. Walter distracts the doormen - not intentionally, you understand - and I just swan in after him. Unchallenged. I fancy a bit of an adventure. So here I am in the Amarillo bar and I tell you what. Those corridors are a bit OTT. Weird ornaments and strange mirrors. Is The Falkirk Stadium a centre for Scientology? Can I have Tom Cruise mixing my cocktail? Apparently not, but I ask the barman anyway for the Latapy Cocktail, which I spotted on the drinks menu. The Latapy Cocktail has dark rum, banana and coconut in it. Basically it is the elixir of eternal life. I am absolutely gutted to be informed by the barman that the Latapy Cocktail is not served on match days. Not served on match days? When is it available then? Mind you, they shouldn't be serving me anything. I'm not supposed to be in here you know.

MISSION DEBRIEFING

Field of Dreams: Falkirk used to play at good old crumbly old Brockville which is now a supermarket, like everything else. The Falkirk Stadium is not as loveable as the old gaff but it is less crumbly and the West Stand is - I have to admit - a very impressive example of stadium architecture. I would say it is not too dissimilar to the main stand at Hampden. All big and shiny. A real monster of a stand. But in a good-looking way. The surrounding mini-stands with the red canopies however, look more like they belong at a horse-jumping trial than a football match. From the main stand, you can look over the top of the horse-jumping crowd for a stunning view of Grangemouth. It is not every football ground that grants you a vista on a petrochemical plant. The flames burn orange and apocalyptic. My God. It is like staring into the eye of Sauron. A sort of Mount Doom scenario. I am not too bothered about having a blast here today, but I would like to have some fun.

Super Pies Me: The Falkirk pie is falling to pieces. It is crumbling away in my helpless hands but I succeed in forcing some of the pie between my jaws before it hits the floor.

> **GAME ON**: Falkirk 0-2 Aberdeen
>
> **ABERDEEN GOALSCORERS**: Dempsey 51, Daal 81.
>
> **FALKIRK**: Higgins, Ross, Dodd, Barr, Twaddle, Thomson, Cregg, O'Donnell, Scobbie (Gow 67), Stewart (Moutinho 80), Stokes.
>
> **ABERDEEN**: Langfield, Hart, Anderson, Severin, Considine, Nicholson, Mackie, Clark, Dempsey, Miller (Daal 77), Foster.
>
> **HEAD COUNT**: 5,812.

Report Card: The first-half of Falkirk v Aberdeen is rubbish of garbage proportions. I almost refuse to watch this refuse. But I have paid my money. Even if I am sitting in the wrong stand. Christ, the lower leagues are better than this. They are more fun anyway. Whit a bore! I wish I'd a face cloth to chew on or something. Matters improve marginally in the second-half. At least they improve for Aberdeen who raise their game slightly to an almost acceptable level. Gary Dempsey drives the Dons in front with a finish into one of the corners of the Falkirk net and substitute Dyron Daal rounds off what turns out to be a profitable day for Aberdeen by delivering the second strike to Falkirk in the same corner of their net. With less than ten minutes remaining it is a fait accompli for Aberdeen which is a fancy way of saying job done. Falkirk's mercurial and evergreen Soca Warrior Russell Latapy might have enlivened proceedings but Latapy has been laid low with a virus and all he can muster is the briefest of warm-ups before he has to sit down again. He should have tried the Latapy Cocktail. Even if they don't serve it on match days, they would have given it to him surely. It is a crying shame that Latapy is not able to play because there are a bunch of Trinidadians here with T and T flags who came specifically to watch the little big man play. (Well, they are not going to come to Falkirk to see the Falkirk Wheel, are they?) I sympathise with them and say so to one of the Trinidad and Tobogganists. I ask him what they are going to do now. 'We are going to party in Falkirk,' he smiles. Party in Falkirk? I should be directing them to Glasgow or Edinburgh for their night out, shouldn't I? But he seems quite excited about a night out in Falkirk. Far be it for me to suggest an alternative. Maybe Falkirk's where it's at. Where is Falkirk again?

Going For Gold: If this is Premier League football you can shove it off a cliff. In an old caravan. I don't like it. I don't like it one bit. Four gold stars for the second-half and that is me being charitable. I am more often than not irritable. And this match has irritated me immensely. Be gone with you. No, not you.

Fanfare: How does that Bjork song go again? 'It's oh so quiet.' With the Falkirk fans it certainly is. Just the few isolated cases bawling at their manager. If Yogi tore their lungs out they would not be shouting anymore. The Aberdeen supporters make up for the lack of singing from the home contingent. 'Staaaaaaaannnd Free, wherever you may be ...' You can always rely on the travelling Dons.

Music To My Ears: 'Local Hero' by Dire Straits. A standard at Scottish football grounds that. All the players should wear Mark Knopfler headbands.

MISSION POSSIBLE 12

SCENARIO: Queen's Park are playing Motherwell in the CIS Cup third round. The only time Motherwell will play at Hampden this season. Queen's Park play here every other week.

DATE: Wednesday, September 20, 2006.

LOCATION, LOCATION, LOCATION: Mount Florida. Which has no Miami vibe whatsoever. It is not even a mountain either. Mount Florida is on the south side of Glasgow. Follow the Flamingos.

CULTURAL NOTES: There is enough to see on a visit to the south side of Glasgow. You have the possibility of the Burrell Collection in the beautiful surroundings of Pollok Park. And there is the magnificent Holmwood House, designed by the famous Glasgow architect Alexander 'Greek' Thomson, who wasn't Greek at all; he was pretending all along.

QUEEN'S PARK PROFILE

KICKED OFF: Queen's Park kicked off before anyone else in Scotland. On July 9, 1867, if you want me to be date-specific. The oldest club in the country. Older than Livingston even. And the second oldest football club in the world after Knots Landing. I mean Notts County.

TRUE COLOURS: White and black hoops. A traditional and exceptional football strip topped off with the Irn Bru logo. Quintessentially Scottish. Like Hampden.

BADGE OF HONOUR: A stripy black and white shield, tilting to the left, with a rampant lion balancing on top of it, and some thistles. The Queen's Park motto 'Ludere causa ludendi' scrolls across the bottom of the club crest. Translated from the Latin it means 'to play for the sake of playing'. Which sounds as if they are not bothered if they win or lose. It is, in essence, an expression of the Corinthian spirit. Queen's Park are the only amateur side in British football. Although one might put the case that there are a lot of teams in Scotland that play like amateurs. But I am not arguing that. Scottish football. It's great. I love it.

NAME CALLING: The Spiders. The arachnoid reference comes from the thin hoops of black and white on the Queen's Park jersey resembling a spider's web. Sort of. If only Queen's Park had Peter Parker on their team, their very own friendly neighbourhood Spider Man. Unfortunately for Queen's Park, few teams in Scotland suffer from arachnophobia.

MORTAL ENEMY: How on earth could Queen's Park, the epitome of the Corinthian spirit, have any enemies? Surely their amateur status lifts them beyond such base concerns as who should be hated and despised. No. They cannot have any enemies. I won't have it. Although I don't think they like Clyde much.

AREN'T WE BRILLIANT?: [deep breath] Queen's Park have won the Scottish Cup ten times, which is none too shabby for a bunch of amateurs. But it does not stop there. Queen's Park once went seven years undefeated. They featured in the first televised football match (their 2-0 defeat of Walthamstow Avenue in London, in 1951). They are twice runners-up in the English FA Cup. Twice. And they provided all Scotland's players for the world's first international football match against England in 1872. Queen's Park. A proper football club, with proper history.

MISSION LOGISTICS

ALIGHT AT: This is dead easy. For me at least. Get on the Cathcart Circle train at Glasgow Central and hop off at Mount Florida. You might have done this trip already if you have been to Hampden for a home international. But you probably don't remember much, what with you being dressed up and pissed up in the Tartan Army manner.

A Pint At: Look no further than the Queen's Park Social Club at Lesser Hampden, which is next to Big Hampden. The pints are cheap with an impressive range of bottled foreign beers in the fridge. Plus. Spider whisky! £2 for a double. And a varied selection of crisps. And TV screens. And a pool table. I ask you, what more could you possibly want from a pub? Spider blinds? Got them. Black and white Venetian. There is a buzzer entry for the social club. Buzz and they may let you in. The Queen's Park Social Club: it's brilliant.

MISSION DEBRIEFING

Field of Dreams: There are a lot of firsts about Hampden. First ever turnstiles in football, first press box, first PA system, first stadium car park, first all-ticket match. Queen's Park retain the title deeds to Hampden Park - or the National Stadium, as the SFA, its tenants, like to call it. The Spiders never quite fill Hampden, like the national team does. Tonight, Motherwell bring a couple of thousand supporters but Hampden remains eerily empty. The average crowd for a Queen's Park league fixture is no more than a few hundred. Some of the Queen's Park members are sitting on plush leather seats. The rest of us make do with non-leather seats but this is still way beyond most clubs in Scotland when it comes to comfort. You are in the main stand at Hampden and hardly slumming it. But I have to go to the toilet. I walk in to the toilets and somehow manage to disturb the peace of some chap having a quiet moment to himself inside a locked cubicle. 'Can I no shit in peace?' he shouts from the other side of the door. There doesn't seem to be an answer to that. So I don't answer. I don't even see how I have interrupted him. All that he would have heard was somebody's footsteps. I leave on tiptoes so as not to further rile Angry Man In Cubicle. I thoroughly recommend Hampden for a Queen's Park match. The ball boys usually have a bit of work to do.

Super Pies Me: The Queen's Park pie disintegrates in my palms (I am having some real problems with my pies lately, it is not like I am doing anything wrong) and I am left with a handful of mince hotter than the sun. Christ, that burns. I never thought pie eating could be such an occupational hazard.

GAME ON: Queen's Park 0-3 Motherwell

MOTHERWELL GOALSCORER: Foran 24, 47, 54 pen.

QUEEN'S PARK: Cairns, Quinn, Whelan (Bowers 66), Paton, Dunlop, Trouten, Canning (Ronald 77), Kettlewell, Ferry, Dunn (Murray 83), Weatherston.

MOTHERWELL: Meldrum, Craigan, Donnelly, Reynolds, Paterson, Lasley (McBride 78) Quinn, Kerr, McGarry, McDonald (McCormack 76), Foran (Elliot 70).

HEAD COUNT: 2,408.

Report Card: Richie Foran forages for a hat-trick and clatters Queen's Park out of the cup at Hampden. The Motherwell striker catapults the visitors in front after twenty-five minutes when he motors clear of a stalling home defence and finishes with aplomb. Foran then bundles in his second goal amid much goalmouth confusion before slamming in his third of a seriously productive evening from the penalty spot after a questionable penalty award. How Queen's Park must regret the chances they missed in the early part of the game. But it is interesting to note the reaction among the Spiders fans to falling behind to a Premier League team. You are an amateur team and you are the only amateur team in the country. And you find comfort from the fact that Motherwell, though they are winning, are not exactly setting Hampden alight with their performance. Yes, they are better than you, no doubt, but at times they look poor. A Motherwell player hoofs an ugly ball into the Queen's penalty box. 'Ooh, that was inventive,' comments one Queen's Park fan with a degree in sarcasm. A decent Motherwell move ends with a shot flying wide of the upright. 'Well done, Motherwell. Whit a team. Brilliant.' A constant drip of sarcasm. A Motherwell player tries his luck from forty yards but his luck is out and so the ball blazes over the crossbar and he looks stupid. 'That was really scary,' says a Spiders cynic and there is solace in such a stance. When you mock the big bully, you don't feel so bad.

Going For Gold: Motherwell are expected to win and they do, though Queen's Park give a good account of themselves and spurn some early chances. I shall give this six gold stars.

Fanfare: They are a select bunch, the Queen's Park regulars, but they are more than the sum of their parts when it comes to noise making. There are chants of 'Black and white army' and 'C'mon the Spiders' and an airing of antipathy towards Clyde ('We hate the Bully Wee') even though they are playing Motherwell.

Music To My Ears: 'Enjoy yourself. It's later than you think.' The Specials. And I have enjoyed myself, but it's getting late. Time to go home.

Hampden Hunt: I take the Hampden tour - and visit the Scottish Football Museum. We congregate for the tour in the Hampden souvenir shop at 2pm. Me and three other blokes with nothing more enriching to do, a young couple, and a nice elderly woman with an excitable grandson. Our guide, who sports a smart anorak with a Scottish Football Association badge, welcomes us to Hampden and delivers some introductory words, but I miss most of them, because a mobile phone goes off. The bloke next to me fishes the offending device from his pocket but instead of answering it or switching it off, stares blankly at it for ages as if he doesn't know what it is. 'It's your phone!' I am tempted to shout at him. Eventually the ringing stops and he puts his phone back in his pocket. '... so, if none of you have any questions, follow me.' We all nod blankly. But whatever was he telling us? That he holds a Masters Degree in Fine Cheeses and that he will be selling samples from his pockets at the end of the tour? That he is the Birdman of Mount Florida and can fly like an eagle? We'll never know.

The tour is off to a fascinating start with the car park. 'Uefa were very impressed with this car park when they chose Hampden as the venue for the 2002 Champions League Final.' We head to the East Changing Room, traditionally taken by Celtic, while Rangers use the West Changing Room. Just like Celtic and Rangers in the city. East and west. The changing rooms (they don't call them dressing rooms) are on a grand scale. In addition to famous footballers, famous pop stars have been here. Hampden is used as a concert venue. I could be standing on the exact spot where Jon Bon Jovi sprayed his hair. Amazing.

'See those stains?' says the guide, pointing at the ceiling. 'Real Madrid players spraying champagne.' Disgusting. You'd think they'd know better. I was fortunate enough to be at Hampden when Zinedine Zidane unleashed that astonishing volley. I remember watching Raul, after the final whistle, acting the matador with a Spanish flag. It was not merely the jubilant Real Madrid supporters who partied that night. All of Glasgow seemed to join in, proud to be associated with such a spectacle.

We move on to the warm-up area. There is a set of goalposts and a speedometer behind the net. We are invited to test our strength and accuracy by taking some penalty kicks. A proud granny cheers her beaming grandson as he easily hits the back of the net. 'Who's next?' The guide throws the ball to me. 'Go on ... have a try.' I tentatively place the ball on the spot. No keeper to beat. Open goal. But I don't want that child upstaging me in the power stakes and the speedometer doesn't lie. I am pathetic. I bludgeon the ball which bounces off the post. I missed. I am mortified and command the artificial turf to swallow me up. But I'm still standing here. Meanwhile, the guide is chasing the rebound down the length of the room. This heightens my embarrassment. Not only am I crap … I am lazy.

We march down the tunnel and our emergence into the Hampden light triggers off a recording of the Hampden Roar and now the Tartan Army is singing 'I'm Gonna Be (500 Miles)'. Time to climb the staircase to collect the imaginary trophy from the imaginary dignitary. The 250 press seats are pointed out. 'And they all write pish,' says the bloke next to me. Sports journalism is a vocation held in such high regard by the general public. It is right up there with estate agent and traffic warden. The Scottish Football Museum is in chronological order. It begins with the Big Bang. No it doesn't. It begins with those pioneers of Scottish football, Queen's Park. I read the minutes of the first meeting. July 9th, 1867. 'Tonight at half past eight o' clock a number of gentlemen met at No. 3 Eglinton Terrace for the purpose of forming a Football Club.' These men knew what they wanted. They didn't want a hat factory. They didn't want a paper mill. They didn't want more tea. They wanted a Football Club.

Within the museum is The Scottish Football Hall of Fame. It features legends such as Jim Baxter, Matt Busby, Kenny Dalglish, Billy Bremner, Bill Shankly, Willie Miller, Dennis Law, Jock Stein, Graeme Souness and Charles Campbell. Not so many will have heard of Campbell. You can tell from his grainy photograph that he hails from the earliest era of the game. There he is in his Spiders shirt and curly moustache. Campbell, a prize-winning sprinter, captained Scotland eight times and won eight Scottish Cups with Queen's Park. He played in both of their FA Cup finals and later became the president of Queen's Park as well as president of the Scottish Football Association. He even refereed the 1889 Scottish Cup Final!

I look at some of the museum exhibits. The match programme from the legendary 1960 European Cup Final when Real Madrid, blessed with the combined artistry of Di Stefano, Puskas and Gento, pummelled Eintracht Frankfurt 7-3 at Hampden. Kenny Dalglish's 100th Scotland cap. A Hibs shirt worn by George Best. A 'See You, Jimmy' hat with sprouting orange hair. Archie MacPherson's sheepskin coat. A seven-inch single of 'We Have a Dream', Scotland's hopelessly romantic anthem for the doomed 1982 World Cup campaign in Spain. An empty Tennents Lager can. A mint green Pringle jumper (donated by a football casual). As I leave Hampden I pass the reception area and there is a six-feet squirrel behind the desk. I know that squirrel. It's Nutz, official mascot of Kilmarnock. What's he doing in Glasgow? Looks like he's foraging for nuts.

MISSION POSSIBLE **13**

OBJECTIVE:
To go to Rugby
Park and watch
Kilmarnock.

SCENARIO: Kilmarnock are playing Inverness Caledonian Thistle in the Scottish Premier League. An Ayrshire-Highlands battle.

DATE: Saturday, September 23, 2006.

LOCATION, LOCATION, LOCATION: Kilmarnock is in East Ayrshire and is roughly the same distance from Ayr as it is from Glasgow.

CULTURAL NOTES: My *Scotland The Braw* guide book gives Kilmarnock short shrift and calls it 'shabby'. I think that's a little bit unfair. Kilmarnock happens to be the home of Johnnie Walker whisky. The locals put a drop in their tea each morning and carry on from there really.

KILMARNOCK PROFILE

KICKED OFF: 1869. Kilmarnock are the second oldest team in Scotland after Queen's Park.

TRUE COLOURS: Blue and white. In alternating vertical stripe format.

BADGE OF HONOUR: What we have here are two squirrels fighting over a football. (There is a squirrel on the town's coat of arms.) We also have this giant hand drawing attention to itself and also to the Kilmarnock motto *Confidemus* which is Latin-speak for 'We trust'. As in, we trust you've enjoyed your afternoon at Rugby Park. I hope so. I've stumped up £19 for the privilege of being here today.

NAME CALLING: Killie. That's it. Don't call them anything else.

MORTAL ENEMY: Ayr United. Although Kilmarnock haven't played Ayr United much in recent years, what with Ayr being pants and all that.

AREN'T WE BRILLIANT?: Kilmarnock have won the Scottish Cup three times, most recently in 1997, but their Scottish league title of season 1964/65 remains the club's finest moment. Kilmarnock edged Hearts on goal average. I say goal average because goal difference did not feature at that time. It was not a deciding factor in those days. If it was, Hearts would have won the league. I reckon Hearts should lodge an appeal.

MISSION LOGISTICS

ALIGHT AT: Kilmarnock station. Trains leave, bearing passengers, both human and canine, from Glasgow Central. This is a slow forty-minute journey. It feels like 400 minutes. From the station it is fifteen minutes' walk to Rugby Park which is in amongst houses.

A Pint At: They will happily serve you a pint at the plush Park Hotel (Kilmarnock's only four-star hotel) which is next door to Rugby Park. But, before that, I pop randomly into the Crown Inn in Kilmarnock town centre. Everybody is watching the Old Firm game on the telly. It is an early kick-off. And at half-time that dreadful Sky Sports advert appears. You know the one. The one where the woman from Inverness points out that the Caley Thistle goalkeeper is the best shot stopper in the league and stopped 72.543287353 shots last season. And then the Kilmarnock supporter says 'and Kilmarnock have the best pies'. One customer jokes 'that's all you can say about Kilmarnock.' Needless to say he won't be running along to Rugby Park today. Next door to the Crown Inn is the fabulous Forum Café. I just thought I would mention it because they have an impressive array of sweeties in jars. So grab yourself a quarter of soor plooms or strawberry bon bons or midget gems. Or pan drops, and suck on them at the game, why don't you?

MISSION DEBRIEFING

Field of Dreams: Rugby Park is never used for rugby but it was treated as a munitions dump during the Second World War. It is an impressive all-seater stadium and the place underwent a great deal of re-development in the 1990s. They rarely come close to filling Rugby Park, unless either of the Old Firm are involved. Much of the time it is less than half-empty and never half-full, no matter how optimistic you are. There is a foul smell, but after a short investigation I reach the conclusion that I have landed in some dog dirt between the train station and Rugby Park and brought it with me into the main stand. Oh well. The Rugby Park tunnel is so narrow that only one team can run out at any one time. It would be funny if both teams made a run for it and they got stuck and they had to call the fire brigade. But then the match would be delayed. So maybe it would be more of an annoyance really.

The sky is bright blue with a few white clouds. These are the colours of Kilmarnock. Perhaps it is an omen. Maybe they will win today. I hope not. I have put on a bet in the bookies in town for a 1-1 draw.

Super Pies Me: In terms of praiseworthy pies, look no further than the Kilmarnock pie. It is widely regarded, in the pie world, the football world, and where the two worlds collide, as one of the best pies on the planet. Or at least in Scotland. And we bake as many pies as any nation. And you know what? The Killie pie does not disappoint. This is an exquisite pie. Exemplary. Comforting tender chunks of steak, lashings of gorgeous gravy, heavenly flaky pastry. This is the best steak pie I know of. And I know lots of pies. It is no wonder some people have two. The Rugby Park stewards have their hands full. Of pies. There are ads for the Killie pie all over the ground. 'Say aye to the Killie pie.' I say aye. Most folks here have been looking forward to their Killie pie. Probably more so than the football.

GAME ON: Kilmarnock 1-1 Inverness Caledonian Thistle

KILMARNOCK GOALSCORER: Nish 7.

INVERNESS CALEDONIAN THISTLE GOALSCORER: Dargo 19.

KILMARNOCK: Smith, Grant Murray, Hay, Lilley, Wright, Fowler, Invincibile (Stephen Murray 76), Johnston, Fernandez (Di Giacomo 84), Wales, Nish.

INVERNESS CALEDONIAN THISTLE: Brown, Tokely, Munro, Dods, McBain, Wilson, Black (Hart 45), Hastings, Rankin, Dargo (McAllister 90), Bayne.

HEAD COUNT: 4,809.

Report Card: Kilmarnock and Inverness both draw blood early on but end up drawing and having to settle for a point each. I don't like draws - apart from this one which wins me money back at the bookies. Draws should be avoided. You do not get draws in tennis. Paper, scissors, stone. They should try that. It may not be a system that is used here in the Scottish Premier League, as it is in the Bulgarian Premier League, but, you know, maybe we can learn something there from our Bulgarian cousins. I think that the SPL must give this matter serious consideration. Paper, scissors, stone. Simple. Colin Nish nods Kilmarnock in front but former Kilmarnock striker Craig Dargo digs one back for Inverness with an emphatic flick into the roof of the

Kilmarnock net from close range. Dargo should seal the three points for the Highlanders but duffs one up by hitting the post, when it might have been easier to hit the roof of the net. Kilmarnock are making heavy weather of the towering Inverness backline but it is like taking on the Cairngorms. Meantime the Kilmarnock defence is at sixes and sevens and eights and nines, but Inverness cannot get that ball over the line. Both teams share the spoils, as they say, from a match that will live not very long in the memory. In fact, I had better write it down now or I'll forget.

Going For Gold: Not a terrible game. Not a terrific game. I will give it five gold stars and that is primarily because I am in a good mood because I correctly tipped the result and made a few quid at the bookies. Thanks Kilmarnock and Inverness, for not getting the better of each other.

Fanfare: Nary a note, nor a peep. All quiet on the Kilmarnock front.

MISSION POSSIBLE

OBJECTIVE:
*To go to Broadwood
and watch Clyde.*

SCENARIO: Clyde are playing Morton in the semi-final of the Challenge Cup.

DATE: Wednesday, September 27, 2006. I really, really do not want to go out tonight. It is too cold. And it is dark. And windy. I would rather stop in with a cup of cocoa but needs must. Must I?

LOCATION, LOCATION, LOCATION: Broadwood is on the edge of Cumbernauld which is not far from Glasgow. Clyde used to actually play in Glasgow, at Shawfield Stadium, where the greyhounds still chase after fake rabbits.

CULTURAL NOTES: After your afternoon at the football, how about a night at the theatre? Cumbernauld Theatre productions have included Bold Girls, Like A Virgin and Losing Alec, a hard-hitting drama about a young left-back who left Clyde to join Partick Thistle.

CLYDE PROFILE

KICKED OFF: 1877. The same year as the first lawn tennis tournament at Wimbledon. Anyone for football?

TRUE COLOURS: What is black and white and red all over? No, not a book. Clyde's strip.

BADGE OF HONOUR: A ship with billowing sails. Reflecting the heritage of the river Clyde. Most probably.

NAME CALLING: The Bully Wee. There are a few credible and incredible theories about the origin of the Bully Wee, none of which I can be bothered detailing, because to be honest, most of them sound like bullyshit. The Gypsy Army is much easier explained. Clyde were compelled to live a nomadic life for a number of years, between departing Shawfield and getting Broadwood ready. They ground-shared with Partick Thistle. And then Hamilton.

MORTAL ENEMY: Partick Thistle. Sharing Firhill for five seasons could not have been easy for either of them. My heart bleeds.

AREN'T WE BRILLIANT?: Would you believe it but Clyde have won the Scottish Cup three times? I wouldn't. The bullying Bully Wee's heyday was the 1950s when they battled Rangers and Celtic and occasionally bloodied both the Old Firm's noses. Which is nice.

MISSION LOGISTICS

ALIGHT AT: Croy (a-hoy!) train station is a short ten-minute train ride from Glasgow Queen Street. The carriages are crammed with commuters with their computers and not Clyde fans with scarves. Alighting is the easy bit. Getting from the train station to the ground is a task that should not be taken lightly. There are occasional passing local buses which go quite near to Broadwood. Otherwise it is a twenty-minute trek on foot with frantic roads and roundabouts to confront. But embrace the spirit of adventure. Walk! And remember your Green Cross Code. The workers in their grey suits go one way to their park-and-ride cars. I go the other way and march towards Cumbernauld in the semi-darkness. I clamber up a hill, follow an overgrown footpath, trample across muddy wasteland and wander through a residential estate, before bumping into Broadwood. Almost by accident. Clyde do not make it easy for the pedestrian, but, hey, I have made it. Naturally, I crave a pint before the match, but I am denied one at the social club ('Members only, I'm afraid.' Arse.) I trudge back through the car park and make my way along a meandering path which forks left and, er, right. I take the left fork and negotiate an underpass and emerge to another fork and yet another choice. This time I go right and encounter another underpass where I bump into a hobgoblin. With a great deal of effort, I manage to shake him off my leg and emerge close to an electrical substation. I go left a bit, right a bit, and in, out, shaking it all about, and collide with a pub and demand some booze, and sink it, before finding my way back to the ground in time for kick-off, largely thanks to the ball of string which I had the foresight to start unravelling at the beginning of my pub quest. Of course, if I had access to a flux capacitor I would have cut out Croy and Cumbernauld altogether and travelled back to the future when Clyde played their football in Glasgow and there would have been no need for any of these countryside shenanigans.

A Pint At: If you can succeed in finding it without getting run over by a car or accosted by a hobgoblin or picked up by a spaceship, Broadwood Farm is a pub near Broadwood (remember your ball of string). Alan Partridge would love Broadwood Farm. If you are feeling peckish you should tuck into the mixed grill of rump steak, chicken breast, pork sausage, gammon steak, fried egg, mushroom, peas, grilled tomatoes, chips and - for an extra 50p - beer-battered onion rings. Wash it all down with a couple of pints of lager and then lie down. You will feel much worse. And then waddle off to the match.

MISSION DEBRIEFING

Field of Dreams: Broadwood Stadium is one of the highest grounds in Scotland. It has seven tiers! It hasn't really. Broadwood is one of the highest grounds in Scotland in terms of altitude. I am either suffering from altitude sickness or having repercussions from the mixed grill. Broadwood is known to some football fans as Ice Station Broadwood and it can be a real test of endurance. I think Ernest Shackleton would have struggled to be honest. There is no stand at the open north end so the ground is exposed to the shifting elements. I am telling you, it can get pretty breezy at Brrrrroadwood. In fact, it is bumfreezingly cold now. In September. As well as the football side of things, Broadwood boasts a leisure centre and a beauty salon. Which is called Beautopia. There is also a series of outdoor five-a-side cages in which blokes of varied shape and size charge about in Rangers tops, Celtic tops, Barcelona tops, AC Milan tops, Liverpool tops, but not Clyde tops.

Super Pies Me: As far as the Clyde pie is concerned, taste is not the issue. Keeping the Clyde pie together and preventing it from falling apart is. Clearly, the bottom has fallen out of the pie market at Broadwood. And collapsibility is not a becoming feature in a pie. The pastry case unravels in my hands and my poor fingers end up coated in gravy. Nurse! Napkin!

GAME ON: Clyde 3-1 Morton

CLYDE GOALS: McGowan 13, Higgins 41, Bryson 79.

MORTON GOAL: 1 Higgins 63 o.g.

CLYDE: Cherrie, McKeown, McGregor, Higgins, McGowan, Bryson, O'Donnell (Masterton 82), McHale, Malone, Ferguson (Arbuckle 76), Imrie (Hunter 89).

MORTON: Gonet, Weatherson, Greacen, Harding, Walker (Finlayson 45), Millar, Stevenson, McLaughlin, McAlistair, McGowen (Templeman 76), Lilley (McClean 86).

HEAD COUNT: 2,296.

Report Card: Clyde show that they have the measure of Morton and reach their first cup final in almost fifty years. Okay, so it is the Challenge Cup final, big deal, but try telling that to these applauding Clyde supporters. They are enjoying this and you want to rain on their parade in the rain. You should be ashamed of yourself. Michael McGowan gets Clyde off to the best available start with a funny goal (funny peculiar). It is basically a kind of cross-cum-shot-cum-goal which flummoxes Morton keeper Stephane Gonet who asks McGowan 'Gonet no dae that' but he is too late to be asking. Clyde's Chris Higgins drops in the second goal for the home side before the very same Chris Higgins delivers a freaky own goal to perk Morton up a bit just when it looks like they have folded over and gone to sleep. But the Greenock club's hopes are extinguished in the Cumbernauld drizzle as Craig Bryson adds Clyde's late third to make this tie safe and put Clyde in the final. And that is that. The highlight of the evening is when a Clyde player tries a fancy sidestep and bamboozles both himself and a Morton defender. The ball trickles out for a Morton throw-in. One unimpressed Clyde fan yells: 'Linedancin's a Tuesday, no' a Wednesday.' Meanwhile, the downpour keeps pouring and the blackened sky fades to a colour beyond black. It seems all the stars have gone out too.

Going For Gold: This cup tie is as frantic as the five-a-side football next door. There is no patience. It is full-pelt-hell-for-leather. Which is not particularly pretty but the game does have its moments, and four goals is not a bad return on the gate money. Six gold stars then.

Fanfare: 'We are the famous Bully Wee, we hate the Jags and we hate Airdrie.' The Clyde fans are absolutely terrified of needles. You'll have real trouble getting them inoculated. The Morton supporters, over on the other side of the pitch, make their response with 'Morton till I die, I'm Morton till I die.' Prompting a Clyde fan to scream 'then die!' But those Morton fans really are miles away. With the stadium three-quarters empty, Broadwood suffers for it. I meanwhile am suffering from the cold. When the Clyde supporters start singing 'Stand Up For The Bully Wee' I stand up. Mainly to restore some circulation in my legs. It is a bitterly bitter night at Ice Station Broadwood. And I left my Kendal Mint Cake at home.

Music To My Ears: Nelly Furtado … Black Eyed Peas … and that 'Paris to Berlin' song. But never mind Paris to Berlin. These Morton fans have done Greenock to Cumbernauld. And they will have to make the return journey in defeat.

Mike Check: 'Would Kevin from Robroyston call his boyfriend Hannah,' announces the man on the mike at Broadwood. Everybody in the main stand sniggers. 'I mean girlfriend Hannah.' We know what you meant.

Additional Travel Report: On my tentative walk back in the pitch black to Croy station, I tumble face-first into a roadside ditch. I survive.

I SPY WITH MY LITTLE EYE SOMETHING BEGINNING WITH PIE

'Larks' tongues, wrens' livers, chaffinch brains, jaguars' earlobes, wolf nipple chips, get them while they're hot, Tuscany fried bats, otters' noses, badgers' spleens …'

'Just a pie please.'

Can you imagine Scottish football without the half-time pie? (Or without the pre-match pie for those who just find it impossible to wait until the interval?) Fact: one in three Scottish football fans has a pie at the match. Which begs the question, what are the other two thinking of?

Cometh the hour, cometh the pie man. If they took the pies out of Scottish football, I'm not so sure I'd take the time to watch Scottish football. Because, when the game stinks, the pie offers crumbs of comfort. It is perfectly-shaped and sometimes perfectly edible.

How about a pie recipe for your curiosity and experimentation? This recipe feeds ten. Or five, if they're greedy bastards.

Ingredients for meat filling:

One pound (500g) of lean lamb, minced.
Pinch of mace or nutmeg.
Salt and pepper.
Quarter-pint (150ml) of gravy.

Ingredients for pastry:

One pound (500g) of plain flour.
Six ounces (175g) of lard.
Six fluid ounces (225ml) of water.

(Taken with a) pinch of salt.
Milk.

Method:

Create the meat filling by mixing the lamb, spice and seasoning. Then make the pastry by sifting the flour and salt into a warm bowl. Form a well in the centre of the flour. Throw a penny in for good luck. And then take it out again and spend it. Melt the lard with the water and, when this bubbles, pour it into the well and mix thoroughly. Take a small amount of pastry and make a ball (keeping the rest of the pastry warm while you make each individual pastry case and have a glass of vodka). Roll each ball flat before shaping your pastry around the base of a glass or jar roughly 8cm in diameter. Make sure there are no cracks in the pastry and absolutely make sure there is no crack in the pastry. Trim round the top of the pastry case to make it even. When this cools, remove the glass, then repeat the process to make the other pastry cases, leaving about a quarter of the pastry for the pie lids. Fill the cases with the meat and add the gravy which is intended to make the meat moist and nothing else. Roll the remaining pastry and use your glass, or jar, to cut the lids. Wet the edges of the lids, place them over the meat and press down lightly. Pinch the edges and trim. Cut a small hole in the centre of the lid thus forming a vent which will allow the steam to escape (that's so clever, isn't it?). Then glaze with the milk (double glaze if you still have enough milk left over for your cereal in the morning) and bake for about 45 minutes, at 275F. Or 140C. Or 408 Kelvin. Or even Gas mark 1. Serve hot, with broon sauce or tomato, depending on which way you swing.

And if you don't make a pig's ear of it, you deserve a round of applause, because you are a better man, or woman, than I. Though I'm a man. To be honest you are probably better off buying your pie at the football ground. Cuts out all that time and mess in the kitchen. Unless you are going to Somerset Park. In which case, you are definitely safer making your own.

So many pies sold these days are mince and when I say mince I mean beef mince. The traditional Scotch pie filling was always mutton. In fact, I messed with a mutton pie once when I bought one from a baker's in Aviemore. As I bit down into the pie, my teeth crunched on bone. Which did not seem a good thing. So I returned the pie, and the bone fragment, to the baker's. 'I've got a bone to pick with you,' I said. And did I receive any sympathy? Not an ounce. A refund? No. I was given short shrift and was scoffed at and laughed at and asked if I had never eaten a Scotch pie before. I guess I hadn't. Silly me.

Most pie merchants keep their recipe a closely-guarded secret. Spiciness is considered to be a good thing in a pie, but not too spicy. Bones aren't good at all. I don't care what they say. The quality of pastry is important and a good-looking pie might be golden brown, texture like sun. They say pies are paler on the west coast. Can't say that I've noticed.

P.S. (Piescript):

Did you know Bovril was invented by a Scotsman? John Lawson Johnston was the man who won a contract to supply one million cans of beef to the French army, in the 1870s, but Britain did not have enough beef to fulfil the order. So, Johnston came up with Fluid Beef (beef extract) which later became Bovril. Since 2004, Bovril has been beef free. It upsets me that. Bovril without beef is like coffee without caffeine. What's the point?

MISSION POSSIBLE

EPISODE **15**

OBJECTIVE:
To go to Central Park and watch Cowdenbeath. Just you try and stop me.

SCENARIO: Cowdenbeath are playing Stirling Albion in the Scottish Second Division. It doesn't get much better than this.

DATE: Saturday, September 30, 2006.

LOCATION, LOCATION, LOCATION: The former coal mining town of Cowdenbeath was once known as the Chicago of Fife. Of course, nowadays, Chicago is regarded as the Cowdenbeath of Illinois.

CULTURAL NOTES: 'Neglected' and 'forlorn' are just two adjectives used by *Scotland The Braw* to sum up Cowdenbeath. I would like to take this opportunity to defend Cowdenbeath. Not every town in Scotland can say it has a well-stocked ironmongers and a proper toy shop.

COWDENBEATH PROFILE

KICKED OFF: 1881. Pablo Picasso is born and later becomes obsessed with Cowdenbeath during his Blue Period.

TRUE COLOURS: Blue and white.

BADGE OF HONOUR: There is a football, a lion rampant, a couple of thistles. But no cow.

NAME CALLING: The Blue Brazil. Coined with tongue planted firmly in cheek. Because there is not really a connection between Cowdenbeath and Brazil. Is there?

MORTAL ENEMY: East Fife. Whose provocative song about the people of Cowdenbeath lacking hygiene and television loads further fuel on the Fife fire of mutual animosity.

AREN'T WE BRILLIANT?: Cowdenbeath won Division Two in 1914 and 1939 and set off both World Wars. The Blue Brazil won the Third Division in 2006 but, thankfully, World War III was averted. Unless it was confined to Fife. And none of us noticed.

MISSION LOGISTICS

ALIGHT AT: Cowdenbeath is on the Fife Circle line and is approximately forty-five minutes from Edinburgh. You get to cross the

Forth Rail Bridge. Woo-hoo! The football ground is only a few minutes' walk from the station. That is, if you don't get waylaid in The New Goth.

A Pint At: There are a fair few pubs on Cowdenbeath High Street. None is more striking than The New Goth. The magnificent signage dares you. It lures you in. As you wonder 'what's in there?' Disappointingly, there are no Goths. There are no visible piercings, no dark eyeliner and no Nine Inch Nails T-shirts. There is that man over there slumped in the corner in the semi-darkness, having a nap behind his half-drunk pint. Maybe he has injected himself with Goth juice. Maybe he is Robert Smith's uncle, but I don't want to wake him up just to ask him that. Tellingly, there are photographs of Jim Baxter on the wall. It looks like he used to drink here back in the day. Maybe Slim Jim, from nearby Hill of Beath, was a closet Goth. I don't suppose the New Goth's prices have changed much since Baxter's day, because the booze is astonishingly cheap. In the end I slink out of the New Goth. You must slink because there is no other way to leave. If you are wanting a drink at the football ground, then there is a bar upstairs in the main stand of Central Park. They do you free sandwiches and a funny smell. I think it's eau d'old socks. You get to order your drink through a hatch. I do enjoy ordering a drink through a hatch.

MISSION DEBRIEFING

Field of Dreams: Scratch those overblown romantic images from your mind right now. Central Park is nothing like Central Park in New York. It is in Cowdenbeath for a start. Being at Central Park is like being an extra in *Escape To Victory*. Is that not Sylvester Stallone in goals? When all the stock cars turn up, before the football has even finished, it becomes more like *Days of Thunder*. I am the least petrol-headed person I know. So I will not be sticking around for the stock car racing. I love the scoreboard though. Best scoreboard I've ever seen. So old. So cool. The Cowdenbeath fans like to stand under it. Other unique aspects of Central Park are the piles and piles and piles of tyres and the large sign which catches your attention as soon as you enter the ground, reminding you 'It's Your Cowdenbeath Open Air Market Every

Thursday 10-330 Also Car Boot Section'. Central Park, Cowdenbeath. Required viewing. Has to be seen to be believed.

Super Pies Me: The Cowdenbeath pie is cheap and cheerful. In fact, it is the cheapest pie in Scottish football, sold at the princely price of 80p. And it is better than some pies that cost twice as much. Still on the subject of food, there is a tempting aroma of curry as you approach the gates of Central Park. This is because there is an Indian restaurant next door.

GAME ON: Cowdenbeath 2-2 Stirling Albion

COWDENBEATH GOALS: Paatelainen 17, Fotheringham 19.

STIRLING ALBION GOALS: Aitken 8 pen, Cramb 24.

COWDENBEATH: Orr, Baxter, Ritchie, Smith, Ellis, Fotheringham, Gomis, Paatelainen, Buchanan, Clarke, Dalziel (McBride 83).

STIRLING ALBION: Hogarth, Hay, McNally, Roycroft, Forsyth, Bell, Fraser, Tomana, Aitken (Taggart 87), Cramb, Shields (Cashmore 82).

HEAD COUNT: 693. All of them here to catch the Blue Brazil. Cowdenbeath are such crowd magnets.

Report Card: The Central Park crowd is treated to a frenetic first half-hour flurry of goals. Takes my breath away, it really does. Stirling Albion's Colin Cramb is crunched in the Cowdenbeath box. Chris Aitken converts the penalty, much to the relief of his team-mates. But much to Stirling's dismay, the Blue Brazil battle back as Markus Paatelainen's downward header finds the Stirling net without the aid of a compass. Cowdenbeath then enable themselves to creep in front as Martyn Fotheringham meets a cross perfectly to slot home. When the ball is threaded through the eye of a needle to Cramb, he does the right thing and slams a shot past the keeper. Stirling Albion have equalised to make it 2-2 after just twenty-four minutes! The rest of the game is not able to live up to this wacky races start, which is unsurprising, really.

Going For Gold: The first twenty-four minutes are gold dust and are worth nine gold stars. But after that it dwindles, so I will deduct one, which leaves a grand total of eight for Cowdenbeath against Stirling Albion. Well done lads. Proud of you.

Fanfare: There is a Cowdenbeath song that I'd like to share with you. It goes something like this (to the tune of 'When the Saints go marching in'). 'On yonder hill, there stands a coo, on yonder hill there stands a coo, it's no' there noo it must have shiftit, on yonder hill there stands a coo'. The Cowdenbeath fans do not hold back when it comes to shouting. They are an angry bunch and they are furious with the referee. Just for being the referee it seems. You are so far removed from the pitch at Central Park what with the fence and the race track being in the way. So you have to shout louder to get your message across. The Cowdenbeath fans shout louder. Curses are thrown. Food is flung. A wasp gets among them and this makes them even more animated as they take turns to try and swat it away. Time stands still at Central Park, but the supporters are never still. They are restless while they switch between joy and anger beneath the ancient scoreboard. Central Park is an essential experience. I am telling you. You should listen.

Music To My Ears: I walk into Central Park and there is an Eighties party in full swing. 'I Think We're Alone Now' by Tiffany. 'Heaven Is A Place On Earth (Called Central Park)' by Belinda Carlisle. I wait for Debbie Gibson but she never arrives. Instead we get Dexy's Midnight Runners. The Eighties spell is broken as the Cowdenbeath team takes the field. To the Champions League theme. First they are the Blue Brazil. Now they think they're AC Cowdenbeath. How about that for self-belief? (Or self-delusion.)

MISSION POSSIBLE 16

OBJECTIVE:
*To go to Tynecastle
and watch Hearts.*

SCENARIO: Hearts are playing Dundee United in the Scottish Premier League. Perhaps this one might live up to its premier billing. They have a lot to live up to after Cowdenbeath and Stirling Albion, I can tell you.

DATE: Sunday, October 1, 2006.

LOCATION, LOCATION, LOCATION: Scotland's capital. Edinburgh. In the Gorgie zone.

CULTURAL NOTES: Apparently Edinburgh has a castle. I wouldn't know. I live in Glasgow.

HEARTS PROFILE

KICKED OFF: 1874. Harry Houdini escapes from his mother's womb.

TRUE COLOURS: Maroon. And white.

BADGE OF HONOUR: The Hearts badge is heart-shaped and there is a saltire involved.

NAME CALLING: Hearts is a nickname in itself. It is short for Heart of Midlothian. Another nickname is the Jambos. A Hearts fan can be called a Jambo but never a Hibee. A Hearts fan might even support the Jam Tarts.

MORTAL ENEMY: The nemesis of Heart of Midlothian is Hibernian of Leith.

AREN'T WE BRILLIANT?: Hearts have won the Scottish Cup seven times. That is not a bad record but it is still three less than Queen's Park. Hearts have been Scottish Champions four times, but the Jambos have not jumped to the top of the pile since 1960.

MISSION LOGISTICS

ALIGHT AT: Edinburgh Haymarket station, rather than Edinburgh Waverley. When you exit the station, hang a sharp right down Dalry Road which eventually becomes Gorgie Road. You will know sure enough when you have reached Tynecastle. It is about fifteen minutes on foot, less if you are on a skateboard. But bear in mind that in some pubs they might refuse to serve skateboarders. I am not looking where I am going as I rush down Gorgie Road and I trip over a dog. Surprised by my fall, I am more taken aback by the fact that the dog is Geoff. He doesn't introduce himself ('Hey, are you alright? Let me give you a paw there. I'm Geoff by the way.') It is Geoff's owner who calls out 'Geoff!' when I fall over Geoff. As if it is Geoff's fault. I would like to make it clear that I am to blame for the pavement collision and take this opportunity to apologise to Geoff if he happens to be reading this. He might even be Jeff.

A Pint At: It is not the nearest pub to Tynecastle, but it is close, and the Athletic Arms, also known as Diggers (because Digger Barnes was a frequent customer before the oil boom in Texas), is a fine hostelry with professional bar staff serving up top-notch beer (and I'm not even a Hearts fan by the way). Diggers is Jambo-packed on match-days but do make the effort to force yourself in there, and do not leave too soon. They have live football on the telly to keep you there too. Pub bliss.

MISSION DEBRIEFING

Field of Dreams: Tynecastle has been the home of Hearts since 1886. It is certainly one of the best grounds in Scotland for atmosphere. Three of the Tynecastle stands were redeveloped in the 1990s, while the main stand - built following the First World War - is a reminder of an older Tynecastle. The seating is cramped but a real benefit of Tynecastle is just how close you feel to the action, and indeed that is the case. I take a pew in the impressive Wheatfield Stand, which is opposite the main stand and is packed full of Hearts supporters, as is most everywhere else.

Super Pies Me: The Hearts pie is a bit overdone. No, scratch that. It is burnt to a crisp. I think this detracts from the enjoyment of a pie but I persist with it, mainly because I am really quite hungry. It is poor fare though to be serving at a football match. A black mark on Hearts. To match the blackened pie crust. Yuck.

GAME ON: Hearts 4-0 Dundee United

HEARTS GOALSCORERS: Archibald 30 o.g, Makela 39, Hartley 89 pen, Mole 89.

HEARTS: Gordon, Tall, Pressley, Berra, Fyssas, Beslija, Hartley, Aguiar, Mikoliunas (Cesnauskis 56), Velicka (Mole 84), Makela (Bednar 61).

DUNDEE UNITED: Stillie, Proctor, McCracken, Archibald, Kalvenes, Conway (Samuel 61), Kerr, Cameron, Robson, Hunt, Duff.

HEAD COUNT: 16,849. More faces than I have been accustomed to these past few weeks.

Report Card: Hearts recover from their midweek Uefa Cup exit to do in Dundee United. Andrius Velicka's shot deflects off Alan Archibald's leg and into the Dundee United net. This represents a goal for Hearts. Finnish forward Juho Makela makes it 2-0 to Hearts, before the break, as he calmly slots the ball past the Dundee United keeper. Hearts make their victory more emphatic in the closing moments of the game. Paul Hartley makes no mistake from the penalty spot and soon after that Hearts substitute Jamie Mole adds insult to United's injured pride in injury time with a simple finish. The Jambos start jumping up and down. At least the Hearts fans go home happy. It must be miserable being a Dundee United fan on a day like this. I am left with a bad taste in my mouth too but I think that it is the Hearts pie.

Going For Gold: Hearts see off Dundee United with relative ease but the scoreline flatters the home side a little bit. Not that their opponents are anything better than dismal. Hearts are entertaining in spells. I will offer them seven gold stars and that is my final offer.

Fanfare: 'Hearts, Hearts, Glorious Hearts' is given a blast before kick-off, accordions and all through the Tynecastle speakers. 'When the Hearts go marching in' follows during the match. And the home supporters spell out their affinity for their club with a performance of 'H-E-A-R-T-S', as they burl their maroon and white scarves in a very Hearts manner.

Music To My Ears: The Beatles' 'Hey Jude'. Hey Hearts. Do you want me to keep an eye on those pies? I think they've been in too long. They need a Pieman to take control of the situation.

EPISODE

MISSION POSSIBLE 17

OBJECTIVE:
To go to Borough
Briggs and watch
Elgin City.

SCENARIO: Elgin City are playing East Stirlingshire in the Scottish Third Division. I have dragged the Family Sutherland along. My mam, my dad, my brother Stewart, my sister Julieann, plus my auntie Ishbel and uncle John are here. And dad-in-law Dave and his pal Charlie whose dad used to play for Elgin City. My Granny Stewart's neighbour Ian McPherson is here too. He rarely misses an Elgin City game. There aren't too many who can say that.

DATE: Saturday, October 14, 2006.

LOCATION, LOCATION, LOCATION: The lovely market town of Elgin in magical Moray. I am not biased or anything, but I was brought up around here.

CULTURAL NOTES: *Scotland The Braw* finds Elgin to be 'an appealing place' and I whole-heartedly agree. But how about some history? Well, let me tell you. Elgin Cathedral was burned down by the Wolf of Badenoch, who wasn't a real wolf. The Wolf of Badenoch tried to torch Pluscarden Abbey, near Elgin, because nobody would take him seriously. ('You're not a real wolf you know.') You can buy honey from the monks at Pluscarden Abbey. They don't make it themselves. They get bees to make it.

ELGIN CITY PROFILE

KICKED OFF: 1893. In a landmark ruling, The United States Supreme Court legally declares the tomato a vegetable. The tomato challenges the decision, insisting it's a fruit.

TRUE COLOURS: Elgin wear black and white vertical stripes. This has the effect of making the team look taller than they are, a sort of optical illusion, while also making them look like Juventus. In a way.

NAME CALLING: Black And Whites. Or City. Personally I prefer the Juventus of the North. Or the Bianconeri of Borough Briggs. Even if I made those last two up myself.

BADGE OF HONOUR: I'm seeing angels instead. And the Latin motto *sic itur astra*. Thus We Reach The Stars. Nothing wrong with a bit of ambition. Even if it is seriously misplaced.

MORTAL ENEMY: Since Elgin are no longer in the Highland League, since they no longer do battle with Forres Mechanics and Lossiemouth, Elgin's sort-of-rivals are Peterhead, even if the Blue Toon is miles away. Not that anyone in the Central Belt realises that. And why should they, eh?

AREN'T WE BRILLIANT?: Elgin City are fourteen-times winners of the Highland League. Some folk would argue that the Bianconeri of the North should be put back in the Highland League. Or put down. Elgin City reached the Scottish Cup quarter-finals in 1968. See! Evidence, if evidence was required, that Elgin City are brilliant.

MISSION LOGISTICS

ALIGHT AT: Elgin train station. Which you can get to via Aberdeen or Inverness. Inverness is closer. But not if you live in Aberdeen. Chances are that if you are coming to Elgin you have embarked on a lengthy round trip. But, like Andie MacDowell almost argues in her L'Oréal adverts, it's worth it. From the train station in Elgin it is a wee walk to Borough Briggs, but a pleasant one taking you past the High Street, where you might want to pop into Cadora for a bag of chips.

A Pint At: Just off the High Street is the Thunderton. And near that is the White Horse which is more of a back-to-basics joint. It would be remiss of me not to mention the social club within Borough Briggs itself. The Family Sutherland and Associates receive a warm welcome and I cannot speak highly enough of the hospitality we are shown. Instead of being shown the door as we usually are when we congregate for a drink.

MISSION DEBRIEFING

Field of Dreams: Borough Briggs. A really good Scottish name that. They used to have a Second World War machine-gun pillbox behind the goals but it is not there anymore. I think the Germans took it away. On a sunny day at Borough Briggs - Moray being blessed with a microclimate and all - you can relax on the grassy bank. Lie back and think of Elgin if you like. The main stand is painted brilliant white and is impeccably neat. A lot of the home fans are quite happy to stand and watch on the far side. Borough Briggs is not exactly the Bernabeu and it is not even the Stadio delle Alpi. But it is full of character and characters. Okay, so it is not full, but you know what I mean.

Super Pies Me: I would dearly like to declare the Elgin pie first past the post in the pie election but I can't. The Elgin pie is decent and that is about it. Maybe if the Elgin pie formed a coalition with other pies they could form a majority and be elected First Pie.

ELGIN CITY GOALSCORERS: Johnston 19, Campbell 23, Mackay 43, Johnston 70, 90.

ELGIN CITY: Renton, Kaczan (Bazie 65), Dempsie, Easton, Dickson, Hind, Campbell, Moffatt (Docherty 83), Johnston, Gardiner (Charlesworth 76), Mackay.

EAST STIRLINGSHIRE: Tiropoulous, Wild, Learmonth, Oates (Livingstone 74), Thywissen, Joe Boyle, McKenzie, Stewart, Ward, Ure, Adam.

HEAD COUNT: 427.

Report Card: Would you believe it? The BBC are here. All the way up from London with their cameras to cover Elgin who will feature on *Football Focus* on *Grandstand* next week (before they pull the plug on *Grandstand*). The only reason that the BBC is here is that they have got wind of Elgin City's seriously bad losing streak - which is in danger of becoming the worst losing streak in British football history. Elgin's current crime record reads Played ten Lost ten. The most terrible results sequence on these isles for seventy-five years. Since Manchester United - of all teams - suffered twelve straight defeats. Elgin are mutating into a freak show, a laughing stock, and there seems to be no light at the end of an endless tunnel. The *Football Focus* reporter pokes her microphone in the face of an Elgin fan and tells him that something impresses her about Elgin City. She thinks it might be the 'resilience' of the Elgin City fans. Is she taking the piss? There is a sort of morbid fascination with today's fixture with East Stirlingshire. If ever a match falls into the must-bloody-win category then it is this one. For Elgin. The Elgin manager, Brian Irvine, has his own column in the local newspaper, the excellent *Northern Scot*. The column is called *Brian's Blog*. But it is not really a blog. Whatever it is it starts very promisingly. 'The football nightmare continues ...' You get the gist. Elgin are in a right state. The Family Sutherland take their seats in the main stand. With this laudable effort I would say that we have doubled the attendance figure with our presence. We watch on ... and wait ... to see ... whit a game! Never in the field of football conflict ... never in a million years would I have thought .... after ten consecutive losses, an effervescent Elgin City engineer their first win of the season to leave a disbelieving bunch of Elgin City fans elated over a comprehensive demolition of East

Stirlingshire. Maybe the presence of the TV cameras shoves rockets up the Elgin City players' backsides, but, in the space of ninety wondrous minutes, Elgin turn from being the most pathetic team in Scotland to being the best team in Scotland. The Juventus of the North's star is rising. Goal Number One. A Martin Johnston header. Goal Number Two. Craig Campbell clatters the ball into the East Stirlingshire net, squeezing it just inside the post. Goal Number Three. Steven Mackay snacks on a strike of his own. Goal Number Four. Johnston loiters at the back post with intent to jump on his second of an increasingly fruitful afternoon. Goal Number Five. Magic Johnston devours his hat-trick shortly before the final whistle sounds and the sound which greets the whistle is one of jubilation. My dad stands up and cheers and ends up the following week on *Football Focus*.

Going For Gold: Borough Briggs blows its lid at every one of those goals that land in the East Stirlingshire net. No one could have predicted this. Sure, East Stirlingshire can be bad most of the time, but Elgin are normally not much better. And, sometimes, they are worse. A few weeks back, East Stirlingshire were the 5-0 heroes against Stenhousemuir. Now, they are the 5-0 fall guys, and Elgin are the heroes. The Third Division is the topsy-turvy division. Watching this with my family makes it an even better occasion. One of my best days ground-hunting yet, I am gratuitously rewarding this game ten gold stars. I am not even sure if it is a gratuitous act. But I am grateful for today. I really am.

Fanfare: There is not much singing from the Elgin City fans. Despite the unexpected turn of events and the sudden upturn in their fortunes. At least my auntie Ishbel doesn't let the side down. She's making a real effort, shouting 'C'mon City!' at regular intervals. No more than a handful of East Stirlingshire fans have been able to take the long road north but one Shire patter merchant harangues the Elgin goalkeeper for a lengthy period (see the 'In The Line Of Fire' section of this book for further details).

Music To My Ears: Bryan Ferry's 'Let's Stick Together'. Through thick and thin.

The Return Journey: I will admit to being terribly drunk once on a train while hunting grounds and it is the train journey from Elgin back to Glasgow. I am already eight sheets to the wind when the train pulls out of Elgin station. This is because after I watch Elgin spank East Stirlingshire, my pre-train pint stop is Elgin's Royal Hotel, across from the station, where I bump into a bunch of holidaying Norwegians, who have been spending the day fishing on the Spey. They relate their fish tales and I regale them with an epic account of Elgin City's incredible performance. The Vikings nod in admiration. I think they wish they hadn't gone fishing. But I could be wrong there. We dram together and after draining the last from our glasses, I say cheerio and stagger hiccupping over the street to catch my train ...

... somewhere between Elgin and Glasgow (round about Montrose, I reckon, but I am too wrecked to be certain of that) I strike up an automatic beer-fuelled friendship with a like-minded lager monster. 'Heeeeyyyyy!' growls this big bear of a bloke, raising his can of lager as a form of greeting. 'Heeeeyyyyy!' I shout back, raising a can of lager I can call my own, and offering an incomprehensible toast to our off-the-rails rail adventure. We are both quite smashed. I reprise my far-fetched account of Elgin City's virtuoso display. 'Heeeyyyyy!' roars my new drinking partner who shall remain nameless, because I never learn his name. He asks if I have any Tunes but he does not seem blocked up (unlike the toilet on this train). But the man means tunes. Music. I search for my music player (I am sitting on it) and we take an earphone each. Both leaning across the beer-splashed sticky table, so that we both can listen, while the train thunders through Perthshire or wherever, we loudly ruin 'Love Will Tear Us Apart' together for the benefit of our fellow passengers, or at least those who have not already fled the carriage terrified and seeking sanctuary. The carriage karaoke continues all the way to Glasgow Queen Street where we both spill onto the platform, hug each other, slur our goodbyes and stumble off separately into the night.

EPISODE

MISSION POSSIBLE 18

OBJECTIVE:
To go to New
Douglas Park and
watch Hamilton
Academical.

SCENARIO: Hamilton are playing Clyde in the Scottish First Division.

DATE: Tuesday, October 17, 2006. Another weekday night in the First Division and again I have my wife's blessing. Clare doesn't seem to mind. As long as I don't come home and talk to her about the game. She can't bear that.

LOCATION, LOCATION, LOCATION: Lanarkshire. South Lanarkshire to be less vague.

CULTURAL NOTES: *Scotland The Braw* is very dismissive of Hamilton. My opinionated guide book says that Hamilton 'has little to offer the visitor'. Well what sort of place is going to give you stuff for free? Just because you turned up? I don't know about horticulture but if you are into horsey culture then Hamilton Park Racecourse is merely a few furlongs from New Douglas Park. So you can have a flutter on the gee-gees, after you have lost all your money on the football.

HAMILTON ACADEMICAL PROFILE

KICKED OFF: 1874. Iceland is granted a constitution and limited home rule.

TRUE COLOURS: Red and white horizontal bands.

BADGE OF HONOUR: Hamilton Academical's badge is based on the Hamilton coat of arms. Looks like three stars, or three flowers, on some kind of shield. Big deal.

NAME CALLING: The Accies. Sounds better than the Hammies. The Hamilton mascot is called Hammy and he's a hamster, naturally.

MORTAL ENEMY: Make that enemies. Motherwell and Airdrie.

AREN'T WE BRILLIANT?: In January 1987, Hamilton created shockwaves when they knocked Rangers out of the Scottish Cup in a third round tie at Ibrox. Adrian Sprott made a name for himself with the only goal of the game and he also made Graeme Souness' moustache bristle. Hamilton have been runners-up in the Scottish Cup on two occasions.

MISSION LOGISTICS

ALIGHT AT: Hamilton West station. Do not bother with Hamilton Central because it is far too far from the ground. You can walk down a lane to New Douglas Park or you can opt to take the slightly longer but less secluded route through a retail park. I go for the latter because it is fairly dark and I am a scaredy-custard, and I do not really know this part of the world too well.

A Pint At: They are poised to pour you a cheap pint at New Douglas Park and my poison today is Tartan Special. I am keeping it real. The Hamilton social club is within the main stand and it is snug and welcoming. There is a dance floor with a glitter ball hanging over it but I am not tempted to do my Moonwalk. Not tonight. I am not wearing white socks and you look daft doing the Moonwalk in black socks. It is also hard to Moonwalk with a pint of Tartan Special in your hand. You end up spilling most of it.

MISSION DEBRIEFING

Field of Dreams: After several seasons as the Littlest Hobo in Scottish football, Hamilton finally moved into their new pad of New Douglas Park in 2001. This is a modern football cathedral although calling it a cathedral is perhaps laying it on a bit thick. You've got the main stand and the north stand - which is also called the Spice of Life stand - and apart from that … there is nothing. It is incomplete. Or at least it looks incomplete. You are at the mercy of the wintry conditions, should there be wintry conditions, and the ground is surrounded by high walls, making it feel prison-like. And beyond those prison walls are supermarkets. There is the orange glow of Sainsbury's and an illuminated giant yellow M which looks like the bat sign except it is a giant M instead of a giant bat. The M is for Morrisons and I have a vivid imagination. Accies' pitch is synthetic which means it's not real and it glistens in the rain. I notice the trackside advert for FieldTurf, but what is it they are suggesting you do? FieldTurf your living room? The ad that really catches my eye is the one on the halfway line. The one that reads 'Tattoo's by Lorraine'. In giant gothic black type on a pink background. It is the apostrophe that does it. Tattoo's by Lorraine. Has she only the one tattoo? And what is it? I'll bet it is 'I Love Accies'.

Super Pies Me: The Hamilton pie is not a success. A wobbly mound of meat encased in unpalatable pastry. Pie sceptics might say that describes any pie. But no. This pie falls short of the required standard.

GAME ON: Hamilton Academical 3-1 Clyde

HAMILTON GOALSCORERS: Offiong 3, 29, Gilhaney 35.

CLYDE GOALSCORERS: Masterton 33.

HAMILTON ACADEMICAL: Jellema, Parratt, Elebert, Easton, McLaughlin (Wilson 41), Stevenson, McArthur, Neil, Winters, Offiong (Wake 88), Gilhaney (McLeod 42).

CLYDE: Cherrie, McGregor, Higgins, Harris (O'Donnell 72), Malone, Bryson, Masterton, McCann (McHale 46), McGowan, Ferguson (Arbuckle 57), Imrie.

HEAD COUNT: 1,253.

Report Card: Tonight's match has been previewed in the paper. Clyde's Neil McGregor is promising his team-mate Stephen O'Donnell 'another smacker' if he scores against Hamilton Accies. Basically, the Clyde pair 'puckered up' after O'Donnell hit the net against Airdrie United the previous Saturday. The only reason the world is aware of this is that the kiss was caught on camera and printed in the papers. 'The boys have been giving us pelters for it,' says McGregor who is keen to stress that he is as straight as a dye and that he has the girlfriend to prove it. But because of the smooch with his team-mate, his girlfriend has been 'taking pelters' too. Poor girl. Everybody is either giving or taking pelters. What are pelters? Some form of currency? The kiss-and-tell footie tale is in the back of my mind as Hamilton and Clyde take to the field and I see O'Donnell is on the Clyde bench. This wouldn't be because of the repeat kiss threat would it? Has O'Donnell actually benched himself because of the heat from the girlfriend? The sub-plot here is an intriguing one. What if O'Donnell is destined to come off the bench and score? What then? Will McGregor carry out his promise and kiss him? Again? Hamilton's Richard Offiong finds the target early Doors (say, Light My Fire) and then bags a second with a looping header. Steven Masterton dwindles the deficit with his jaw-dropping free kick flying into the top corner. But Mark Gilhaney's pile-driver piles more misery on Clyde and restores Hamilton's two goal advantage. O'Donnell is a late substitute for Clyde and his first act is to blast a shot way over the Hamilton crossbar. Did he do that on purpose? Because if he scores, his team-mate will kiss him, and the pelters will be given and taken all over again. In the meantime, McGregor seems to have switched from central defence to midfield. Is he trying to assist for a kiss? I decide to banish all this stuff from my head. I am reading far too much into this. I should not have skim-read that newspaper. Is there a hat-trick in the offing for Offiong? That's a better question. No. This time he fresh airs. Soon after that, Offiong is off. But he has put in a tremendous shift and he has been suitably rewarded with his two goals.

Going For Gold: The football is much better than the pie. And better than some Scottish Premier League games I have seen. At least the first-half is. I'll give this one seven gold stars.

Fanfare: 'Oh Ricky, Ricky, Ricky, Ricky, Ricky, Ricky Offiong.' There are slim pickings for songs at New Douglas Park tonight. At one point the Hamilton fans in the main stand, and the Clyde fans in the Spice of Life stand, begin to trade insults and it starts to hot up a bit. 'Scum!' 'Gypsies!' 'Scum!' 'Gypsies!' They used to share this ground. Then one of the Hamilton fans calls the Clyde supporters 'sheepshaggers'. That is a new one on me. I know that Aberdeen and even other teams from the north and the rural regions get called sheepshaggers. But Clyde? They play in Cumbernauld!

Music To My Ears: Tom Jones. Cover version after cover version after cover version. At least we are not subjected to his mistreatment of Prince's perfect 'Kiss'.

MISSION POSSIBLE 19

EPISODE

OBJECTIVE:
To go to Balmoor Stadium and watch Peterhead.

SCENARIO: Peterhead are playing Alloa Athletic in the Scottish Second Division.

DATE: Saturday, October 21, 2006.

LOCATION, LOCATION, LOCATION: The north-east fishing port of Peterhead. Where my dad used to fish from.

CULTURAL NOTES: Peterhead is 'best avoided' says my increasingly derisive *Scotland The Braw*. But why spurn the delights of the Maritime Heritage Museum? Have a look at the harbour, the high-security prison and power station. There is loads to keep you occupied.

PETERHEAD PROFILE

KICKED OFF: 1891. The building of the Trans-Siberian railway begins. From Peterhead to Vladivostok.

TRUE COLOURS: Blue and white.

BADGE OF HONOUR: A fish heads a football into the net. Or the net catches both the fish and the football. I'm really not sure.

NAME CALLING: The Blue Toon is the nickname and it refers to Peterhead and its football club. Rather than a reflection on the average temperature in Peterhead, it is supposed to have something to do with fishermen wearing blue stockings but that doesn't sound right to me. My dad was a fisherman and I never saw him wearing blue stockings. At least not in public.

MORTAL ENEMY: Fraserburgh. Except that the Blue Toon have left the Broch behind in the Highland League. You could make a case for enmity towards Elgin City, but it is not the strongest of cases, as Elgin isn't that close, but it will have to do.

AREN'T WE BRILLIANT?: Peterhead gained admission to the Scottish Football League in 2000 and after five campaigns in the Third Division won promotion to the Second Division in the summer of 2005. Expanding the timeline, Peterhead, conceivably, could be crowned champions of Scotland in 2015. But don't all rush out and place bets on that.

MISSION LOGISTIC

ALIGHT AT: It is not much use taking the train to Peterhead. The nearest station is thirty-two miles away. In Aberdeen. This makes Balmoor the furthest football ground from a train station in Britain and this is of no great comfort to me, right now, what with me being so heavily reliant on the rail service. Almost totally reliant on it actually. I am going to have to bite the bullet and board a bus. A Magical Mystery Bus Tour from Aberdeen to Peterhead. I once saw a band called Magic Bus. They had women in cages. At the very least, I have company. Having taken the early morning train from Glasgow to Aberdeen, I meet Brian at Aberdeen bus station. He has agreed to come with me to the game. I already know Brian. I didn't just meet a stranger at Aberdeen bus station and ask them if they wanted to come to the Blue Toon with me. That would be nuts. I am not that desperate for some companionship in my ground-hunting. Brian and I are on the Magic Bus now to Peterhead. Via Cruden Bay. Brian points out points of local interest. Such as Slains Castle which helped inspire Bram Stoker to write Dracula. I would like to get off the Magic Bus and have a closer look at the castle but we are bound for Balmoor I'm afraid. You know, *Dracula* would have been a very different book had Bram Stoker gone to Balmoor instead of Slains Castle. Five miles from Peterhead, the Magic Bus breaks down. Evidently it is not a Magic Bus. We kick our heels by the roadside, until another bus comes along and picks us up and transports us to Peterhead, past the golf ball power station, and the gates of the prison. Not through the gates of the prison, but past them. From the main bus stop in the Blue Toon (there is no bus station as such), we are left with a twenty-minute walk to Balmoor. Brian and I can hardly contain our excitement. We are very fortunate, and we have the hour-long bus journey back to Aberdeen to look forward to, but only after absorbing a Scottish Second Division football match. I hope it's absorbing. It better be good. After the lengths we've gone to in getting here.

A Pint At: Peterhead FC have a social club that they can be proud of. It is inside the main stand at Balmoor and it is spacious and clean with super-efficient service. There are half-a-dozen bar staff and they all seem to want to serve Brian and me and to pour us our well-deserved pints of lager. After the game, on our way back to get the bus, we nip into the Station Bar, which we also quite like. I dig the patterned carpet.

MISSION DEBRIEFING

Field of Dreams: Standing in front of the turnstiles at Balmoor is a sailor boy. They send them to sea at a young age in Peterhead. It turns out that he is not a sailor boy, but a sea cadet, and he is fundraising. Brian and I make our cash contribution. Balmoor is a smart stadium with two similar stands facing each other and nothing behind either of the goals apart from some bushes at one end. Peterhead's previous ground, Recreation Park, was bought by a supermarket chain. The move to a more modern Balmoor occurred in 1997. You can tell you are in Peterhead judging by the maritime look sported by some of the crowd. I clock Captain Birdseye. Or it might be Captain Ahab. He has given up chasing the white whale. He wants to hunt grounds like myself and has come to watch Peterhead chase promotion. Maybe I shouldn't be hunting grounds. Maybe I should be harpooning them. I have to mention the sign for the toilets. Brian wants me to. It is a sign on a grass hill pointing to another patch of grass. TOILETS. Maybe they do it al fresco in the Blue Toon. They are a hardy bunch of souls in Peterhead.

Super Pies Me: The Peterhead pie is a peculiar pie on initial discovery. I am surprised to find, packed within the light pastry, the kind of mince your granny used to make. Lots of gravy. Mm. After one bite, I decide that I really like it, though it is a different kind of pie to any I've tasted before. I wolf it doon in the Blue Toon. Brian has scoffed his already. He has gravy dribbling down his chin. You can't take him anywhere. Honestly.

GAME ON: Peterhead 1-2 Alloa Athletic

PETERHEAD GOALSCORER: Tully 60.

ALLOA ATHLETIC GOALSCORER: Brown 75, Payo 80.

PETERHEAD: Mathers, McInally, Camara, Tully, Perry, Gibson (Wood 51), Sharp, Buchan, Gilfillan, MacKay (Bavidge 51), Linn (Youngson 71).

ALLOA ATHLETIC: Creer, McKeown, Ovenstone, Malcolm, Forest, Grant, Hamilton (Payo 62), McClune, Brown (Clark 89), McAnespie (Comrie 90), Sloan.

HEAD COUNT: 491.

Report Card: After a rotten first forty-five minutes which feels like 450 minutes it is goalless at half-time. Brian and I are behind the goals with an elderly bunch of Peterhead fans. The game is poor but the banter is supreme. Peterhead are set to be shooting in our direction in the second-half. 'We'll just bide here for the avalanche,' says one wit-dry Peterhead fan. As the match wears on, and we feel worn out watching it, the Blue Toon look ever less likely to win. And a home substitution is made. 'It's nae substitutes they need. It's prostitutes,' says the same Peterhead sage. I wonder what he means. Is this to do with scoring? Eventually the comments become even more surreal. As the low standard of the match plummets further, the Peterhead joker turns to his pals and announces 'I watched Magic Roundabout last week and it was far better than this.' We have now entered a new realm of absurdity and I cannot quite get my head round it. Brian, on the other hand, is killing himself laughing. The home side seem to have lost all interest in kicking the ball towards the Alloa penalty box. Ball after ball gets launched out of sight. Ball number one. Booted over the roof of the main stand. Ball number two. Goes the way of the first ball. Ball number three. Fired in the direction of the harbour. Ball number four. Straight into the bushes. 'They'll need a lot a bas the day by the looks o it,' sighs our match random commentator. Ball number five. 'It's nae oot' …. [ball clears the wall] … 'it's oot noo.' Surely it would be easier putting the ball in the Alloa net but the Blue Toon just do not seem at all interested in anything as purposeful as that. I'm thinking the players have got a sweepie going. Predict how many balls exactly they can sweep out of the ground before the ninety minutes are up. Then, suddenly, after an inconsequential hour of football manure, Peterhead dare to push ahead through Craig Tully's header. Naturally, a headed response from Graeme Brown hauls Alloa level. You wait for a goal and then three come along because Alloa substitute Javier Payo makes Peterhead goalkeeper Paul Mathers pay for a poor goal-kick by circling him three times and shooting into the empty net, which is now no longer empty, because, of course, there is a ball in it. Alloa take their tardy but merited victory at Balmoor. The Peterhead fans are appalled by their team's late collapse and one guy takes off his bunnet and throws it. Before picking it up again.

Going For Gold: The Blue Toon thought they had at least a point in the bag but they get stung by the Wasps. For the sake of the eventful finale, I can stretch to five gold stars for this one.

Fanfare: They don't sing much or shout much at Peterhead games. The fans tend to keep it mostly to themselves but, if you keep your ears peeled, rather than your eyes pricked, you likely will hear some odd gems of wisdom and nonsense. Brian and I are fortunate enough to get in tow with some fine exponents of sarcasm and surrealism. In terms of making an actual noise, there is one man who has been keeping a rattle inside his coat and he pulls it out and surprises us all by giving it a whirl when Peterhead score. But when Alloa score their second the only rattle sounding for Peterhead is the death rattle.

Mike Check: There is a problem with the man on the mike at Balmoor. He is filling up half-time with his act but we cannot make out a word of what Mr MC is saying. Maybe he is mumbling. Maybe the volume is not high enough. Maybe those speakers are crap. But his words are unintelligible. And it is not the Blue Toon dialect that is causing all the confusion, because the natives are none the wiser either. 'Is that fir Polish fowk or fir us?' demands one perturbed Peterhead fan. 'Kiz a canna mak oot a word o' it. He'd be as weel stickin' thone microphone up his erse, kiz that's fit he's talkin' oot o.'

Fish Tale: Before Brian and I board our bus back to Aberdeen, we join the early evening queue at Zanre's fish and chips shop. This is a prize-winning fish and chips shop and it is worth the wait (as long as you don't miss that last bus). Zanre's once featured on *Blue Peter*. There is a plaque on the wall highlighting *Blue Peter's* visit to the Blue Toon and the fish and chips shop. 'Go on,' says Brian, giving me a nudge while we wait for our fish suppers. 'Ask them for a *Blue Peter* badge.' I glare at him. 'I don't think it works like that, Brian.'

Betting Scandal: For an account of Brian, the spawny git, scooping the half-time draw at Peterhead, see the 'All Bets Are Off' section.

MISSION POSSIBLE 20

OBJECTIVE:
To go to Cappielow and watch Morton.

SCENARIO: Morton are playing Peterhead (eh?) in the Scottish Second Division. The Blue Toon two games running. It's not possible.

DATE: Saturday, November 4, 2006. The day before Guy Fawkes. Perhaps there will be some fireworks.

LOCATION, LOCATION, LOCATION: The town of Greenock in Renfrewshire.

CULTURAL NOTES: Greenock had the first dock on the Clyde. You can take a boat cruise from Greenock to the likes of Dunoon, Largs, Rothesay, Millport and Barbados.

GREENOCK MORTON PROFILE

KICKED OFF: 1874. The year Winston Churchill was born.

TRUE COLOURS: Royal blue and white. Vertical bands.

BADGE OF HONOUR: Another ship. Clyde have one too. This one seems to be navigating choppy seas.

NAME CALLING: The Ton. Sounds heavy.

MORTAL ENEMY: The Ton's least favourite Buddies. St Mirren. The people of Greenock puke on the Paisley Pattern. They do not take kindly to that panda either. If it choked on its bamboo breakfast, the Morton fans wouldn't mind one bit.

AREN'T WE BRILLIANT?: Greenock Morton (to give them their full title) have been involved in more promotions and relegations than any other club in Scotland. This is a fact and this means that there is rarely a dull moment at Cappielow. Well in theory, anyway. The Ton won the Scottish Cup in 1922, beating Rangers 1-0.

MISSION LOGISTICS

ALIGHT AT: Cartsdyke is the closest train station to Cappielow. You will see Cappielow to the right just before the train draws into the station. Cartsdyke is on the Glasgow Central to Gourock line but not all trains make a stop at Cartsdyke so do check before you board the train. It is about a forty-minute rail journey followed by a ten-minute walk to the ground.

A Pint At: On the street corner, as you turn up towards the gates of Cappielow, is the Norseman pub, which is above a chip shop. Interestingly, the pub sells Pot Noodles. Well, I find it interesting. From the windows of the Norseman you can see the shipyard cranes. The pub has a good selection of malt whiskies and there is the ubiquitous Carling lager on tap.

MISSION DEBRIEFING

Field of Dreams: I have heard people calling Cappielow 'Crappielow' but maybe that is just the way St Mirren fans pronounce it. Cappielow used to be a real dump and while it is not the finest stadium in Scotland it does not look as bad as it once did. The Cowshed especially has been improved. It is almost unrecognisable from its former guise when it really did look like a Cowshed. It is mostly terracing but with seating at the front and it can feel really crowded, which makes for a great atmosphere. Morton draw on a strong support wherever they are in the Scottish divisions. The Wee Dublin End of the ground is unused while the Sinclair Street End where you come in (with the gigantic Caledonian MacBrayne billboard - 'We're supporting a ferry good team') is selected by a few Morton fans to stand on and there are lots of children roaming about. One of them slips on a step and lands flat on his back. Dunt. Ouch. There is a lot of litter strewn around Cappielow, paper cups, chip papers etc. It is not one of the cleanest grounds that I have encountered, but having said that they have hand-wash in the toilets at the back of the Cowshed which is very posh.

Super Pies Me: I have a confession to make. I don't have a Morton pie. I am not feeling up to the task today. I had been greedy and polished off some left-over stew for lunch and now my stomach can't stomach the Morton pie. Really. I couldn't even face one wafer-thin after-dinner mint. I would explode. So instead I ask a Morton fan eating a pie what he thinks of his pie. He looks at me like I'm simple but he sees that I'm not going to go away and he volunteers that his pie is 'okay' before getting back to the job in hand. There you go. The Morton pie. It's okay.

GAME ON: Morton 4-2 Peterhead

MORTON GOALSCORERS: McGowen 43, Weatherson 61, McLaughlin 88, Finlayson 90.

PETERHEAD GOALSCORERS: Bavidge 5, Tully 27.

MORTON: McGurn, Weatherson, Macgregor, Harding, Greacen, McLaughlin, Millar, Stevenson (Walker 89), Lilley (Templeman 60), McGowen (Finlayson 60), McAlistair.

PETERHEAD: Kelly, McInally, Cameron, Tully, Perry, Gibson (Youngson 82), Sharp (Linn 62), Buchan, Bavidge, Wood (McKay 67), Gilfillan.

HEAD COUNT: 4,418.

Report Card: Whit a game! Morton storm back from two goals down to draw level and then, to top it all, they net twice more in the final two minutes to win a fair see-saw of a game. I suppose it is a game of two halves but every game of football is a game of two halves. Martin Bavidge bashes in an early counter for the Blue Toon and Craig Tully's header furthers the guests' lead. That's how it stays at the break and Morton appear to be in serious trouble. But somehow they recover. With a vengeance. Interventions by Paul McGowan and Peter Weatherson make it 2-2, and Peterhead are rocking on their feet, and with a couple of minutes remaining, Scott McLaughlin's magnificent volley fires Morton in front for the first time. The Cowshed erupts. Kevin Finlayson finishes off dumb-struck Peterhead with his header. 'Easy, easy' chant the Morton fans. But it has been anything but. The home heroes wave to the Cowshed. Drams are ordered in the Norseman. It is the day for it. Because of the weather partly, but mostly for that dramatic winning outcome.

Going For Gold: An amazing comeback from Morton and an incredible collapse from Peterhead. It is one of those games where, if you are daft enough to leave before the final whistle, you have missed everything that matters. One of the most engrossing games that I have witnessed so far. Easily nine gold stars. Yet again a lower league game offers better value for money than a fixture in the top division. I am not being all romantic and clichéd about it and siding with the wee teams but, in my experiences so far, the lesser lights are being more entertaining, even if their strength and skill are inferior.

Music To My Ears: 'Live is life, na-na, na-na-na.' Bloody Hell, it's Opus! Live Is Life. What does it mean? What it means is the Morton cheerleaders performing to Live Is Life, carefully building their pyramid in front of their proud mums in the main stand. Sensibly the smallest cheerleader is placed on top of the pyramid. The crowd applauds a fantastic feat. Later, for the benefit of the Cowshed, the Cappielow cheerleaders perform their foot-stomping, pom-pom-pomping interpretation of Kenny Loggins' 'Footloose' in the heavy Greenock rain. A very Scottish football sight to behold. Pale young girls dancing in the rain for podgy blokes eating pies.

EPISODE **21**

MISSION POSSIBLE

OBJECTIVE:
To go to Easter Road
and watch Hibernian.

SCENARIO: Hibs are playing Hearts in the CIS Cup quarter-final. A nice tame affair then.

DATE: Wednesday, November 8, 2006.

LOCATION, LOCATION, LOCATION: Where the sun shines. Leith. Which, for hundreds of years, was distinct from Edinburgh. It's still different.

CULTURAL NOTES: Down in the Port of Leith you can step aboard the Royal Yacht Brittania at Ocean Terminal where you can also indulge in some retail therapy. I'm not sure though that shopping qualifies as culture. In fact it doesn't.

HIBERNIAN PROFILE

KICKED OFF: 1875. Hans Christian Andersen's life comes to a fairytale end.

TRUE COLOURS: Green and white.

BADGE OF HONOUR: A harp indicates the club's Irish roots. *Hibernia* is the Roman name for Ireland. A ship signifies the Port of Leith. A castle acknowledges Edinburgh. While a football shows that Hibs can play football.

NAME CALLING: The Hibees. Pronounced Hi-bees. Not how my pal Paolo calls them. The Hibes (rhyming with vibes), but he's Italian so he doesn't know any better.

MORTAL ENEMY: The big city rival of the Hibees are the Jambos. Now have you got that?

AREN'T WE BRILLIANT?: Hibs were actually the first-ever British club to enter the European Cup. In 1955. They have been Scottish Champions four times (thrice in a five-year period between 1947 and 1952 when the Famous Five were in their pomp) and they have also won both the Scottish Cup and the League Cup.

MISSION LOGISTICS

ALIGHT AT: Edinburgh Waverley. Your main walking route might include Princes Street, London Road and Easter Road. The walk could take you twenty minutes. If you walk briskly.

A Pint At: There are plenty of pubs in the vicinity of Easter Road. The Albion bar is very close to the ground while The Four In Hand has The Proclaimers on the jukebox and The Proclaimers on the wall and a pint's-worth of lager on my lap because the Hibs fan next to me has knocked my glass into my lap with his elbow. I am soaked through. Wonderful. I tell him it doesn't matter but I still expect him to at least offer me a fresh pint. But he doesn't. Cheers mate. I pop my head in the door of another local pub which I expect to be full of Hibs fans except that it is heaving with Hearts fans singing 'all Hibees are gay'.

MISSION DEBRIEFING

Field of Dreams: Easter Road has seen plenty improvement in recent years and is one of the best stadiums in the country. Not that I am saying that it is better than Tynecastle or anything. They are both equal in my eyes. The East Stand is the one remaining old stand. It is seated now but not that the Hibs fans know it. They prefer to stand on their seats. Or more accurately, they prefer to stand on the seat of the person in front of them. And they won't stand for any nonsense - like someone like me trying to sit down in their own seat. I have never been to Easter Road before and I am unfamiliar with these intricacies of the seating, or rather standing, arrangements in the East Stand. When I arrive at my numbered seat there is a Hibs fan standing on it. So I say to him 'excuse me, you're standing on my seat.' He ignores me and I try again. 'Eh, excuse me, but you seem to be standing on my seat.' He looks down on me. He looks like a cross between Begbie from Trainspotting and one of the Chuckle Brothers. He looks cross and he is not chuckling. 'If you want a fucking seat go and fucking sit somewhere else.' Gulp. Okay. He casts me a more withering glance and expands on his initial advice. 'You fucking stand on the seat in fucking front of you.' He says this as if I am the most stupid person on the planet and, in his angry eyes, I am the most stupid person on the planet. This standing-on-the-seat-in-front-of-you business is illogical behaviour. Surely there is a far better solution, such as standing on your own seat, for instance. Or even sitting in it. But taking everything into consideration, I consider it to be wise not to pursue this line of conversation with the man on my seat.

So I just do what he does. I stand on the seat in front of me. And the bloke in front of me does not seem to care, as he is standing on the seat in front of him. We are all happy! Gradually I get into the swing of things. The East Stand at Easter Road. It is different. I had been told that you could see Arthur's Seat from Easter Road but I can't see it. Possibly because Arthur's arse is in the way.

Super Pies Me: The problem with the Hibs pie is not one of quality but the fact that it is so dark at the back of the East Stand - where the pie stall is - that I cannot see what I am dealing with. I start eating but I can't see my hands and I can't see the pie. I should have brought a torch.

GAME ON: Hibernian 1-0 Hearts

HIBS GOALSCORER: Jones 32.

HIBERNIAN: Malkowski, Whittaker, Martis, Jones, Murphy, Brown, Stewart (Beuzelin 14), Thomson, Zemmama (Benjelloun 90), Sproule (Fletcher 73), Killen.

HEARTS: Gordon, Goncalves, Berra, Pressley, Tall, Neilson (Barasa 55), Mikoliunas (Mole 66), Aguiar, Hartley, Zaliukas (Makela 83), Velicka.

HEAD COUNT: 15,825.

Report Card: Hibs win a hot Edinburgh derby and hop over Hearts and into the CIS Cup semi-finals. Hibs defender, Rob Jones, scores the only goal of the game, knocking the ball into the Hearts net from a corner kick in the first-half. The East Stand ignites - and turns into a moshpit. I feel like I'm at a Mudhoney concert. Leaping supporters spill several rows forward because of this peculiar standing-on-seats arrangement. I get half a knuckle in the face but I grin and bear it. I have to. This is absolute madness. Sheepdog whistles and all. (Who'd bring a sheepdog to a football match?) There is much jumping, kissing, shouting, screaming, falling and bedlam. Eventually, after about an hour of this, the scene calms down again. Hibs remain largely in control throughout this Edinburgh derby match and they carve out some further good chances late on. But the solitary strike suffices and at the final whistle I think 'here we go again' and sure enough I have to hang on for dear life; but it is useless when some 20-stone geezer is toppling on top of you. I am all bumps and bruises but when it is all over I start thinking 'that was brilliant'. As well as watching the game you have to watch yourself at Easter Road. Or you might get flattened. There is no denying the rush of adrenalin though. It is basically the sense of being shit-scared.

Going For Gold: The game itself is a bit of a let-down. Hibs are better than Hearts but it is not a football classic. I take most from the atmosphere and from the barmy nature of the East Stand. The match itself can have six gold stars.

Fanfare: 'We are Hibernian FC, we hate jam tarts and we hate Dundee.' Presumably, they mean Dundee cake, if they hate jam tarts. 'Hi-bees … Hi-bees … Hi-bees' is the constant cry and there is of course the obligatory interval airing of 'Sunshine on Leith' with scarf-waving compulsory, except that I don't have a scarf. It is an emotive moment, I won't deny it. 'Steven Pressley wank wank wank' is directed at, well, Steven Pressley, while 'in your Gorgie slums' would suggest that Leith is a more salubrious part of Edinburgh. (Why is it these days that 'you find a Big Mac and you think it's a treat'? Whatever happened to finding a fish supper?) 'Hearts, Hearts, glorious Hearts', in the capable hands of the Hibs supporters, becomes 'shite, shite, glorious shite' and when Rob Jones scores he is duly serenaded by the happy Hibs fans who perform Spandau Ballet's 'Gold' – a difficult trick to pull off that – in an adaptation with a re-titling of 'Jones' with the song building to the crescendo of 'he's indestructible, oh, always believing in, Jones'. They repeat this over and over again. Tony Hadley would be pleased. Lastly, I notice the prominent sign in the East Stand that reads 'Chanting which challenges the sexuality, religion or race of individuals or groups is an offence, the police and the club will take action against offenders.' How do you round up the entire East Stand?

21 matches down … 21 to go … Time for that half-time lottery!

And the winning number in this week's 50/50 draw is …

… 12024.

If you, dear reader, are in possession of that winning ticket, then you might want to spend some of your winnings on the perfect present for that special someone in your life. Try …

THE SCOTTISH FOOTBALL GIFT LIST

(Selected items available from all good, and relevant, club shops.)

For the Albion Rovers fan in your life …

The Albion Rovers golf set. Comprising two markers and a pitch repairer. Offering your partner the strongest hint that they could be engaged in something more worthwhile on a Saturday afternoon.

For the Alloa Athletic fan in your life …

The Alloa Athletic teddy bear. Cuddlier than a wasp.

For the Arbroath fan in your life …

Danny's Bearded Army postcards and they are only 20p each. When Celtic legend Danny McGrain was manager of Arbroath, the Arbroath supporters took to wearing false beards in a hirsute tribute to McGrain. Some of them may have gone the full hog and cultivated their own beards. Sadly, there are no beards, real or fake, available in the club shop. Just postcards. But 'wish you were here' from Gayfield sounds good.

For the Ayr United fan in your life …

An Ayr United woolly hat. It is white, white, white and, to be honest, it looks a bit girlish, but then the most important thing is keeping warm, isn't it?

For the Celtic fan in your life ...

A bottle (or case) of BIN 67 Cabernet Sauvignon. Lions Lager available soon. If you are after a non-alcoholic present you could pick up the Celtic mascot Hoopy Hound. I don't believe he has a drink problem. Hoopy is tagged at a bargain price of £14.99. But please remember, a dog's for life, not just for Saturday night and losing him on the way home.

For the Clyde fan in your life ...

There is a broad range of goods on offer at Broadwood. First up, the Clyde jester's hat and I am not joking. You want your partner to look like an arse? Get them one of these. You could also get them a 'Roy Who?' T-shirt, commemorating Clyde's shock defeat of Celtic and Roy somebody-or-other in the Scottish Cup a couple of years ago.

For the Dundee fan in your life ...

Something for you both to share. The Dundee FC headboard. Available with duvet and valance. (The valance is the skirt thing that goes around the bed). Lie back and think of Dundee. Then wake up from your nightmare screaming.

For the Dundee United fan in your life ...

The Dundee United car sticker. 'Wee Terror On Board.' Bless. You could always add a bag of tangerines to make your gift seem more generous and thoughtful and healthy. Can you feed a child tangerines?

For the Dunfermline Athletic fan in your life ...

Dunfermline Athletic black and white face paint. Actually that would do for St Mirren and Ayr United and Gretna and Elgin City and Queen's Park and East Stirlingshire ...

For the East Fife fan in your life ...

An East Fife ruler, with which you can rule the world.

For the East Stirlingshire fan in your life ...

Now this is class. The East Stirlingshire baseball cap. Black and mean looking. Bearing the legend of 'The Shire'. Looks real hip hop. I reckon Ice Cube would wear it. Were he into The Shire at all. Actually, East Stirlingshire should get MTV to Pimp My Ground.

For the Falkirk fan in your life ...

The Falkirk mug. With the slogan 'Falkirk's a braw place to play'. Go on. Have a cuppa.

For the Gretna fan in your life ...

A whole host of possibilities. Rocky the Raydale Rooster (scaled down). Guaranteed to get you up in the morning. A giant foam finger. What are you supposed to do with that?

And a bottle of Living The Dream whisky. Tank that in one go and you will be living the dream.

For the Hearts fan in your life ...

The Hearts dog fleece. In maroon. But be aware that a Hibs fan might report you to the RSPCA.

For the Hibernian fan in your life ...

What will it be? A Proclaimers CD (well I never)? A Frisbee (not the Proclaimers CD)? Or a green bear? A really, really spooky-looking green bear.

For the Kilmarnock fan in your life ...

Well, there is the Kilmarnock beach towel. It comes in blue and white and you will get great use out of it during summer outings on the Ayrshire coast. If you are not fussed about the beach towel, you could turn your attention to a shrunken Nutz the Squirrel.

For the Motherwell fan in your life ...

The Motherwell car set. Tremendously exciting. This package has got absolutely everything. Freshener, window scraper, key-ring. And the keys to a new Mercedes.

For the Partick Thistle fan in your life ...

The Partick Thistle articulated lorry. I am being serious. It is a long toy in a very long box. I do not see what articulated lorries have to do with Partick Thistle. Unless they get a lot of truckers at Firhill these days. I suppose if your fan-base was long-distance lorry drivers then your away support might be reasonably strong. Distance would not be a deterrent for truckers. A convoy of Jags fans. Honk-honk.

For the Queen of the South fan in your life ...

The best gift of them all. To be worn with pride and to raise a smile from a passer-by. If they happen to notice. The Queen of the South T-shirt. A sharp piece of apparel which is not exactly suited to the Scottish climate but does borrow brilliantly from *Trainspotting*. 'Choose Queen of the South, choose to be the only team in the Bible, choose big Jim Patterson, choose big Jim Thomson, choose Ted McMinn, choose Basher Houliston, choose Dougie the Doonhamer, choose to be part-time and still beating you, choose to have a wheelbarrow, choose to travel hundreds of miles every other week ...' I believe every team in Scotland should set about producing their own version of this clothing classic.

For the Rangers fan in your life ...

Or for the Rangers animal in your life, the Rangers dog bowl. Or the Rangers cat bowl, if you happen to be more of a cat person. I'm more of a dog person personally. Wire Fox Terriers. They're great.

For the Ross County fan in your life ...

A scarf, but not just any old scarf. The Staggies' scarf! Wrap that around your neck and go out!

For the St Johnstone fan in your life ...

A wax jacket. Oh, they've already got one, have they? Get a St Johnstone baby bib for your baby then. 'Saints Mad Just Like Dad'. Proven to soak up the spewings. Did you know that you can buy a bag of tatties from the farm next door to McDiarmid Park?

For the St Mirren fan in your life ...

The St Mirren sweatbands are ace. You need at least two of them. No point buying one. They are plain black and white with the letters SMFC in big bold letters. The St Mirren sweatbands are very heavy metal. Reminiscent of old AC/DC sweatbands.

For the Stirling Albion fan in your life ...

Take shelter under the Stirling Albion umbrella. Sold in red and white and no other. You know it is folly not to bring a brolly to a Scottish football match.

I would like to point out that not all club shops were open (so when do they open?). In the shops that were open, I had to sift through an awful lot of crap. Anyway, on with the second-half ...

MISSION POSSIBLE 22

OBJECTIVE:
To go to Raydale
Park and watch
Gretna.

SCENARIO: Gretna are playing Queen of the South in the Scottish First Division. Crikey. A Borders derby.

DATE: Saturday, November 11, 2006.

LOCATION, LOCATION, LOCATION: the border town of Gretna, which is distinct from Gretna Green which is several miles away.

CULTURAL NOTES: Weddings became a Gretna tradition because of runaway couples eloping north of the border for a quickie. Marriages were made over the anvil at the blacksmith's shop, horseshoes were straightened and the rest is history.

GRETNA PROFILE

KICKED OFF: 1946. Gretna were only admitted to the Scottish Football League in 2002 but they have been making up for lost time by running like the clappers through the divisions.

TRUE COLOURS: White and black.

BADGE OF HONOUR: The Gretna badge consists of a horseshoe and an anvil. Wedding stuff.

NAME CALLING: Black & Whites. Or Borderers. Neither nickname is particularly stirring.

MORTAL ENEMY: Queen of the South. Whom Gretna are always trying to depose. Recently with some success. Doon with the Doonhamers! But those are not my words.

AREN'T WE BRILLIANT?: Gretna have fast-tracked themselves through the divisions, reaching the Scottish Cup final in 2006, which they lost to Hearts at Hampden, but qualifying for the Uefa Cup. A lot has been said and written about Gretna but I would like to mention Dennis 'Touchy' Smith. He was a Gretna striking legend (though he did not like being reminded of missed chances). Dennis scored more than 100 goals for Gretna in a single season. The Carlisle and District League must have been crap.

MISSION LOGISTICS

ALIGHT AT: Gretna station. Turn left for Gretna. Don't turn right for Gretna Green. Unless you are planning on getting hitched before the match. It is about a fifteen-minute walk to the football ground from the train station. You pass through a long tunnel and then through a field. On my way to Raydale Park, a horse and carriage passes by, the carriage containing two happy-looking newlyweds. Ah, bless! I would shower them with confetti but if I rip up my return train ticket I'll have to buy another one.

A Pint At: I would not say that Gretna is the best place for a pint because I can't seem to find any pubs. There is a hotel near Raydale Park, so you can head in there for a drink, but I make it into the Gretna social club at Raydale Park for the sake of 50p on the door. Not having ever spent much time in this part of the world, the biggest thing I find is re-tuning my ears to the local accent, but everyone is very friendly and the social club is very busy.

MISSION DEBRIEFING

Field of Dreams: Raydale Park is packed to the rafters for the derby with Queen of the South whose fans are packed like sardines in the low covered enclosure across from the main stand. Raydale Park is a ramshackle affair and there is barely room to move in the ground but this is a special derby occasion. The match has attracted a sell-out crowd. In fact this has caught me out. I have to sweet-talk my way in. 'No tickets? But I've come from Glasgow. I'm hunting grounds. I'm writing a book about this. You might manage to squeeze me in? Oh thanks. That's brilliant. Thanks a lot. I'll write good things about Gretna. I mean that.' One unusual aspect of Raydale Park, regarding the toilets, is that there is a gap between the roof and the wall. This gap lets the wind in but it also means that you can see out (and presumably in). By positioning myself at the corner of the, um, urinal, if I lean back far enough, while still concentrating on the task in hand, I can still watch the game, while dealing with the necessaries. I do not imagine that there are too many grounds in Scotland where you can do this. Meanwhile the Gretna manager Rowan Alexander is being hugged by a rooster. This is Rocky, Gretna's mascot. There is also a woman dressed up as a rainbow handing out balloons. Gretna eh?

Super Pies Me: It takes me about a day to locate the pie counter at Raydale Park and I spend another three days queuing (admittedly it is derby day so that is understandable). When I reach the head of the pie queue, there is only one pie left. And it appears to have aged in the interim. It is more the remnants of a pie really. For a savoury snack, it looks distinctly unsavoury, as it lies there alone in the heated cabinet. I decide not to bid for it, and settle for some Capri Sun instead. Which soon has me back in the toilets, but I do not miss anything of the match. I've got a room with a view.

GAME ON: Gretna 5-0 Queen of the South

GRETNA GOALSCORERS: Tosh 7, Graham 17, McMenamin 26 pen, Paarpalu 68, McMenamin 74.

QUEEN OF THE SOUTH GOALSCORERS: There aren't any.

GRETNA: Main, Townsley (Jenkins 75), Granger, Tosh, Canning, Innes, Paarpalu, Nicholls, McMenamin (Grady 77), Graham (Deuchar 77), Skelton.

QUEEN OF THE SOUTH: Corr, Paton, Scally (Thomson 53), Lauchlan, McCaffrey, McKenzie (Moon 46), Swift, Weir (O'Connor 72), Barrowman, O'Neil, Gibson.

HEAD COUNT: 2,193.

Report Card: The match was in some doubt because of heavy rain but it is going ahead even if the pitch is almost waterlogged. Gretna run riot against their local rivals and restore themselves to the top of the First Division table where they think they belong. Steve Tosh opens Gretna's account brilliantly with a curler into the top corner. It really is brilliant. One of the best goals of my season. David Graham grabs Gretna's second while Colin McMenamin manages the rampant hosts' third from the penalty spot. Eric Paarpalus pouches the fourth with a Thunder Cat thunderbolt and McMenamin goes on to make it five from close range and Gretna are well out of sight.

Going For Gold: All-guns-blazing Gretna make Queen of the South greet. This match is a downer if you are from Dumfries but if you are a floating neutral much like myself then there is plenty of good football from Gretna to keep you entertained. Eight gold stars but all of them for Gretna on this occasion.

Fanfare: If it was a contest of noise between the two sets of fans, then the Queen of the South fans, though they are outnumbered, and their team is getting trashed, would win hands down. Gretna are not great when it comes to building an atmosphere. One of their fans makes an attempt at background noise with the odd chant or two, not that anyone joins in. 'I'd rather be from Baghdad than Dumfries,' doesn't say much about Dumfries and is surely an exaggerated matter of opinion. When the Queen of the South mascot, a border collie (or more accurately a bloke dressed up as a border collie) called Dougie Doonhamer walks away after the fifth Gretna goal goes in, the cry goes out - 'Where's your doggie gone?' Probably gone off into a quiet corner to lick his wounds. Or his balls.

Music To My Ears: The Gretna team runs out at Raydale Park to The Proclaimers. It must feel like 500 miles for some teams visiting Gretna. Not for Queen of the South though. At the end of the game the fans make their way to the exit to the accompaniment of 'Nothing's Gonna Stop Us Now' by Starship - as featured in the critically-acclaimed film Mannequin. All together now ... 'and we can build this dream together ... standing strong forever ... nothing's gonna' - Stop!

Falkirk's Field of
Dreams. 'If you build
it, they will come '...

Box Office Gold.
'Kilmarnock and Caley
Thistle? Must be a
romantic comedy.'

Got any ID? The intimidating bouncers at Borough Briggs in Elgin.

Captive Audience. The Peterhead Six cheer their team to, um, defeat.

Snow Patrol. A bleak afternoon in wintry Alloa.

Shield your Eyes. The crowd struggles to watch as the sun lights up the magnificent Brechin hedge.

Bent as a Corner Flag. Just a mild wind at Arbroath then.

Back To School. Peterhead's badly fitted-carpet mascot gets his sums wrong.

Sheepdog Trial. Dougie Doonhamer protests his innocence in Dumfries.

Pandamonium. Ayr's rattled panda demands his bamboo back from a young fan.

Game's a Bogey. Ross County's Staggie flagrantly picks his nose in Dingwall.

Lock up your Daughters. Wullie the Warrior plunders and pillages at Ochilview.

Wheel of Fortune. Hamilton's Hammy the Hamster hams it up.

Hidden Treasures. The Glebe Park Emporium gears up for some brisk trading.

Live on Ayr? The Beechgrove Potting Shed, live from Somerset Park.

Berwick Bonanza. Shop till you drop with the Wee Rangers.

Hard Sell. Peterhead cunningly abandon their club shop on match day.

Cordon Blue Toon. The *a la carte* menu at Balmoor.

Meat Market. Hungry men queue for minced cow at Cowdenbeath.

Odd One Out. Have a go. It's the Dunfermline bridie, superior to the Ayr United deep-fried horror to i right, and below, the delapidated offering from East Stirlingshire or the half-eaten pie from Elgin City

AFC CLUB SHOP

New Stock in the club shop

The club shop has recently found a new supplier of mugs. The Jamie Bishop and Ian Dobbins mugs that were previously in stock, had to be ordered in batches of 12. The new supplier will make a single mug which means that you can order a mug with any player gracing your mug.

Also available are the 36-0 mugs, which show the team as it was when history was made.

Mouse mats are also available with the 36-0 team pictured on them. A limited number of these three items is available today and more can be ordered as required All are priced at £6.

The new scarves are also now in stock, priced £9.

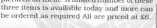

Remember you can order your copy of any home game on DVD priced at £8. Order with Karen in the club shop and your DVD will be ready in a couple of weeks.

Mug Shot. Arbroath may not have many cups. But they have plenty mugs.

Web Chat. Invest in an insect. Bid for an arachnid. Sponsor a Spider!

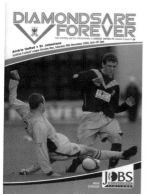
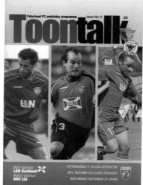

Top Shelf. Quality reading material. Beats J K Rowling any day.

The Charms of Cowdenbeath. Shop in the open air market (and car boot section) and drink in the darkness of The New Goth.

Frankie Goes to Gayfield. Welcome to the Pleasure Dome, Arbroath.

Last Orders. The 42nd hole at Arbroath. End of hunt. Mission accomplished. Cheers!

MISSION POSSIBLE 23

SCENARIO: Airdrie United are playing St Johnstone, slayers of Partick Thistle, in the Scottish First Division. Are the Saints going to destroy the Diamonds? This is the question that the entire country has been asking.

DATE: Saturday, November 18, 2006.

LOCATION, LOCATION, LOCATION: The town of Airdrie in Darkest Lanarkshire. I mean North Lanarkshire.

CULTURAL NOTES: The observatory in Airdrie is one of the few observatories in Britain that is open to the general public. So make the most of it. Darkest Lanarkshire offers ideal conditions for star-gazing. A few swigs of Buckfast will have you seeing stars. In fact, too much of the stuff will probably result in you discovering new planets.

AIRDRIE UNITED PROFILE

KICKED OFF: 2002 (following the demise of Airdrieonians). In 2002, a new insect order, *Mantophasmatodea*, was announced. *The Sun* rushed out a twelve-page special pull-out.

TRUE COLOURS: White. With a Big Red Diamond.

BADGE OF HONOUR: Wow, an eagle with two heads!

NAME CALLING: The Diamonds (duh). Famous Diamonds include Neil Diamond, Anne Diamond and Dominik Diamond.

MORTAL ENEMY: Motherwell ... and Hamilton. Nothing like a heavy dose of Lanarkshire loathing.

AREN'T WE BRILLIANT?: Airdrie United might be 21st-century boys, but in their second season of existence they were crowned Second Division champions.

MISSION LOGISTICS

ALIGHT AT: Drumgelloch. Which is one stop after Airdrie. Trains operate from Glasgow Queen Street and the journey time is approximately half-an-hour. From Drumgelloch station, it is about ten minutes to the ground on foot. Less if you are on a pogo stick.

A Pint At: There is a spacious and sociable supporters' bar within the Jack Dalziel Stand. Which is incredibly convenient, because there do not seem to be too many drinking holes in the vicinity of New Broomfield. And I have a keen nose for pubs. It glows bright red.

MISSION DEBRIEFING

Field of Dreams: Excelsior Stadium or New Broomfield. Which sounds less silly? New Broomfield. Whatever you want to call it, I got locked in there once. (New Broomfield, where no-one can hear you scream.) I lingered too long on writing my match report for a Sunday newspaper; I may have fallen asleep, and was shut in by the groundsman who, to be fair, had already issued three warnings. I was forced into scaling the stadium wall with my laptop, which, quite frankly, is a useless piece of climbing equipment. I then had to straddle the barbed wire, ripping my breeks in the process, and deal with a dramatic drop on the other side. Still, I survived. In the cold light of day, I will acknowledge that New Broomfield is a smart stadium with four well-sized stands all seated. But there are many more seats than there are punters. Which is often a problem in Scottish football. Both sets of fans, Airdrie and St Johnstone, are accommodated in the main stand which leaves three stands with banks and banks of empty seats. Which is an extremely dispiriting sight. On a more upbeat note I like the contrast between two pitch-side advertising boards. One for a lap-dancing club. The other promoting the benefits of root vegetables.

Super Pies Me: Have you ever dealt with a contaminated pie? The Airdrie pie is a good, honest pie, and a bargain to boot. I have no beef with the Airdrie pie. Not a problem. The only thing is that my Airdrie pie is somewhat marred by the sickly brown sauce, but then again, the pie did not pour the sauce on itself. I did it. And I am regretting it now. As I focus on scraping the sauce from my pie, I enjoy hearing this conversational exchange at the New Broomfield pie counter.

Woman Behind Counter: 'Whit dae ye take in yer tea?'

Airdrie Fan: 'Broon sauce. Naw ... milk.'

GAME ON: Airdrie United 2-1 St Johnstone

AIRDRIE UNITED GOALSCORERS: Barrau 38 pen, Smyth 59

ST JOHNSTONE GOALSCORER: Milne 85.

AIRDRIE UNITED: Robertson, Smyth, McGowan, Taylor, Christie, McDonald, McDougall, Holmes, Prunty (McKeown 73), McPhee (McKenna 90), Barrau (Lovering 84).

ST JOHNSTONE: Halliwell, Lawrie, Stanic, Mensing, McManus, Anderson (McLaren 60), Lawson (Sheridan 71), Hardie, Milne, Scotland (MacDonald 65), Sheerin.

HEAD COUNT: 1,550.

Report Card: New Airdrie manager Kenny Black gets off to a flyer with this victory over St Johnstone. The home side's Xavier Barrau picks the deadlock from the penalty spot after Saints keeper Bryn Halliwell brings down Bryan Prunty for having an 'a' in Bryan. Marc Smyth smacks in Airdrie's second goal to put further daylight between these two teams before Steven Milne curls one in for Saints, but it is all too little too late too insufficient for the Perth side.

Going For Gold: A fairly satisfactory First Division fixture. Six gold stars is about the measure of it.

Fanfare: 'Wise men say, only fools rush in, but I can't help falling in love with you.' Elvis has left New Broomfield. But that does not prevent these quiffed Airdrie fans in white jumpsuits from covering The Big E. When not invoking The King with 'Fools Rush In', the Diamonds-daft supporters go all Roy Orbison on us with their mass-crooning of 'Only The Lonely'. It makes for a unique atmosphere. I'm quite enjoying this. The home supporters also indulge in this really weird tribal grunt thing ('a-wooh a-wooh'), which reminds me of that bit in *Indiana Jones And The Temple of Doom* where that poor bloke has his pumping heart ripped out of his chest.

Music To My Ears: Another 'Local Hero'. More Dire Straits.

MISSION POSSIBLE **24**

OBJECTIVE:
To go to Recreation
Park and watch Alloa
Athletic.

SCENARIO: Alloa Athletic are playing Raith Rovers in the Scottish First Division.

DATE: Saturday, December 2, 2006. Only 23 days until Christmas.

LOCATION, LOCATION, LOCATION: Alloa. Near Tillicoultry, near Stirling.

CULTURAL NOTES: *Scotland The Braw* helpfully describes Alloa as 'non-descript'. Despite Alloa Tower being one of the largest surviving medieval tower houses in Britain. Queen Mary once spent the night there, after a match.

ALLOA ATHLETIC PROFILE

KICKED OFF: 1878. Cleopatra's Needle arrives in London. I'm sorry. I've lost the thread.

TRUE COLOURS: Gold and black. Waspish.

BADGE OF HONOUR: A wasp. Alloa don't have a mascot but they do have a wasp outfit, but no-one will wear it. Come on lads! Someone. Please. Put it on and run about like a daftie. You might get a buzz out of it.

NAME CALLING: The Wasps. Score a goal against them and they'll STING you.

MORTAL ENEMY: Bees. And Stirling Albion.

AREN'T WE BRILLIANT?: Alloa lifted the Bell's Challenge Cup in 2000. No, they didn't steal it. It was won fairly and squarely by the Wasps. In 2005, Alloa achieved their greatest-ever win when they thrashed Selkirk 9-0 in the Scottish Cup. Selkirk still insisted on playing rugby. They'll never learn. But can I tell you about an Alloa playing legend? Wee Willie Crilley, whose era was the 1920s, and whose height was five-feet-and-a-bit. It is claimed that Crilley once nipped through the legs of a defender and, with just the keeper to beat, asked the Alloa fans behind the goals which corner of the net he should place the ball in. Crilley duly obliged. And then levitated on the penalty spot.

MISSION LOGISTICS

ALIGHT AT: Well, the nearest train station to Alloa is Stirling train station. If, like me, you are deranged, then you will hop on the next bus to Alloa which, if I recall correctly, was, I think, the number 63. From the bus stance in Alloa town centre, it is really no more than a ten-minutes-uphill-walk to the football ground. Upon arrival, simply state your business and you shall receive your medal for intrepidness. No less than you deserved either.

A Pint At: The Thistle bar, just along from the bus stance, has beer on tap and football on the telly and is flanked by fast-food outlets should your gut need stuffing.

MISSION DEBRIEFING

Field of Dreams: Recreation Park is a smashing sporting moniker for a smashed-up football ground. Nah. It's not that bad. The place has had a lick of paint. It looks all right. From the outside. Everything is yellow. Yellow fence. Yellow turnstiles. Yellow doors. The die-hards (i.e. mentalists) huddle at the Clackmannan Road End. Which now boasts something of a roof which offers partial shelter from the inevitable rain. The wonderful view of the distant Ochil hills remains. You will have to stump up additional pennies in order to get into the main stand but I am quite happy standing here with these wound-up Wasps.

Super Pies Me: The Alloa pie is waterlogged. Call it off. So soggy. And I haven't even left it out in the rain either. Bleuch.

GAME ON: Alloa Athletic 1-2 Raith Rovers

ALLOA ATHLETIC GOALSCORER: Brown 51.

RAITH ROVERS GOALSCORER: Davidson 19, Thorarinson 59.

ALLOA ATHLETIC: Creer, McKeown, Clark (Hamilton 46), Malcolm, Forest, McColligan (Stuart 80), Grant, Ovenstone (Bolochoweckjy 87), Brown, Payo, Sloan.

RAITH ROVERS: Brown (Fahey 43), Wilson, Fotheringham, Andrews, Campbell, Davidson, Fairbairn, Silvestro, McManus, Thorarinson (One 83), Curry (Bonar 60).

HEAD COUNT: 786.

Report Card: A winning start for new Raith Rovers manager John McGlynn after a game that sees both sides have a man sent off. Iain Davidson's header delivers Rovers the early lead but Graeme Brown nods Alloa level. Raith's Kevin Fotheringham is booked twice in two minutes, and two wrongs do not make a right, but two yellows make a red, so he's off. Then Hjalmar Thorarinson hammers a shot under the Alloa crossbar and over the line and ten-man Rovers are ahead again! And we are not done yet. Oh no. Alloa's Steve McKeown is dismissed and two red cards do not make it right, but they do make it a level playing field again, even if Raith Rovers are going to run out winners on this occasion, swatting the Wasps aside.

Going For Gold: Three goals and two dismissals make for a diverting day of football. I think that, oh, six-and-a-half gold stars is an accurate reflection on this eventful encounter.

Fanfare: 'Singing ooh-ah Alloa, singing ooh-ah-Alloa.' That is seriously funked up. But that is what these Alloa fans are singing. There really is no shortage of singing or swearing at the Alloa end, and it gets even more interesting for the second-half, when the Raith Rovers fans run over from the other side of the pitch and try to cram in under the same small roof, because their team is now shooting this way plus they want to escape the heavy rain. But the Wasps are not for budging, because this is their nest. Non-niceties are exchanged and it gets a little tense and steward and police segregation is required. At an Alloa-Raith Rovers match! This is crackers. The Alloa Athletic fans sing 'ooh-ah-Alloa' again. Recreation Park Under A Groove. 'When The Wasps Go Marching In' is the less funky B-side. But in reality the older Alloa fans are not singing and it is the kids who are performing these Alloa greatest hits and they are sounding pretty high-pitched. And the adjacent Raith Rovers fans find the soprano singing funny and deliver their damning and drenched response to the home efforts. The Raith Rovers fans are not afraid to mock the children with (to the tune of Go West) 'Come back ... when your baws have dropped'. Which is put across in a heavy baritone. Which I'm not sure is deliberate or not.

Music To My Ears: Before the match, the Alloa team runs out to the A-Team Theme! Pity the fools who think they can leave Recreation Park with three points. Except that Raith Rovers do leave with the three points.

Mike Check: The man on the mike at Recreation Park is playing to the gallery. 'And one other half-time score that might interest you ...

Peterhead 2 ... Stirling Albion ZERO.' That zero could not be more emphatic. The Alloa fans sound chuffed that their nearest neighbours are getting beaten, although their vicarious joy will be short-lived. Stirling stage a winning comeback in the Blue Toon while Alloa are capitulating on their own patch of grass. Not so gloating now.

EPISODE **25**

MISSION POSSIBLE

OBJECTIVE:
To go to Stark's
Park and watch
Raith Rovers.

SCENARIO: Raith Rovers are playing Ayr United in the Scottish Second Division.

DATE: Saturday, December 16, 2006. Nine days till Christmas!

LOCATION, LOCATION, LOCATION: Kirkcaldy, in Fife, is the twelfth-largest town in Scotland. The ancient royal burgh has a long history and a long esplanade. Kirkcaldy is known as The Lang Toun and the people of Kirkcaldy can be called Langtonians without them taking offence. Former Prime Minister Gordon Brown is a Langtonian and honorary president of the Raith Rovers supporters' club.

CULTURAL NOTES: Kirkcaldy 'doesn't hold a great deal of interest' for *Scotland The Braw*. That book is so down on Scottish towns sometimes. I don't know why they called it *Scotland The Braw*. They should have called it *Scotland The Bad* or something. Back to Kirkcaldy though. The steps at nearby Ravenscraig Castle interested John Buchan and are said to have inspired his novel *The Thirty-Nine Steps*. And if you are in the Lang Toun in April, look out for Links Market, which isn't a sausage festival but a week-long funfair that dates from the fourteenth century. Well I never.

RAITH ROVERS PROFILE

KICKED OFF: 1883. Krakatoa erupts and Stark's Park is out-of-bounds for a few weeks.

TRUE COLOURS: Navy blue and navy white.

BADGE OF HONOUR: A lion. The lion is either holding a shield or a steering wheel. It is most likely a shield come to think of it. What business would a lion have with a steering wheel? I suppose if it kept to the mane roads. (I really am truly sorry about that.)

NAME CALLING: The Rovers. Which genius thought that one up? Ring Raiths would be good if they wanted a Tolkien angle.

AREN'T WE BRILLIANT?: Raith Rovers have a few trophies to their alliterative name. They lifted the League Cup in season 1994/95 (at that time it was called the Coca Cola Cup). Rovers beat Celtic on penalty kicks at Ibrox. The Kirkcaldy club were also First Division champions in season 1992-93 and then also in season 1994-1995 which means they must have been relegated in between, but they don't mention that, do they? No. Whitewash the embarrassing bits and boast about your achievements.

Interestingly, Raith Rovers hold the British record for the most league goals scored in a single season. They fired in 142 in their 1937/38 campaign. Bizarrely, in 1923, the Raith Rovers team was shipwrecked off the Canaries.

MORTAL ENEMY: Fellow Fifers Dunfermline.

MISSION LOGISTICS

ALIGHT AT: Coming from Edinburgh the train hurtles right past Stark's Park and you will need to wait until the train stops at Kirkcaldy train station before you get off. It is about fifteen minutes' walk to the ground passing Beveridge Park and you will no doubt be looking for a pre-match beverage. With that in mind …

A Pint At: Stark's Bar is just down the hill from Stark's Park. You really can't get much closer to Stark's Park than Stark's Bar and the away supporters catch on pretty quickly. It gets quite busy in the run-up to kick-off. It is also all very seasonal and tinselled when I turn up. They have their Christmas decorations up. There is also a picture of Homer Simpson behind the bar with the line 'Stark Raving Mad' next to the custard fool. There is some of that Premiership football on the box but when you look at it, it is a pale imitation of what goes on in the Scottish Second Division.

MISSION DEBRIEFING

Field of Dreams: Stark's Park offers a stark reminder of the 1990s drive to build 10,000-seater stadiums to satisfy bonkers criteria. There are many more seats here than a club like Raith Rovers needs. The Raith fans like to sit up at the back of the South Stand, and from that high vantage point you get a great view of the Lang Toun and its spires. You also get a real aerial view of the match. The small band of Ayr United fans seem miles away in the North Stand. The Railway Stand is empty apart from a giant flag bearing the slogan *'stregati da una fede'*. The Raith fans have borrowed the slogan from Torino in Italy. It essentially means 'bewitched by our faith'. Whereas I thought it was some kind of Italian soup with beans in it. The odd-looking Main Stand is the most memorable part of Stark's Park and there are actually some home fans in it. The press shed is hilarious. But then journalists are a funny bunch. The book library at Stark's Park deserves a special mention. It is situated in the South Stand. It is mostly football books and the deal is that you borrow a book for £2 including a £1 deposit that you get back when you return the book. There is a book on Maradona and one on the late John Peel among lots of other titles. The book library at Stark's Park is a great idea.

Super Pies Me: The Raith Rovers pie is quite tasty. Hats off to the club for also offering an excellent alternative to pies. Stovies! Now that is what I call proper food. Get stuck in.

> **GAME ON**: Raith Rovers 1-0 Ayr United
>
> **RAITH ROVERS GOALSCORER**: Campbell 84
>
> **RAITH ROVERS**: Fahey, Wilson, Pelofi, Campbell, Lumsden, Silvestro, Thorarinson (Curry 46), Bonar, McAvinue, One (Tulloch 89), Kilgannon (Manson 77).
>
> **AYR UNITED**: McGeown, Caddis (Miller 64), Lowing, Forrest, Campbell, Robertson, Strain (Walker 82), Stevenson, Vareille, Weaver, Dunn.
>
> **HEAD COUNT**: 1,186.

Report Card: Raith Rovers are having a terribly barren time of it at home. They have not won a single match at Stark's Park in nine months. But because I turn up, they put to bed their home hoodoo, not that I receive any thanks for it. Defender Mark Campbell's late scrambled goal sums up a scrappy game. It is a curious match-winner with players fresh-airing and everything and the ball taking an eternity to crawl past a despairing Ayr keeper and into the corner of the net. The South Stand stands to attention and applauds and there is a palpable relief about the place. From boredom to bedlam in the space of a few seconds.

Going For Gold: I am deferring to Henry Kelly for a definitive ruling on this one. Henry is of the opinion that this was a terrible game. And I agree. Not that Raith Rovers are too bothered about the manner of their much-needed victory. They and Ayr United can have three gold stars, but to be frank it is more than they deserve. An almost joyless afternoon until the moment that made all the difference for Raith Rovers.

Fanfare: 'Come on you Rai-aith … come on you Rai-aith.' This is still better than all the Christmas carols which are inflicted upon us at half-time. Bah bumbag. The Raith striker Armande One (pronounced o-nay rather than one) seems to be a bit of a cult figure with the Raith Rovers fans. Being viewed as a cult figure is not always the compliment that it sounds. But anyway, the words 'big man' have never appeared more apt for a man. One is one giant among smaller men (and his shorts are too small). He can't really jump very well and is capable of losing aerial battles with opponents half his size, but, occasionally, One's toes turn all twinkly and he dazzles for 2.3 seconds before losing the ball again. He is a perplexing sight which I suppose may explain how he became a cult figure. There are at least two songs at Stark's Park that honour One and I am party to them both. The first ode to One is really a variation on the hokey cokey. It builds to a rousing climax of 'Ooooohhhhhhh Armande Armande One. Oooooohhhhhh Armande Armande One. Ooooooohhhhhh Armande Armande One. See how the big man runs runs runs.' And if that isn't silly enough for you, there is the other Armande aria (to the tune of Walking In A Winter Wonderland). 'There's only one Armande One. There's only one Armande One. He used to be shite but now he's all right. Walking in an One wonderland.' The Raith supporters time their rendition of this to perfection with One flying a header over the Ayr United crossbar. Moments later Armande's arse halts an Ayr free kick. Ayr are awarded another free-kick and it happens again! Raith Rovers don't need a wall. They just need an Armande One.

EPISODE **26**

MISSION POSSIBLE

OBJECTIVE:
To go to McDiarmid
Park and watch
St Johnstone.

SCENARIO: St Johnstone are playing Ayr United in the Scottish Cup third round. That time of year again. The romance of the cup. Sure.

DATE: Saturday, January 6, 2007. A new year, the same Scottish football season.

LOCATION, LOCATION, LOCATION: The Fair City of Perth, which, for several centuries, was Scotland's capital. Perth is situated on the banks of the River Tay.

CULTURAL NOTES: In Perth, you will find the Fair Maid's House (which was the setting for *The Fair Maid of Perth* by Sir Walter Scott). The Museum of the Black Watch is in Perth. As is the Caithness Glass Factory. And, in August, Perth Agricultural Show is Livestock And Uncut from Perth. Better get your tickets now. Near Perth is Scone Palace. It's next to the Pancake House.

ST JOHNSTONE PROFILE

KICKED OFF: 1884. The siege of Khartoum. Where's that? Is it in Fife?

TRUE COLOURS: Blue and white.

BADGE OF HONOUR: Another one of those two-headed eagles. With a lamb to the slaughter inside the stomach of the two-headed eagle.

NAME CALLING: The Saints. Or Saintees.

MORTAL ENEMY: Sinners. Both Dundee clubs.

AREN'T WE BRILLIANT?: St Johnstone achieved their highest-ever league finish when they ended up third in the Premier League after their strong 1998/99 campaign. The Perth club have won the First Division title four times and they have been League Cup finalists twice as well. And they once knocked Hamburg out of the Uefa Cup. And St Johnstone are the only senior club in Britain with the letter J in their name. Jambos does not count.

MISSION LOGISTICS

ALIGHT AT: Perth train station is approximately 208 miles from McDiarmid Park. It takes me an absolute age to walk to the football ground, and in hindsight I should probably have never even attempted to walk such a distance. On the return leg to the train station I give my sore legs a rest and catch a local bus which would have been a more sensible thing to do in the first place. If you want my advice, take a bus or take a taxi and don't even consider doing it on foot. Perhaps it would not have crossed your mind in the first place because you are eminently more sensible. I doff my cap to you sir.

A Pint At: It is all in the name. The 208 Bar, on Crieff Road, acknowledges the 208 miles between the train station and the stadium. Walking on my last legs, I manage to stagger into the 208 Bar and croak for a pint of the coldest lager which I raise to my dry lips with the maximum of effort before passing out in a corner of the room. When I open my eyes the strange décor reminds me of Stanley Kubrick's *Eyes Wide Shut*. So I shut my eyes again and try to retreat to a place in my mind where there is no pain. Why the hell did I not take the bus? I have gone too far this time. Christ. This game had better be good.

MISSION DEBRIEFING

Field of Dreams: Old McDiarmid had a farm. Eee-eye-eee-eye-oh. And on that farm they put Britain's first purpose-built all-seater stadium. Eee-eye-eee-eye-oh. St Johnstone's ground is neat. Not in the American sense. Just neat. It still looks sort of like a mini Ibrox but it is not that grand. McDiarmid Park replaced St Johnstone's old ground of Muirton Park. There is an electronic scoreboard in one corner which runs the latest scores from across the nation. It feels like sitting at home on a Saturday afternoon watching the vidiprinter. Except that you are at a match. And the results are going across the screen rather than up the screen. Like so many all-seater grounds in Scotland, with so many empty seats, it is hard to get too worked up about being at McDiarmid Park, but it is comfortable.

Super Pies Me: I have an important announcement to make. Gather round and listen up. The St Johnstone pie is simply superb. It is a high-quality pie. It has all that you could possibly want from a pie and I don't ask for much. The other thing is that it is a steal at £1.10. I rate this as one of the best pies I have ever tasted. It is a landmark moment for me. And a landmark ruling. The best pie yet. They've set the bar high. I'm not sure this can be beaten.

GAME ON: St Johnstone 0-0 Ayr United

ST JOHNSTONE GOALSCORERS: I wish.

AYR UNITED GOALSCORERS: Likewise.

ST JOHNSTONE: Cuthbert, Lawrie, Dyer (McLaren 80), Mensing, McManus, Anderson, Sheerin, McInnes, Milne (Jackson 69), Scotland (MacDonald 46), Stanic.

AYR UNITED: McGeown, Caddis, Lowing, Forrest, Campbell, Robertson, Strain (Hyslop 90), Casey, Vareille (Friels 85), Wardlaw, Dunn.

HEAD COUNT: 2,173.

Report Card: This is a new low. And the first blank. My first goalless draw at ground-hunting. St Johnstone and Ayr together fail to provide any semblance of entertainment whatsoever, as this tedious cup tie grinds to a numbing halt. There really is not too much that can be said about this terrible advert for football. This is supposed to be a cup tie. There should be shooting opportunities, some drama, a goal even, maybe a winner. But there is no winner and we are all losers. St Johnstone and Ayr will have to do this all over again in a replay. I just could not face that and fortunately I won't have to. I would rather sit and watch dry paint do nothing. This stinks like a skunk that has accidentally fallen into a vat of egg sandwich mix and then dragged itself out only to land in a puddle of fish. You would need the patience of a Saint to put up with this. It is beyond tedium. Give me a game of backgammon any day. Or tiddlywinks. Or rugby. I take that back. Not rugby.

Going For Gold: What, some gold stars? I wouldn't even waste some gold farts on this nonsensical non-event. It ranks as one of the most rank matches I have ever had the displeasure of witnessing. It makes me so angry just thinking about it. I'm going to stop thinking about it and I'm going to try and remain calm. And I walked 208 miles, all that way to watch this ....

Fanfare: You will not catch the St Johnstone fans singing. We are in Perth. So there is a dearth of vocals. Oh, hang on a minute. What's that? .... 'when the Saints go marching in, I want to be in that number ...' I want to be out of here. Thank you St Johnstone and Ayr. For using up ninety minutes of my life, ninety minutes that I will never be able to fill in a form for and claim back. Half-time is okay because I get to enjoy my pie. I will hold on to that at least. 'We love you Saintees we do … we love you Saintees we do …' well you really must truly love them because on tonight's evidence it must be hard to love them. The weird thing is St Johnstone have been having a good season. By all reports they have been playing some good football. They have left it out tonight. A few of the Ayr fans are leaving, but not of their own accord. They have been causing some discord and are being helped by the police. Some of the Ayr fans are doing the bouncy and I can see that some of them are shirtless. In January. Maybe the police are going to wrap them up in blankets.

IN THE LINE
OF FIRE

Hunting grounds? Gurning grounds more like. Welcome to the Theatre of Screams. The Stadium of Stick. The Arena of Abuse. Roll up! Roll up! Get wound up. Goad the goalkeeper. Hound the referee. Lash out at the linesman. Let it all out - that's it. Decry the defending. Slam your useless striker and rage against the goal machine who is destroying your own team. The world is full of injustice but, at a football match, you can fight against inequality, without fear of falling foul of the law. Goal kick! Corner kick! Free kick! Penalty kick! Kick him! Howl yourself hoarse. Roar yourself crimson. Slander a stranger. Curse like a tinker. Shout 'arsehole!' and 'Wullie, ye're shite!'

Scottish football offers no hiding place for the perceived wicked. Especially in the lower divisions where the crowds may be smaller, but they are madder and nearer and they do not hold back, whether it is filthy invective, serious sarcasm or beyond-Dali-surrealism.

Who are the targets of fury? The objects of ire? Well, it really depends.

THE THROW-IN TAKER

Hark at the Beardman. At Firs Park in Falkirk. His team is East Stirlingshire and the enemy - for today at least - is Stenhousemuir. My friend Matteo is insisting on calling him the Beardman on account of him having a beard. The Beardman is a grandmaster of mockery and he is further unnerving an already nervous opposition and causing bother almost to the point of interrupting the game.

A Stenhousemuir player is taking a throw-in. But the Beardman is loitering behind him. With intent. Only the low wall divides player and punter. The Beardman leans forward. It looks as if he is about to snatch the ball from the player's hands. But no. He is having a word in the player's ear. Naturally. In fact he is shouting in the player's ear. He is shouting: 'Whit's your name? Whit's your name?' The player ignores the question; he isn't answering that, and he looks totally bemused, as he should. And the question is put to him once again. 'Whit's yer name?' An uncomfortable, interminable pause. The player appears paralysed. Frozen. Freeze frame.

The Beardman answers his own question. 'It's on the back o' yer shirt!' The player takes the throw-in and bolts as far from the touchline and the Beardman as he can, fleeing his bearded abuser. But the thing is there is no name on the back of the player's shirt. This is the Scottish Third Division, where players do not have names on the back of their shirts. Which begs another question: what was the Beardman going on about? Was he merely trying to rattle the player? Because, if he was, he succeeded.

THE STENHOUSEMUIR TEAM

Let us remain at Firs Park for a moment. The Beardman is training his sights on the entire Stenhousemuir team. They all take the brunt of his random pronouncements. Now he is concocting a curious blend of two different songs which contain the same message. A damning of the pretensions of a supposedly superior team. Stenhousemuir are top of the table and East Stirlingshire pretty much prop it up. But East Stirlingshire are winning right now and the Beardman knows better. 'Championi, Championi ... oh no, oh no, oh no ... you're havin' a laugh.' If ever there was a twelfth man, it is the Beardman.

THE GOALKEEPER

A few weeks later, in Elgin, I encounter the Beardman again. East Stirlingshire are having an away day at Borough Briggs. First I can hear him, but can't see him, then I see him. Standing on the grassy knoll (fittingly for a Lone Gag Man), behind the goals, his mischievous gaze and his lacerating humour focused completely on the Elgin goalkeeper, who, it must be said, is wearing a pink shirt. Shocking pink. 'Hey!' shouts the Beardman. 'Goaalie!' The pink object of the Beardman's, um, obsession, is in the process of placing the ball on the edge of the six-yard box in preparation for a goal-kick. The Elgin keeper is not listening to the Beardman but the Beardman's words never fall on deaf ears. They are too loud.

'Hey! Rent boy! Where did ye get yer pink shirt?' There is no response, unsurprisingly, from the man in pink who is doing his utmost to focus on the act in hand of launching the ball into the air. But the Beardman is not for giving up. 'Did ye get it at Top Man? Top Man goalie? Top Man in Elgin?' Which is a cue for the Beardman to burst into song. His lyrics are highly original, though the familiar melody is appropriated from the popular Cuban folk song 'Guantanamera'. 'Top Man in Elgin! You're the Top Man in Elgin! Top Man in Eellll-gin! Oh you're the Top Man in Eellll-gin!'

You couldn't make it up, but the Beardman can.

Goalkeepers are obvious targets. At Somerset Park in Ayr, a terracing sniper fires this snippet of information to the Berwick Rangers goalie. 'Yer wife's a hoor, keeper.' To the keeper's credit, he acknowledges this comment and smiles, before calmly taking a sip from his water bottle. Sticks and stones and all that.

As the Edinburgh derby rages at Easter Road, a fat Hibs fan screams at the Hearts keeper, Craig Gordon. For being skinny! And for playing for Hearts, let us not forget that. Up in Inverness, the Celtic keeper Artur Boruc is a figure of fun for one Caley Thistle fan. 'Oi bourach! Bourach! Fit a bourach min!' Boruc is Polish and is none the wiser about this Invernesian implying that Boruc sounds like bourach and bourach means mess and Boruc is making a mess of things. Which he isn't. Still it has some of these Inverness supporters in stitches.

THE INJURED PLAYER

Heaven help you if you are a footballer and you happen to get hurt. Because these Scottish audiences can be ultra-unsympathetic. They can be downright callous. A Kilmarnock player collapses to the turf at Celtic Park, clutching his face, after a nasty-looking head collision. 'Dig a hole and bury the c***!' shouts a Celtic supporter. Sound medical advice, that. We have a doctor in the house. Never mind nurse, scalpel. It's nurse, shovel.

THE INJURED PLAYER WHO'S NOT REALLY INJURED

Scottish football crowds love effort but loathe effete actors who drop like flies. Because diving is not a Scottish trait. Oh no. It's those foreigners. Or at least anyone on the other team. If your man goes down it is a stone-wall penalty and a red card to the hacker on the other team. If the man on the other team goes to ground then he deserves a severe talking to from the referee. And probably a red card. When the man on the other team falls to the turf, he is supposed to jump straight back on his feet again because everything is okay. Or this happens. 'Get up ye big fanny!' This unforgiving attitude towards malingerers is detectable at Peterhead when an Alloa player goes down like a box of fish. The Alloa physio races on to the pitch in order to treat the stricken player. It so happens that the Alloa physio is both female and blonde. As she rubs the dying man with her magic sponge, one elderly and cynical Peterhead fan observes: 'He's nae injured. He's jist needin' a feel!'

A STENHOUSEMUIR PLAYER AGAIN

A throw-in for Stenhousemuir. But don't worry too much. The Beardman's not here. Stenhousemuir are hosting Elgin, not East Stirlingshire. An Elgin player jumps up and down in front of the home throw-in taker in an annoying attempt to put him off. 'Nail it in his bastardin' face,' cries a humanitarian in the main stand at Ochilview.

THE COCKY TEENAGER

Ah, the impudence of youth. This is Albion Rovers against Stenhousemuir. (Look, I am not a Stenhousemuir fan, honest. It is just that I have seen them a lot recently and I have no idea why that is.) Stenhousemuir's teenage tyke, David Templeton, who looks about eight-years-old, brazenly tries his luck from the halfway line, lobbing it like Beckham with the ball landing just wide of the Albion Rovers post. It is an admirable and audacious effort but one spluttering Albion Rovers supporter is none too impressed: 'Try that again when your pubes grow!'

KAJAGOOGOO IN THE FANCY BOOTS

What is it with the youth of today? Eh? Why must young Scottish footballers wear white boots, blue boots, red boots or golden boots? What exactly is wrong with black boots? And what possesses them to dip their hair in bird shit and backcomb it through a hedge? Honestly. It is like a Kajagoogoo convention out there. And there goes Limahl, scurrying down the left flank, none too shy. A footballer's fussy mane, for the fulminating fan, is like a red rag to a bull. The sculpted follicles of these spotty posers enrage even the most mild-mannered of supporters. 'Nice hair-do ya wee fanny!'

THE MANAGER

Dick Campbell doesn't have a hair-do. He has a bunnet. Dick once told me a joke. What do you call a man who is nearly home? Hamish. Well, I thought it was funny. Every single manager will get it in the neck from their team's fans at some point or other. And I see, and hear all too well, Partick Thistle manager Dick Campbell (now ex-Partick Thistle manager Dick Campbell) getting bombarded with abuse at Firhill, while St Johnstone are enthusiastically humping Thistle 5-1. Spleens are vented in the Jackie Husband Stand, I can tell you. 'Aye Campbell, yer a dumpling. Yev no' goat a bloody clue.' These words are articulated with far more than a hint of venom. Why is it that the loudest accuser at a football match always sounds like Johnny Vegas playing the part of an Orc in *The Lord Of The Rings?* And, tell me, why is it that these noise merchants cup their hands round their mouth, as if their hands have just taken on the properties of a loud-hailer? All that it does is to muffle their words of hatred. Which is probably a good thing. 'What a shambles Campbell.' Reviling in rhyme, that is good. 'Here, Campbell! A've got a spare leg if ye want it.' The implication being? That the Partick Thistle manager has not got a leg to stand on? That you have been blessed with an additional leg and you do not mind donating it to someone who needs it more than you? Some of the thorny insults directed at the Jags boss are much worse than could be printed on this page. New swear words are invented. I later read a newspaper interview with Campbell, where he reflects on the bile that is barfed in his direction on a routine basis. 'If it was my family carrying on like that, they would get a skelpit arse.' That should have been the deal. The Thistle fans could have shouted whatever they wanted at Dick Campbell. On condition that he could skelp their arses afterwards. With the skelping highlights to be shown on TV.

THE REFEREE

Invariably, the ref is a fanny. (Well, let's face it. He is never going to be fantastic. Is he?) His task is to officiate, whilst the fans salivate. He whistles and they bristle. The referee cannot win. So he helps the other team win. And that is simply not fair. He has to be brought to task. He has to be called an arse. So much of the filth which spills from the stands is intended for the man in black. Or the man in cobalt or blue or aquamarine or turquoise, or whatever the flip it is, that garish colour they are dressing the referees in nowadays. I hear one fan describing it as stupid blue prick but I think he is commenting more on the man than the hue of his shirt.

The referee spots a spot-kick when no-one else sees one and he denies a penalty when it is obviously one of those stonewall thingies. He nitpicks over the positioning of a free kick (although players do often take liberties in this regard). He sends a man off for nothing. Nothing. And allows the actual offender to commit GBH, rewarding their ultra-violence by keeping his yellow and red cards close to his puffed-out chest. A cynical challenge or a swan-like dive? The reward of a free-kick or points for flamboyancy? There is only one man with a whistle. (Actually, they should give players whistles as well; that would alter the face of football.) The referee succeeds in holding the game up, while messing it up, before he leaves the field to a torrent of abuse and an avalanche of insults, a barrage of belligerence. Language you have never heard the like of in your life. Unless you have been to a football match. Maybe it was you who was shouting.

At Central Park, one Cowdenbeath supporter is so irate at the referee's dreadful decision (the awarding of a goal-kick to the other team when it clearly should have been a corner) that he throws the rest of his cheeseburger onto the pitch. It's half a cheeseburger at least!

If you are a pot-bellied match official, if you're looking out of shape, and the worse for wearing your shirt, you will certainly not be spared. 'Do the SFA only have one size of shirt ref ye fat bastard?' Often the jibes are stunning in their simplicity. 'Referee! Ya cock!' This could never be viewed as an expression of admiration. 'Shut yer puss ref' is hardly a term of endearment either. Really, who would want to be a referee?

Realms Of The Ridiculous Regarding Referees And Remonstrators:

Exhibit A (Broadwood, Cumbernauld, one dark night): A fat bald fan calls the ref a 'fat bald bastard'.

Exhibit B (Broadwood, Cumbernauld, same dark night): Man with his son sitting next to him labels the ref 'a fucking disgrace'. Oh, the irony. This is actually quite depressing.

On the question of referee bias: sometimes, when you sit with the supporters of another team, you start to come round to their way of thinking. Take Dunfermline versus Rangers at East End Park. 'Welcome to games against the Old Firm,' smiles a weary Dunfermline fan next to me. 'This ref's not bad either.' He is not at all happy with the referee but, on balance, he thinks the referee not as bad as referees usually are when Rangers or Celtic come here. Some of these Dunfermline fans are being driven demented by the number of refereeing decisions which are going against them. They feel that Dunfermline are not only playing Rangers. They are playing the referee. And after a while it starts rubbing off on me. This ref is behaving outrageously. How does he think he will get away with this?

THE LINESMAN

Call him the linesman or the assistant referee. One Alloa fan calls him the assistant prick. Flag-wavers are in the frontline on the touchline. They are much closer to the crowd than the referee. The linesman (look, I am calling him the linesman: okay?) never seems to see anything going on in the game but he must hear everything going on behind his back. If you have ever wondered why a referee does his job (even if he seems not to be doing it) you really have to contemplate these poor souls running the gauntlet with their little flags. What is their motivation for turning up on match day? How Can They Be Bothered? The view among some supporters is that they don't bother. They just turn up and make it up as they go along.

Patrolling the perimeter of the pitch, with his back to the baying audience, the linesman requires thick skin. And maybe a helmet. My friend Brian tells me of a linesman running to keep up with the play when a fan reaches out and plucks the flag from the linesman's hand. The linesman carries on running. I don't witness any flags getting pinched, but the flag is, without doubt, a focal point for much of the anger heaped on linesmen. 'Does yer flag no work, linesman?' is a common shout. A more creative call I hear is 'Stick it up yer erse, sideways.' Nice suggestion, but surely too ambitious.

At Stair Park, there is a Stranraer supporter staring at the linesman. He is unconcerned at how his team are faring against Morton. No interest whatsoever. His undivided attention is planted on the linesman. Every time the linesman goes remotely near this supporter he is assailed with short-and-to-the-point insults. 'Big clown.' 'Eejit.' 'Headcase.' 'Clown.' 'Arse.' 'Big eejit.' 'Big arse.' It is a remarkable performance and one that reminds me very much of Father Jack in *Father Ted*.

THE HATCHET-MAN (A.K.A. THE HAMMER-THROWER)

Here it comes. The tackle to end all tackles and quite possibly someone's career. 'Yer a fucking animal!'

THE FOREIGNER

Bananas aren't chucked at black players any more in Scottish football, but xenophobia is alive and kicking. 'Fuck off you fucking foreign fuck.' An invitation to leave the country, to one of Hearts' Lithuanian players, during the cordial Edinburgh derby at Easter Road.

ALEX RAE

The Dundee player-manager seems to get singled out an awful lot at First Division grounds. Ostensibly for the crime of being seen to be on the pitch. 'Ye wee baldy hoor!'

THE TIMEWASTER

A Dundee corner at Victoria Park in Dingwall. They are taking their time about it and the Jailend is getting restless. 'Hurry up ye nugget!' Nugget?

THE ENGLISH

When a Berwick Rangers player is adjudged, by opposition fans, to have hoodwinked the referee, the Berwick Rangers player is not just 'a cheatin' bastard' but 'a cheatin' English bastard'. Even if he is Scottish.

NOT IN THE LINE OF FIRE: The Victorious Forfar XI

The antidote to all the negativity. The Loons lamp the Blue Brazil 2-0 at Station Park. As the happy Forfar heroes traipse off the pitch, a delighted Forfar fan acclaims each one of them individually and with admirable sincerity. 'Well done Willie Stewart! Well done Gregory! Well done Sandy Wood!' It is very refreshing to hear. Sounds like some throw-back to an earlier era but it makes a change from the usual and it is nice to end on a sweet note after all that sour.

EPISODE **27**

MISSION POSSIBLE

OBJECTIVE:
*To go to Pittodrie
and watch Aberdeen.*

SCENARIO: Aberdeen are playing Hibernian in the Scottish Cup third round. I hope very much that this is an improvement on St Johnstone and Ayr United taking the piss in their third round tie. It would have to be.

DATE: Wednesday, January 10, 2007.

LOCATION, LOCATION, LOCATION: The Granite City, The Silver City, Furryboots City, The Oil Capital of Europe, The Energy Capital of Europe. Enough!

CULTURAL NOTES: 'One detests Aberdeen with the detestation of a thwarted lover.' Thus wrote the writer Lewis Grassic Funky Gibbon. *Scotland The Braw* describes Aberdeen as 'soulless'. What is soulless about gazing at the stars from a Belmont Street gutter at three in the morning? When in Aberdeen, you should do as the locals do and have a buttery (or three). It's the Scottish croissant, don't you know.

ABERDEEN PROFILE

KICKED OFF: 1903. The Tour de France kicks off. Or sets off.

TRUE COLOURS: *Beaucoup rouge*. Which is French for lots of red.

BADGE OF HONOUR: Goalposts and a football form the letter A in AFC. Conceptual, min. And can I just say that Aberdeen, along with lots of other clubs, were only too happy for me to use their badge in this book. I guess Celtic are special.

NAME CALLING: Aberdeen are nicknamed The Dons due to the nearby river Don. Another sobriquet is Sheep Shaggers because of the fans' rumoured fondness for fondling fleece.

MORTAL ENEMY: Rangers. No-one else comes close.

AREN'T WE BRILLIANT?: The Dons were at their dandiest when they beat Real Madrid to win the European Cup Winners' Cup in 1983. This was The Glory of Gothenburg. Aberdeen have been crowned Scottish champions four times and are the only club outside the Old Firm and Inverness Caledonian Thistle never to have been relegated from the top flight. Stuff that in a fact sandwich and eat it.

MISSION LOGISTICS

ALIGHT AT: Aberdeen train station. The relevant thoroughfares are Union Street and King Street, and if you end up on Pittodrie Street then that provides the clue that you are pretty much there. It is a reasonable hike to Pittodrie on foot, but you can always catch a bus on Union Street and get off further along King Street. Watch out for the seagulls and HGVs heading harbour-wards.

A Pint At: The Pittodrie Bar on King Street is a reliable old-fashioned booze den. If you would much prefer to be necking your pint three minutes before kick-off, without missing any of the football action, then the Broadhill Bar is a mere throw-in from the Richard Donald Stand, though the pub's doors are supposed to open only to home fans; but since I'm a neutral I pretend I'm a home fan and I'm all right for a drink then. Thanks for letting me in. Now ... which Rangers songs could I sing to entertain everyone?

MISSION DEBRIEFING

Field of Dreams: Pittodrie means 'hill of dung' in Gaelic. It also means 'chilling your bum beside the North Sea'. Giant Winged Beasts, possibly seagulls, swoop down on the pitch at the final whistle. Aberdeen's pad is something of a Scottish football classic. It was the first all-seater ground in the country, just beating Cliftonhill to that accolade. The Richard Donald Stand is the biggie structure looking somewhat taller than the rest of the stands. Next to Pittodrie there is both a golf course and a graveyard.

Super Pies Me: The Aberdeen pie excels at being average. There is a noticeable and worrying gap between the pie pastry and the pie meat (well it worries me). I am not sure what the gap means (maybe it's a sign) but I notice it, so it must be something that most other pies don't do.

GAME ON: Aberdeen 2-2 Hibernian

ABERDEEN GOALSCORERS: Brewster 58, Nicholson 89.

HIBERNIAN GOALSCORERS: Sproule 43, Killen 73.

ABERDEEN: Langfield, Hart, Anderson, Considine (Brewster 45), Foster,

Nicholson, Severin, Dempsey (Maguire 45), Clark, Miller (Lovell 77), Mackie.

HIBERNIAN: McNeil, McCann (Stevenson 64), Jones, Martis, Murphy, Whittaker, Shiels (Benjelloun 74), Stewart, Beuzelin, Sproule, Killen.

HEAD COUNT: 7,905.

Report Card: Sprightly super-sub Craig Brewster springs off the Aberdeen bench and helps his team to an Easter Road replay. Aberdeen keeper Jamie Langfield spills the ball in a comical manner and Ivan Sproule says 'thank you very much goalie,' but the evergreen Brewster (wearing red) levels the tie with a powerful header into the Hibernian net. Chris Killen is capable of restoring Hibs' lead and the Kiwi striker does, with a voluptuous volley, before the gangly Brewster tees up Barry Nicholson who smashes the ball home to rescue the tie dramatically for the Dons and ensure that there will be a cup re-run in Edinburgh.

Going For Gold: Not enough fans bother to pitch up at Pittodrie on this nippy northern night (the game's also on the telly) but those who can be arsed to attend are treated to a stirring contest. Note to both St Johnstone and Ayr United - this is a cup tie. You are supposed to look for goals. They help you progress into the next round. Neither Aberdeen or Hibernian have made it into the next round, so it's still annoying for there not to be a proper conclusion, but the thing is that these teams at least tried to get the better of one another and in the process they were able to entertain a bit. Seven gold stars.

Fanfare: The atmosphere is not exactly buzzing; however, there are mitigating factors. This is a wintry Wednesday night in January and the stadium is two-thirds empty when, normally, it is half-full, which still isn't great. The most vociferous Dons fans are up the back of the Richard Donald Stand (formerly the Beach End) but the Aberdeen supporters truly excel on away days when they are always on song. Any of their songs here peter out before they even reach the pitch. The giant flags swirling in the wind add some colour to the occasion though. I especially enjoy the Willie Miller/Che Guevara flag. As far as the singing goes, we first off get the lyrical complexity of 'Aberdeen, Aberdeen, Aberdeen ... Aberdeen, Aberdeen, Aber-dee-een'. But to be fair to the Aberdeen supporters, there are other and better songs in their repertoire. 'Sssttaaaaaaannnnd free, wherever you may be, we are the famous Aberdeen, and we don't give a f-' Ahem. The Dons fans manage to then make it abundantly clear where they stand on the subject of Glasgow Rangers. 'We hate Glasgow Rangers ...' And when the strangely subdued Hibs supporters start chanting 'Hiii-bees, Hiii-bees, Hiii-bees, Hiii-bees' the cantankerous Aberdeen fans respond to drown them out with a rapid-fire 'shiteshiteshiteshiteshite' which sounds like the really-fast-speedy-up-bit in Fat Boy Slim's 'Funk Soul Brother'. The Dons also do a round of the 'Northern Lights of Old Aberdeen' and there is a run-through of the far less traditional 'Red and White Barmy Army'. Good effort from those who have come along tonight and are trying to make the best of it. There's a drum too but they don't beat it too loud, so it never gets really annoying. Not like a Livingston drum.

Music To My Ears: In the run-up to kick-off, we get AC/DC's 'Back in Black', otherwise Angus the Bull, the Aberdeen mascot, would have taken the huff. He head-bangs along to it and performs some of his air guitar histrionics. Daft bovine. I would have quite liked to hear 'Move Any Mountain' by The Shamen, but you can't have everything you know.

MISSION POSSIBLE 28

SCENARIO: Rangers are playing Dundee United in the Scottish Premier League. The weather all across Scotland is atrocious today so I am playing it safe by picking a match closer to home. I do not want to be travelling two hours on a train to arrive and to learn that the game has been called off. So Ibrox it is then.

DATE: Saturday, January 13, 2007.

LOCATION, LOCATION, LOCATION: The Govan area of Glasgow, in the south-west of the city. Not far enough from Celtic Park.

CULTURAL NOTES: Ibrox Stadium is within walking distance of the Glasgow Science Centre. You can't miss all that titanium. Once inside the Glasgow Science Centre there is lots of fun to be had and you don't have to be a kid, although that probably helps. Again not far from Rangers' ground is Bellahouston Park which is the home to the House for an Art Lover, which was built from drawings by architect Charles Rennie MacKintosh. There is also a dry ski slope so you can pull down your breeks and bum surf to the bottom.

RANGERS PROFILE

KICKED OFF: 1872. Thomas Hardy anonymously publishes *Under the Greenwood Tree.*

TRUE COLOURS: Red, white and blue.

BADGE OF HONOUR: A lion rampant inside a football with the Rangers motto 'Ready'. Which is a bit like the Scout motto 'Be Prepared'. I think Rangers should change their motto to 'Relax' and see how they get on. They can always change it back again. I asked Rangers if I could use their badge in this book. They took a similar approach to Celtic. They made me wait for a bit. And then they said no. Hurray for the Old Firm.

NAME CALLING: Rangers are the Gers and they are also the Teddy Bears. Rangers fans are called Bluenoses. You can say it to their face as well and they won't mind at all. I'm sure they do mind being called the Orcs by some Celtic fans, but that's Celtic fans for you. The truth is that they all love each other dearly.

MORTAL ENEMY: That would be Celtic then. I think we've been over this a few times. Why can't they all just get along?

AREN'T WE BRILLIANT?: Rangers won the European Cup Winners' Cup in 1972 when they beat Moscow Dynamo 3-2 in the Nou Camp. The Ibrox club celebrated Nine-in-a-Row in the 1990s when the Scottish League title seemed to be exclusively their domain.

MISSION LOGISTICS

ALIGHT AT: Ibrox Subway station. You can catch the Subway from Buchanan Street or St Enoch. It is a circular line so it doesn't matter much which direction you go in. You will get there in the end unless you fall asleep. The Subway can be pretty packed on a Rangers match day. Not quite Tokyo during rush hour but busy nonetheless. It is not two minutes' walk to the ground and you will be offered hats, badges and scarves and other Rangers-related paraphernalia.

A Pint At: Directly opposite the entrance to the Ibrox Subway station is the Stadium Bar which, as the name suggests, is extremely close to the stadium. The Stadium Bar is a practical choice as long as you don't expect anything fancy (like a cocktail) because the Stadium Bar is nothing fancy. The carpets have a lot of history in them. They are rather sticky and you can also feel the rumble as the Subway trains pass. The beer is served in plastic glasses. And a charming man points at the empty seat next to me and asks 'Is any c**t sitting there?' At least he is direct about it and does not dance around the subject. He just wants to sit down. He only asked a question. 'Help yourself mate,' I encourage him.

MISSION DEBRIEFING

Field of Dreams: Ibrox Stadium is one of only a dozen stadiums in Europe accorded five-star status by Uefa. But this doesn't mean there is a swimming pool. Unless there's one in the dressing room. The ground is an impressive blend of the old and the new. There is the red-brick façade of the main stand which is a listed building that harks back to an earlier era. Inside the front door is the marble staircase, but you probably will not be climbing up that on match day or sliding down the banister like Dick Advocaat used to like to do. The Flying Dutchman Down The Banister. You can arrange a tour of Ibrox, just like you can tour Celtic Park. The corner areas of Ibrox are filled in these days with additional seating and there are big screens too. It is a magnificent ground but my seat isn't that great. I had trouble getting a ticket with the home fans for this one. Even a match with Dundee United draws a large crowd. I manage to pick up a ticket for the West Enclosure with restricted viewing. The view is restricted by a low beam in front of me which means I can see the pitch, but if the ball is punted in the air I lose sight of it and I can't get a proper sense of the crowd either. Keep the ball on the ground guys. I am either having to duck down or rush forward out of my seat. I can't sit at peace. If I do I'll miss something. I am sitting next to the match-day doctors who also keep rushing out of their seats, but to attend to any fans in distress. I was warned about the restricted view but it's still a bit of a pain.

Super Pies Me: At Ibrox they serve simply the best. Champions' Food. I wouldn't say that my pie is champion exactly. It's passable, but not a contender for any title.

GAME ON: Rangers 5-0 Dundee United

RANGERS GOALSCORERS: Adam 23, Burke 36, Boyd 59, 68, Ferguson 88.

DUNDEE UNITED GOALSCORERS: Don't be daft.

RANGERS: McGregor, Hutton, Hemdani, Svensson, Murray, Burke (Sebo 74), Ferguson, Clement, Adam, Prso (Novo 41), Boyd.

DUNDEE UNITED: Stillie, Dillon, McCracken, Kenneth (Archibald 46), Duff, Samuel (Hunt 52), Kerr, Cameron (Gomis 81), Robertson, Conway, Daly.

HEAD COUNT: 50,276.

Report Card: Walter Smith's second spell as Rangers manager gets off to the ideal start as the buoyant home side comprehensively destroy Dundee United in front of a chuffed Ibrox crowd. United keeper Derek Stillie abandons his penalty box and is punished by Charlie Adam thumping a shot into the untended net from forty yards. Then Chris Burke's header enlarges Rangers' lead. In the second-half, Rangers goal machine Kris Boyd bags himself a double, one with his head, one with the flash of his boot. Rangers captain Barry Ferguson rounds off a routine thrashing with a nice finish for Rangers' fifth. At one point a freak gust of wind, more a typhoon, flies in the corner gate and just about knocks over a dozen police who are trying to remain on their feet. It is as if there are firemen outside the ground who have trained their power hose on the police. It's fun to watch but it can't be fun to be involved in a very strange phenomenon.

Going For Gold: As good as Rangers are, Dundee United are garbage. Only one side in it. One-sided. I will proffer this game seven gold stars. Some of those goals are pretty good.

Fanfare: Before the game some blue-themed tunes are pumped through to the Ibrox crowd to get the Bluenoses going. 'All the bluebells are blue, all the bluebells are blue' … … 'we'll keep the blue flag flying high' … 'it's the blue, blue, blue, sea of Ibrox' … 'I found my thrill, on blueberry hill' … 'blue moon, you saw me standing alone' … no sign of Blue Monday though. 'Super Ally' is tackled when Rangers assistant manager Ally McCoist emerges from the dug-out and there are a couple of Follow, follows. 'When I was walking down the Copland Road' comes up on the big screen, with the lyrics there encouraging the fans to join in, and it becomes a weird sort of sing-along.

Music To My Ears: Naturally there is 'Simply The Best' by Tina Turner. And almost as predictably for any kind of football match 'Let Me Entertain You' by Robbie Williams. The Rangers fans have been entertained and they even get to see Robert Prytz at half-time when the former Rangers player takes part in the 50/50 draw on the pitch. He's still got his hair.

MISSION POSSIBLE

OBJECTIVE:
To go to Palmerston
Park and watch
Queen of the South.

SCENARIO: Queen of the South are playing Dundee in a Scottish Cup third-round replay.

DATE: Tuesday, January 16, 2007. This is an awkward one. An evening game and the last train back to Glasgow leaves Dumfries around the time that the match should finish (in the event of there being no extra-time). I am not entirely happy about the situation but it is a chance I'm willing to take, even if I might have to leave the game early. I am just hoping for a clear result either way so that I can flee Palmerston with a clear conscience and catch my train and not be worrying about missing a game that builds to a dramatic goals-filled climax and then spills into extra-time and concludes with a tense, decisive penalty shoot-out. Of course, this is exactly what happens, isn't it?

LOCATION, LOCATION, LOCATION: The ancient Borders town of Dumfries, the 'Queen of the South' on the banks of the River Nith.

CULTURAL NOTES: Dumfries is an 'architectural hotchpotch' says *Scotland The Braw*. But it is a Borders town with strong literary connections however. Robert Burns spent the last few years of his life in Dumfries. He used to drink at the Globe Inn and so can you. There is a Burns statue on Dumfries High Street and you can also visit the Robert Burns Centre. James Barrie, the Peter Pan creator, studied at Dumfries Academy and was granted the Freedom of Dumfries. The annual Guid Nychburris (Good Neighbours) Festival culminates in the crowning of The Queen of the South. Helen Daniels won it one year.

QUEEN OF THE SOUTH PROFILE

KICKED OFF: 1919. Romania annexes Transylvania.

TRUE COLOURS: Royal blue and white.

BADGE OF HONOUR: The Queen of the South badge features intricate QOSFC lettering with the town motto 'A Lore Burn' which means roughly 'to the muddy stream'. Not to infinity and beyond, we don't need to go that far; let's just go to the muddy stream. It'll be good.

NAME CALLING: Queen of the South is sometimes shortened to Queens for convenience. The main nickname of Queen of the South is 'The Doonhamers'. This is said to stem from workers from Dumfries on the railway lines and in the shipyards of Glasgow referring to Dumfries as 'doon hame'. And I'm not going to argue with them about that.

MORTAL ENEMY: The Doonhamers seem to have a downer on the Clayholers of Stranraer and they also get terribly worked up about their close neighbours Gretna. There is also a suggestion of some historical beef with Ayr United so the Doonhamers keep themselves fairly active when it comes to letting off steam.

AREN'T WE BRILLIANT?: Time for some Bible bashing. Queen of the South are the only football team mentioned in the Bible. You probably already know that, but if you don't I'm telling you. Look up Matthew 12:42. 'The Queen of the South shall rise up in the judgment with this generation, and shall condemn it: for she came from the uttermost parts of the earth to hear the wisdom of Solomon; and, behold, a greater than Solomon is here.' I've memorised it. The Queen of the South players gather in a huddle in the centre circle before every match and recite Matthew 12:42. That is the gospel truth. Queen of the South won the old Division Two in 1950-51 and the Dumfries part-timers won the modern Second Division in 2001-02.

MISSION LOGISTICS

ALIGHT AT: Dumfries train station. But it is nearly two hours from Glasgow Central on the slow train (the only train) so I am in this for the long-haul. I need to make sure that I get that last train back too. Exiting the station I take a walk down Lovers' Walk on my own and eventually cross the High Street, nodding to the Burns statue and crossing the bridge over untroubled waters, and I have still got a wee bit to go yet. Damn. I'm going to have to leave the game earlier than I thought. At this rate I'll have to leave at half-time. I hope either Queen of the South or Dundee are three goals up by then. Oh well, I am here now.

A Pint At: There are a plethora of pubs in Dumfries but I head straight for the ground and to the Palmerston Lounge which is in the main stand at Palmerston Park. And it is already bustling with Doonhamers. The Palmerston Lounge is one of the very best football social clubs in the country. Lots of booth action. And lots of Queens memorabilia on the walls. There is also a plaque showing the Bible reference.

MISSION DEBRIEFING

Field of Dreams: Palmerston Park is frayed around the edges but it is a cracking ground actually, even if it is falling somewhat apart. The Portland Bill Terrace behind the goals is full of Doonhamers making a fair old din. There is a boy here with bagpipes too. On the roof of the stand is a giant clock with the words 'Time To Visit'. The newer East

Stand is split between home and away fans while the terrace behind the other set of goals is not in use. Palmerston retains its tradition and can provide the platform for a great atmosphere. It's a good day out. It's a good night out. Or a good half-a-night out in my case. I would say that the floodlights dominate the neighbouring houses so much that they must light up your living room and save you some of your electricity bill.

Super Pies Me: The Queen of the South pie is very meaty. You would think I was a food critic, wouldn't you?

GAME ON: Queen of the South 3-3 Dundee (Queen of the South win 4-2 on penalties)

Told you this would happen.

QUEEN OF THE SOUTH GOALSCORERS: Dobbie 40, 69, O'Connor 86.

DUNDEE GOALSCORERS: Lyle 48, Deasley 82, Lyle 87.

QUEEN OF THE SOUTH: Corr, McQuilken, Lauchlan, Thomson, Paton, Scally, Burns, O'Neill (Robertson 62), Gibson, Dobbie (Weir 80), O'Connor (Henderson 105).

DUNDEE: Roy, Griffin (McDonald 77), Dixon, MacKenzie, Smith, Rae, Shields, Robertson (Mann 119), Swankie (Campbell 115), Lyle, Deasley.

HEAD COUNT: 2,037.

Report Card: Whit a game! Pity I end up missing much of it. Stephen Dobbie delivers the lead to the Doonhamers just before the break, with an excellent finish, but then Derek Lyle equalises for Dundee at the back post shortly after half-time. Then Dobbie strikes again, the ball slipping under the culpable Dundee goalie, and I am looking at my watch and I'm going to have to leave in a minute to catch the last train back to Glasgow. I depart at 2-1 to Queen of the South and imagine that they might hold on. Yes, in fact I'm sure they will hold on. I probably won't miss a thing really. When I get back home hours later I put on the TV and check the final score. Shit! Here is the summary of what I managed to miss. Bryan Deasley gets Dundee back in it at 2-2 before Sean O'Connor nudges Queens ahead again. Only for Lyle, the scorer of Dundee's first, to make it 3-3 in the dying seconds. After a scoreless period of extra-time (I have no idea how dramatic or otherwise it was, because I wasn't there) Queens triumph in the penalty shoot-out, their keeper, Barry John Corr, the penalty-saving hero by all accounts.

Going For Gold: I can't really issue any gold stars for a match I never saw completed. A match where I only saw half of the goals and none of the penalties and missed most of the fuss. I imagine it's a nine or ten but I sure as hell can't award them. I wasn't even there for it.

Fanfare: The Doonhamers fans don't need to come out of their shells. They're already out and they are shouting like mad. One of the few songs I can make out is 'When the South go marching in'. But I probably miss about a dozen songs they sing in the second-half or in extra-time. I know that Queen of the South have this one song about a wheelbarrow and the point of the song seems to be that the wheels come off. Hmm. When the Queens mascot Dougie Doonhamer appears the fans point at him repeatedly and shout 'Dougie! Dougie! Dougie!' and Dougie laps it all up like a good dog enjoying the attention. But he looks like he wants fed too. A couple of the Dundee fans seem to be getting lifted by the police but the troublemakers are removed swiftly from the stand because the police have cranes for this sort of thing.

Request To The Rail Service Provider: Can't you have trains running later than 21.44 from Dumfries to Glasgow on weekdays? Especially if there is a game on at Palmerston? I was gutted when I got home, although I would have been more gutted had I stayed and watched the conclusion of the match and missed the last train back and had to spend the night in Dumfries. Only kidding. Dumfries is a lovely place.

MISSION POSSIBLE 30

OBJECTIVE:
To go to Station
Park and watch
Forfar Athletic.

SCENARIO: Forfar Athletic are playing Cowdenbeath in the Scottish Second Division.

DATE: Saturday, January 20, 2007. God, is it still January? It has been a long winter and it is not over yet. Not by a long chalk.

LOCATION, LOCATION, LOCATION: Did you know that the Royal Burgh of Forfar, in the heart of Angus, is the ancient capital of the Picts? I didn't either. The Queen Mother spent her early childhood in Glamis and is said to have seen her first football match at Station Park. She could not have picked a better one. Forfar versus Brechin in the Forfarshire Cup. She had three bridies.

CULTURAL NOTES: Forfar is 'hardly thrilling' says *Scotland The Braw*. But it must have been pretty exciting in the 1660s when the Forfar Witch Hunts took place. One witch admitted to roasting a goose for the devil, before she was roasted herself by a bunch of fair-minded locals.

FORFAR PROFILE

KICKED OFF: 1885. The year Dr Emmett 'Doc' Brown is sent back to in *Back to the Future* after lightning strikes his DeLorean in 1955.

TRUE COLOURS: A sky blue and navy combination.

BADGE OF HONOUR: Let's see here. There is a tree. There is a castle. There is a cow. There is a stag. Have I missed anything? Nope, don't think so.

NAME CALLING: The Loons. Not that they are mental or anything. Loons means boys in some parts of the country. It is a colloquialism, not an insult. The reason Forfar are called the Loons is because once upon a time a youthful second XI broke off from Angus Athletic to form Forfar Athletic.

MORTAL ENEMY: Brechin City. You could add Montrose and Arbroath to that list.

AREN'T WE BRILLIANT?: Forfar's finest moment was racing away with the Second Division title during the 1983-84 season. They were the first club in Britain to clinch a title in that season. There was once a rumour put about that Forfar had changed their name to Forfar Nil. Sadly there was no truth in it. The Loons have run Rangers close in cup competition a few times. And it is interesting to note that Forfar legend Jim Black not only played for Forfar and managed Forfar but refereed Forfar. Hmm.

MISSION LOGISTICS

ALIGHT AT: This is a little bit awkward, but persevere. Get off at Dundee rail station and get yourself to Dundee bus station. From there take the bus to Forfar. It is not a long bus journey and in fact it is a rather nice one through appealing countryside.

A Pint At: The Caledonian bar is very close to Station Park. It is a traditional boozer with quite a friendly atmosphere, it seems, and there is other football on the TV if you need it.

MISSION DEBRIEFING

Field of Dreams: Station Park is next to the Forfar Mart. Like with a lot of lower division Scottish grounds, there is room to roam at Station Park. You are given the freedom to sit or stand anywhere you like. I sit in the main stand for a bit and then hang out behind the dug-out with the hardcore Forfar followers. At another point I stand on the terrace behind the goals and, during a quiet moment in proceedings, count sheep in a close-by field. Station Park is a very pastoral setting. It's really pleasant.

Super Pies Me: Here comes the bridie! Here comes the bridie! She's huge, but she's quite hot. I have to be honest here … [deep breath] … for me, the famous Forfar bridie is a bit of a let-down. I had never had one before and perhaps I had built it up in my mind, but, essentially, it is a hybrid of a pie and a sausage roll. The novelty value soon wears off. As I stand at the counter and squirt broon sauce on my Forfar bridie, a man behind me in the queue nudges his son and points at me. 'Look at that!' exclaims the dad. I panic a little and mutter an apology, believing I have committed some heinous Forfar faux-pas by lavishing sauce on my bridie. Except it turns out that the man is merely admiring my bridie and complimenting me on my choice of condiment. I relax slightly and bite into my bridie - which is triangular and the size but not the shape of a cow.

> **GAME ON**: Forfar Athletic 2-0 Cowdenbeath
>
> **FORFAR GOALSCORERS**: Lombardi 57, Gribben 80.

FORFAR ATHLETIC: Wood, Trialist (Fraser 88), King, Allison, Lumsden, Coyle, Trialist, Tade, Tosh, Gribben, Lombardi.

COWDENBEATH: Hay, Baxter, McBride (Dalziel 77), Lennon, Hill, Hannah, Fusco, Fotheringham (Weir 25), Buchanan, Clarke, Scullion (Trialist 59).

HEAD COUNT: 377.

Report Card: Strikes by Michele Lombardi, the moonlighting Formula One driver, and Darren Gribben fetch bottom-club Forfar victory over 10-man Cowdenbeath. Lombardi opens the scoring from close-range shortly before the hour-mark while Gribben grabs the second by chesting the ball down and dipping his volley beyond the Cowdenbeath keeper who is caught out by the bounce. Steven Weir is given the red card by the referee near the end (for a late tackle) but it is really silly of the referee to give Weir the red card. What if the referee wants to send somebody else off? He will check in his pocket and there will be no red card because he has given it to Steven Weir who has disappeared down the tunnel. My main problem at Station Park is keeping warm because it is freezing here. I wish I had worn my second coat and maybe even a third coat and today I have forgotten my silver long johns. The Forfar number nine is running about in short sleeves. All the other players are long-sleeved and some of them are wearing gloves. Paul Tosh must be the hardest man in Scottish football. I have no idea how he manages to cope but he seems to be coping fine.

Going For Gold: It is a welcome win for Forfar but this is not one of the better games I have had the privilege to watch. I will settle with six gold stars from this outing in Angus.

Fanfare: The Forfar fans are few but they seem committed to the cause although they don't have any songs to sing. So I have invented for them … a canon. The Partick Thistle canon was based on 'London's Burning', but this one borrows the template of the popular French canon 'Frère Jacques' and goes something like this. Actually it goes just like this:

Frère Forfar, frère Forfar,
Bridie noo, bridie noo,
Sunny Loons of Angus, sunny Loons of Angus,
Station Park, Station Park.

Music To My Ears: Before the game 'I Don't Wanna Be Your Lover', by Texas, rings round Station Park. I wouldn't mind so much but they play it twice. In a row. We later get a bit of Springsteen. The Forfar team runs out to, yes, 'Local Hero' by Dire Straits.

MISSION POSSIBLE 31

OBJECTIVE:
To go to East End
Park and watch
Dunfermline Athletic.

SCENARIO: Dunfermline are playing Rangers in the Scottish Premier League.

DATE: Sunday, January 21, 2007.

LOCATION, LOCATION, LOCATION: The auld grey toun of Dunfermline, deep in the kingdom of Fife. Scotland's capital until 1603 and the Union of the Crowns. Which preceded 'Union of the Snake' by Duran Duran.

CULTURAL NOTES: You might want to stop by the impressive Dunfermline Abbey and, if you have the time and the inclination, you can regard the only remaining, but dramatic, façade of Dunfermline Palace, which is next to Dunfermline Abbey anyway.

DUNFERMLINE ATHLETIC PROFILE

KICKED OFF: 1885. Scottish vet John Boyd Dunlop invents the pneumatic tyre.

TRUE COLOURS: Black and white stripes. In a vertical direction.

BADGE OF HONOUR: The Dunfermline badge looks like something out of Sleepy Hollow. I think it may be the seriously creepy tree in the background. And the outline of hills which somehow look like bats. And there is a tower and I don't want to go in there. I'm scared.

NAME CALLING: The Pars. There are numerous suggestions for the origin of this moniker. And none of them are to do with golf. My favourite explanation of The Pars is that the players used to perform in such a manner that observers suspected they were paralytic.

MORTAL ENEMY: The Dunfermline-Falkirk rivalry is not the most edgy football rivalry of all-football-time, but it does constitute a rivalry nonetheless, in that they don't like each other.

AREN'T WE BRILLIANT?: In the 1968/69 season, Dunfermline reached the semi-finals of the European Cup Winners' Cup, three years before Rangers won the competition. The Pars have won a couple of Scottish Cups. Sometimes the Pars have been found to be distinctly above par.

MISSION LOGISTICS

ALIGHT AT: The stations of Dunfermline Queen Margaret and Dunfermline Town are both within fifteen minutes' walk of East End Park. Dunfermline Town is perhaps a better jumping off point if you fancy a pint before the game. But wait until the train stops before jumping off and then head up the awfully steep hill towards the town centre in search of a libation.

A Pint At: The award-winning Commercial Bar (off the High Street) stocks guest ales and even welcomes guest supporters. Good spot for a pint. Over at East End Park there is actually a bar inside the main stand. It is called Legends, and it is for the home fans, but I ask nicely and they let me in. Elvis is the first to greet you as you enter the bar, and up on the walls are portraits of Pars legends from Istvan Kozsma to Norrie McCathie and Jim Leishman. Legends goes for American sports-bar look, booths with TVs, but the sheer convenience of location helps it work for me. Legends has a mezzanine level. Which is a fancy way of saying there's an upstairs bit.

MISSION DEBRIEFING

Field of Dreams: East End Park has been redeveloped plenty in recent years. It remains a rather likeable ground with the old main stand holding up tradition. The views are good and the atmosphere can be decent, depending on whom Dunfermline are playing that day. Behind the North Stand there is a cemetery. What is it with Scottish football grounds and cemeteries? Off the top of my head, I can think of Celtic Park and Pittodrie, and there are more, I'm sure of it. Yes. Brechin. Dunfermline flirted with an artificial pitch which did not prove popular and mercifully the Fifers reverted to an old-fashioned, no-nonsense plain-as-grass surface.

Super Pies Me: I ignore the pies on offer and go straight for the Dunfermline steak bridie. Though I don't lunge over the counter for it. I ask nicely and receive. The Dunfermline steak bridie is divine. I am all too aware that I have verbally trashed the Forfar bridie, or at least not raved about it. Having slighted the Forfar bridie, I am now going to enrage the Forfarians further by declaring the Dunfermline steak bridie to be a superior bridie. There. I've said it. The Pars bridie is a bridie par excellence. At the steep price point of £1.90, it costs more than your average half-time feed, but this is not an average feed. Flaky, golden pastry, generous soft chunks of steak with glorious gravy. Frankly, it's one of the best things I've ever eaten.

GAME ON: Dunfermline Athletic 0-1 Rangers

RANGERS GOALSCORER: Adam 9.

DUNFERMLINE ATHLETIC: De Vries, Shields, McGuire, Wilson, Morrison, Ross (McIntyre 77), Mason, Ryan (Hamill 46), O'Brien (Muirhead 77), Hamilton, Crawford.

RANGERS: McGregor, Hutton, Svensson, Weir, Murray, Burke (Buffel 70), Ferguson, Hemdani, Adam, Novo (Sebo 90), Boyd.

HEAD COUNT: 7,868.

Report Card: Rangers scrape the scrappiest of victories over Dunfermline with the only goal of the game arriving early through Charlie Adam sweeping Nacho Novo's cross into the Dunfermline net without the aid of a broom. The hacked off Dunfermline players then take to brandishing shovels about the pitch (one of them even commandeers a pitchfork from the groundsman) but the Pars are unable to dig themselves out of defeat as they also have a couple of penalty claims turned down. Jim Hamilton wastes the best chance to level for the home side, but his header flights over the Rangers crossbar and lets the visitors off the hook. Another league win for the new Rangers management team of Smith and McCoist.

Going For Gold: Another Premier League classic in that it lacks class. I wouldn't say I'm pining for Cowdenbeath, and the steak bridie alone makes this trip to Dunfermline worthwhile, but I expected better than this. Hit me with a dose of proper top-tier football or at least football that contains an element of enjoyment. Four gold stars. Please allow me to sulk.

Fanfare: 'Ole, ole, ole, ole, we are the Pars, we are the Pars.' This is par for the course for Dunfermline and is about as inspired as their fans get when it comes to singing songs of praise and heart-felt loyalty to the cause. They do manage to improvise at one point with a derisive round of 'Walter Smith … quack, quack, quack'. Except that it's not quack, quack, quack.

Music To My Ears: Billy Ocean. Billy Ocean? 'Into The Valley' by Dunfermline punk band The Skids is the anthem which has the Dunfermline team emerging from the East End Park tunnel; although the Dunfermline team would surely have emerged from the tunnel at some point, because they have a match to play, and if they don't run out they'll be docked three points.

ALL BETS ARE OFF

Maybe if I was a betting man, I would have fared better. Or squandered more money than I did.

The stakes were high. Sometimes I would throw caution to the wind and wager AS MUCH AS THREE POUNDS on a match. At other times I might prefer to hedge my bets and risk a more meagre amount, say, a pound. Losing it still hurt.

I am not a betting man. A betting man does not walk into a bookies and go 'ooh, orange juice!' There is a pitcher of the diluted sweet stuff on the counter next to a tower of paper cups. That's nice, I think. Such unexpected hospitality. So I pour myself a stiff measure.

The bookies. Used to be something secret and illicit. You never could see inside any of these places. I often wondered what went on in there. Occasionally, gruff blokes would stagger out (clouds of smoke behind them: had the building caught fire?) and into the pub conveniently situated next door. Moments later, here they were again, lurching out of the pub, looking ever the worse for wear, and straight back into the bookies. It seemed to be a peculiar existence - and not one which particularly appealed to me. 'Son, what do you want to be when you're older?' 'A gambling drunk mum, if that's okay with you.'

Bookies these days are free from fag reek. They are well-lit and clean and remind me of airport departure lounges. Except that instead of the next flight to Faro on the board it is the 3.15 from Musselburgh. I stand shoulder-to-shoulder with betting zombies, staring at the banks of colourful screens. But I can make neither horse's head nor horse's tail of it. All these hundreds of bright numbers are sending me into a trance.

Being a betting novice, I thought it would be a good idea to get my brother involved. My brother knows as much about betting as I do. But I like to get him involved now and then. Keeps him busy. My plan is for my brother to provide me with tips. Off the top of his head. This turns out to be a bad idea. However, until I realise it, ahead of each match I call Herb. My brother's not really called Herb. I've just been calling him Herb all these years and can't seem to stop.

Herb! What's your hunch?

3-1 to Albion Rovers.

Are you sure?

Aye. 3-1.

Herb is a man of few words. But his latent curiosity has been piqued.

Where's Albion Rovers?

Coatbridge, Herb. I'm there right now in the bookies.

Coatbridge eh? I was thinking of going there my holidays next year.

I can't decide whether Herb is being serious or sarcastic. It's hard to tell with Herb.

In any event, Stenhousemuir defeat Albion Rovers 2-1. Shortly after the final-whistle, I receive a text message from my brother. SORRY. HERB.

But I stick by him. I don't want to be too heavy on him, he's my brother. He'll come good in the end.

I'm on my way to Falkirk. They are playing Aberdeen. I call Herb while I'm on the train.

What'll it be today Nostradamus?

4-1 to Aberdeen.

You really think so?

No. 4-1 Falkirk.

4-1 to Falkirk?

No. 1-1.

Only if you're sure now Herb.

I'm sure.

Aberdeen win 2-0. After the game Herb gets in touch again. SORRY

GARY. WILL BUY U 2 JARS OF BEETROOT 4 EACH POUND U LOST.

I don't really need six jars of beetroot. I text back my brother telling him not to bother with the beetroot. But he's not taking no (beetroot) for an answer.

Looking back over the costly course of the season, it's amazing how I persevere with Herb and his hopeless hunches for so long. Brotherly love must be blind. He comes close on one occasion. The day I go to Tynecastle.

Cheers for the beetroot Herb.

No problem Gary.

What do you reckon?

Oh I think it'll be great beetroot. It's Baxters.

No, what do you reckon about the match?

4-1 to Hearts.

Any particular reason?

Dundee United are pish.

Hearts win 4-0. Had Dundee United been marginally less pish they might have scored, and Herb's prophecy would have come true. Instead, it's another couple of pounds down the drain. Oh well.

To Herb's credit, he comes up with a fresh method of match prediction. One that doesn't involve asking him what the outcome of a match will be.

Hello Herb.

Gary, I've had an idea.

Let's hear it then.

Deanna.

Your dog.

Aye, we'll ask her.

Ask her what?

Ask her what the score will be.

You mean ask a German Shepherd to predict the outcome between Elgin City and East Stirlingshire?

Aye.

And how does that work Herb?

I'll feed her crackers.

You're crackers.

No, listen. I'll give Deanna crackers and however many she eats that's how many goals Elgin are going to score.

And East Stirlingshire?

Well, I'll give Deanna some water. And then start feeding her more crackers.

?

I take my hat off to Herb and salute him. He's a genius. We are going to take the bookies to the cleaners with this dog-betting business. It is amazing no-one has ever thought of it before.

You will be glad to learn that no German Shepherd was force-fed crackers during the making of this book. We keep Deanna out of it. Indeed, after Herb's crackpot crackers scheme, I keep my brother out of it and go it alone for the first time, tipping Elgin to win 2-0. Despite the fact that Elgin have lost their past ten league games. I am ripping up the form book and I am laughing at it in an exaggerated evil character from Scooby Doo manner. And the woman behind the counter in the Elgin bookies is laughing at me. '2-0? To Elgin? Ha-ha-ha.' You might mock me. But you'll see. You'll all see. Mwa-ha-ha-ha-ha.

It turns out I'm not bold enough. There is a real turn up for the books and Elgin win 5-0!

One day my boat does come in. Or is it my ship? I find the brilliant foresight to foresee Kilmarnock drawing 1-1 with Inverness Caledonian Thistle at Rugby Park. After the final whistle, I skip all the way to the bookies to collect my winnings. All £7 of them. From an audacious £2 stake at 7-2 odds. I am simply made up, a made man, and I dream of ways of spending this totally unexpected windfall. I settle for a pair of pints and a single malt.

After my long-awaited breakthrough at the bookies, I become ever more adventurous in my relentless pursuit of a crazy cash bonanza. I begin delving into the Byzantine world of accumulators. You know the sort of thing. Raith Rovers to beat Ayr United, Manchester United to beat

Everton, Real Madrid to beat Barcelona and the sun to set fire to the moon. Except that the sheer number of possibilities soon makes my head hurt. My concentration becomes so impaired that I am unable to focus on the game of football I have paid to see. So I bin the bookies, jack in my chance of the jackpot and go cold turkey. Well, almost.

There is always the 50/50. I hold on to that particular cause. However lost it is.

The 50/50 half-time draw is part and parcel of Scottish football. You need to have a pint or two, buy the match programme, buy your 50/50 ticket, buy a pie and watch your team get humped. While singing badly and swearing abusively. That's Scottish football in a pie case.

'Get your 50/50 ticket!' I am like a moth to a flame or a mouse to some cheese or a fish to bait. I'll take two please. 'Aye,' laughs the 50/50 seller at Cliftonhill, 'just like Charlie and the Chocolate Factory.' You mean to say that the prize is a trip to a chocolate factory? In that case, I'll take ten.

At Firs Park, the home of East Stirlingshire, I find the 50/50 seller after the turnstiles. Two please. The man grins and points an index finger to his temple. 'It's all in the mind,' he whispers. So ... this transaction isn't taking place; you are nothing but a figment of my rampant imagination and East Stirlingshire aren't playing Stenhousemuir today. I might as well go home then.

Here's the thing about the 50/50. You don't have a 50/50 chance of winning. Unless the only entrants are you and one other punter and you have both bought the same number of tickets. 50/50 tickets are so called because half of the money goes to the club and the other half becomes the total prize money.

Another aspect of the 50/50 is that the prize money varies. Stirling Albion offer up a cash pot of £75 for the half-time draw at Forthbank. Ross County boast a bumper £600 the day I turn up at Victoria Park (alas I do not depart with £600 in my wallet). After they break it to me at Cliftonhill that the prize isn't a tour of a chocolate factory, they inform me that if I win the 50/50 I might be able to treat myself to a pie. That is one very modest prize or a truly expensive pie. Ultimately, the size of the 50/50 handout depends on factors like the size of the crowd and the willingness of fans to have a flutter.

Each half-time of every match, all season, I grasp those 50/50 tickets in my hands but my number never comes up. Robert Prytz, or whichever football legend, fishes the winning ticket from the tombola and the winning number is announced to the crowd and Robert Prytz leaves the pitch to warm applause - and I slope off and join the pie queue, having torn up my tickets.

Then my friend Brian joins me at the match between Peterhead v Alloa in the Blue Toon. I remember us passing through the turnstiles at Balmoor and there is the 50/50 man and I scramble for change in my pocket while Brian hands over a £5 note and waits for change. My 50/50 is bought after Brian's 50/50. If only it had been the other way round. If only. Had I just been that little bit quicker on the draw. Damn.

'It's not the sunniest of places, Peterhead, is it?' says Brian. The day is indeed gloomy. Yet Brian's disposition will be exceedingly sunny once half-time comes around. (The bastard.)

Here is how they stage the 50/50 draw at Balmoor. It is most unusual. The Peterhead FC mascot, resembling a badly-fitted carpet (Brian and I christen it Carpet Monster), shuffles sheepishly round the perimeter of the pitch, while holding aloft a blackboard bearing the all-important winning 50/50 number in white chalk. Brian and I are both stationed behind the goalposts and have to wait ages for Carpet Monster to pass us and for that moment of truth to occur. The tension increases as the dishevelled creature (which looks kind of like a dog) ambles towards us, displaying the prized information. Brian points out that Carpet Monster is sporting brown brogues. I am squinting at the chalk number on the board. And staring at the number on my 50/50 ticket. I am really close. In fact, I am one number out. And Brian has stopped studying Carpet Monster's brown brogues and has realised that he is right on the money and that he, Brian, is in possession of the winning ticket. Now Brian is jumping up and down at Balmoor like a man possessed, and he is thumping the air with delight. You lucky shit.

The Peterhead fans around us recognise the commotion - and they seem full of goodwill and congratulate Brian. I pretend that I am full of goodwill towards Brian and pat him on the back. Although it is more like a punch. 'Well done,' I grimace, through gritted teeth. I have missed out on the 50/50 for the umpteenth time and I had always reminded myself, well, you're not supposed to win; it is a million to one shot (kind of). And there is Brian. Winning the 50/50 at the first time of trying. The fortunate grinning idiot. He runs over to the main stand to collect his winnings and he sprints back with an extra spring in his step and an extra £200 in his pocket and still the stupidest smile on his stupid face. 'How do you split £200 eight ways?' asks one of the Peterhead fans. Brian laughs. Is that nervous laughter? Maybe he is ripe for a mugging. Maybe I should instigate it. I give up my 50/50 fix after the Balmoor Travesty, and stick to the football.

Betting. It's a mug's game.

MISSION POSSIBLE **32**

SCENARIO: Ross County are playing Dundee in the Scottish First Division.

DATE: Saturday, January 27, 2007. Still January! Are the months stuck or something?

LOCATION, LOCATION, LOCATION: Not as northerly as Wick Academy, or IFK Reykjavik for that matter, Ross County are the second northernmost team in senior football in Britain, after Elgin City. Ross County are situated in the Ross-shire town of Dingwall, not far from Inverness. Not far enough for Ross County fans.

CULTURAL NOTES: *Scotland The Braw* describes Dingwall as 'tidy, but dull'. Maybe if they had gone back when the weather was better. Perhaps the compilers of *Scotland The Braw* failed to find out that Dingwall is actually the birthplace of Macbeth. There was rarely a dull moment in his life. You can still bump into his ghost about town. Or is it Banquo's?

ROSS COUNTY PROFILE

KICKED OFF: 1929. Popeye makes his debut in a cartoon. Not for Ross County.

TRUE COLOURS: Dark blue, dark white and dark red.

BADGE OF HONOUR: A stag's head. Taken from the crest of the Seaforth Highlanders, the regiment for which a lot of local people fought and died during the First World War.

NAME CALLING: The County. Or the Staggies, which is much more romantic and conjures up a stereotypical image of the Highlands. Strangely enough, on the way up to Dingwall, I glimpse a stag from the train. And when I reach Dingwall there is a stag party in one of the pubs. Later, in the street, I spot a few staggeringly drunk people staggering about who are not involved with the stag party. Maybe this is just something they do in Dingwall on a Saturday afternoon.

MORTAL ENEMY: Inverness Caledonian Thistle.

AREN'T WE BRILLIANT: The Staggies won the Highland League title three times before they were admitted to the Scottish Football League in 1994, along with Caley Thistle. County have not enjoyed quite the level of success of Caley Thistle. But they did win the Third Division title in season 1998/99 and, in November of 2006, won their first ever national cup competition, when they defeated Clyde on penalty kicks in the Challenge Cup final.

MISSION LOGISTICS

ALIGHT AT: In the time it takes me to get to Dingwall, I might have made it to Damascus. But at least when the train does pull into Dingwall station, several hours after my dawn departure from Glasgow (with a change of service in Inverness) there is a pub right here on the platform. Alight for a pint and suddenly everything's all right. An additional bonus is that the football ground is just over the bridge from the train station. We're all set then.

A Pint At: I'm not going to duck the issue. The Mallard's the name of the aforementioned pub on the station platform. And it has been taken over temporarily by Dundee fans. There is an advert for a karaoke night by Andy Candoo. I bet he never cancels. For the sake of variety, I also pop into a couple of other pubs in the centre of Dingwall, such as it is. They are a bit of a mixed bag to be honest but my curiosity has been satisfied.

MISSION DEBRIEFING

Field of Dreams: A policeman approaches me outside the gates of Victoria Park and I just happen to be hanging about the Jailend of the ground. The Jailend is the home terrace behind one of the goals. Behind the Jailend is Dingwall sheriff court. Maybe this is it. I am going to get lifted and locked up. The policeman wants to know why I'm taking photographs. I tell him that I'm hunting grounds and the pictures are documentary evidence. He seems satisfied with this explanation and explains that he only asked me because 'you cannot be too careful in this day and age.' I am all in favour of proper vigilance and homeland security, yet still I'm thinking 'but we're in Dingwall'. The West Stand is a dandy all-seater affair. And opposite the West Stand with their backs to the Cromarty Firth there are a few hardy boys on an exposed bit of uncovered corner terracing, unflinching in the bitter northern cold. They look as if they might be tossed into the firth, if they are not careful. In the interests of experimentation I head over there and stand with them for a minute, but I only last a minute. Unlike them I have not the patience nor the endurance of an emperor penguin. For the most part I stand in the Jailend with the Jailenders. At least it provides shelter and it feels like just about the most fun you can have with your clothes on at Victoria Park.

Super Pies Me: The Ross County pie passes the pie test with flying colours. Nice pastry. Tasty, quite spicy mince. Nae sauce on the scene though.

> **GAME ON**: Ross County 0-0 Dundee
>
> **ROSS COUNTY**: Samson, Smith, Moore, Dowie, Keddie, McCulloch, O'Carrol, Anderson (Scott 79), Higgins (Gunn 64), Cowie, McKinlay (Robertson 75).
>
> **DUNDEE**: Roy, Shields, Dixon, McHale, MacKenzie, Smith, McDonald, Robertson, Lyle, Davidson (Trialist 68), Swankie.
>
> **HEAD COUNT**: 2,175.

Report Card: Whit a bore! The drabbest of draws in Dingwall with neither side remotely rising to the occasion. Both teams mining hidden depths. One of the few moments that I remember from this drearathon is Dundee's Scott Robertson powering an inaccurate blast over the Ross County crossbar. That really is about it. So pitiful it's pathetic. The poorest game I have had the gross misfortune to watch since St Johnstone and Airdrie. I'm actually feeling quite depressed about this dour Dingwall occasion. Another black mark on the First Division. I think the Premier League is dragging it down. The one thing that's interesting is that Ross County are in a dark blue shirt with white shorts and Dundee are in a white shirt with dark blue shorts and they look like a negative print of each other. But I wouldn't bother developing any photos from this match.

Going For Gold: I travel all that distance. For this. I want my money back. I want my day back. Gold stars two. Both of them for the Jailend experience, nothing for the foul football.

Fanfare: 'Glad to, glad to be, glad to be a Staggie!' I'm glad for them. All the action is at the Jailend. These people need locked up.

Music To My Ears: We are treated to a half-time Burns tribute with it being near Burns Night and all that.

MISSION POSSIBLE

OBJECTIVE:
*To go to the Tulloch
Caledonian Stadium
and watch Inverness
Caledonian Thistle. Phew!*

SCENARIO: Inverness Caledonian Thistle are playing Celtic in the Scottish Premier League.

DATE: Sunday, January 28, 2007. It can't still be January.

LOCATION, LOCATION, LOCATION: The city of Inverness, hub of the Highlands, is on the banks of the River Ness which is the subterranean home of Careful-Ness, Ferocious-Ness, Lovely-Ness, Sporty-Ness and all the other members of the Family Ness, discovered by Angus and Elspeth in the children's cartoon series of the early 1980s.

CULTURAL NOTES: Inverness is 'busy and prosperous' according to *Scotland The Braw*. Is that good or bad? Hey! Check out the pink castle! Learn some Highland history at the Inverness Museum and Art Gallery. You're not far from the battlefield at Culloden either.

INVERNESS CALEDONIAN THISTLE PROFILE

KICKED OFF: 1994 (following the painful merger of Inverness Thistle and Caledonian FC). The lead singer of Nirvana, Kurt Cobain, is found dead in his Seattle home.

TRUE COLOURS: Blue and red.

BADGE OF HONOUR: A thistle, which is apt. With a majestic eagle landing on top of it. Like that happens every day. An eagle landing on top of a thistle. They've just made that up.

NAME CALLING: Caley Thistle, Caley, Caley Jags, Jags, Super Caley, ICT, Inverness, Inverness Caley … oh what's the use, whatever anyone says they're going to get it wrong somehow.

MORTAL ENEMY: Ross County. The supporters of Caley Thistle (or whatever they wish to call their team) can't stomach the Staggies.

AREN'T WE BRILLIANT?: Inverness Caledonian Thistle have never been relegated from the top flight. Which makes Inverness Caledonian Thistle officially Brilliant. And, on top of that, they boast the most letters of any club in Scotland. 26! Caley Thistle are also noted for knocking Celtic out of the Scottish Cup once, a fair feat which sparked a Mary Poppins style headline about Caley being both super and ballistic, while deeming Celtic atrocious.

MISSION LOGISTICS

ALIGHT AT: Inbhir Nis train station. Where the heck are we? Oh. Inverness. It's a long slog from the station to the ground, but it can be done. Longman Road is a long road man but I persevere. And a number of Caley Thistle fans seem to have the same idea, so I cannot be too misguided. It does get rather dicey negotiating the hectic road of traffic heading to and from the Kessock Bridge, but there is a policeman at the crossing point who seems to have the super-human capacity to stop cars with the mere raising of one hand. After the match you can always hop aboard one of the double-decker buses which wait outside the ground to ferry fans back to the city centre.

A Pint At: Not far from the train station is the Innes Bar on Innes Street. It's quite popular with Caley Thistle fans but they are not letting Celtic fans in today. They have got tables and chairs and wardrobes pushed up against the door. Since I am only a harmless floating neutral ground-hunter they let me in but I have to climb in the window. Later on I pop my head in the door of the Citadel next to the harbour and it is heaving with Celtic fans. The main drawback with the stadium's location, magnificent though it is, is that there is not a pub anywhere nearby.

MISSION DEBRIEFING

Field of Dreams: The Tulloch Caledonian Stadium is beautifully positioned right by the Moray Firth. Though if you are sitting in the big impressive main stand you will not see anything of the firth because it's behind you. Which sounds very pantomime. You're able to wander out to the wings of the main stand and to look back at the views of the firth, and I recommend that. The Kessock Bridge, which you can't miss, was modelled on a bridge over the river Rhine in Düsseldorf. So there you go. Plenty of Caley Thistle fans head for the North Stand (or Bridge End) so that's where I go and it is very friendly. People you don't even know say hello to you. And that's rare in Scottish football. There are a lot of families present. Inverness have the widest pitch in Scottish league football. It's wider than it is long. A lot of visiting teams do find that a 2-6-2 formation works best. Other ground points are that there are a lot of seagulls and there's a salt depot next door.

Super Pies Me: The Inverness Caledonian Thistle pie is a bit arid. I'm not sure if you can describe food as arid, but I'll go for it. Arid.

GAME ON: Inverness Caledonian Thistle 1-2 Celtic

INVERNESS GOALSCORER: Bayne 57.

CELTIC GOALSCORERS: Riordan 37, Vennegoor of Hesselink 90.

INVERNESS CALEDONIAN THISTLE: Fraser, Tokely, Dods, Munro, Hastings, Wilson, McBain, Duncan (Black 74), Rankin, Bayne, Wyness (McAllister 2), McAllister (Paatelainen 84).

CELTIC: Boruc, Telfer, Pressley (O'Dea 39), McManus, Naylor, Nakamura, Gravesen, Lennon, Riordan, Vennegoor of Hesselink, Beattie (Miller 45).

HEAD COUNT: 7,484.

Report Card: Yon Avenger of Hesselink is the thorn in Caley Thistle's side. He wreaks a whole lot of havoc in injury time to clinch three points for Celtic. Hasselhoff runs off and kisses the delighted Celtic fans behind the goals but his celebrations are short-lived as the referee, who seems jealous, books Hasselhoff, who has already received a yellow card so he is hassled off the park. Not that he misses much. The game is over. Earlier on, Derek Riordan puts Celtic ahead with an uncomplicated tap-in, after some bad home defending, but Graham Bayne responds correctly with a header for Inverness who then think that they have one point in the bag. Fools. They have reckoned without Yon Avenger bloke.

Going For Gold: I feel quite sorry for Inverness but take nothing away from Celtic even if they take everything away from Inverness. It is a dramatic end to a good contest. I'm going to go with seven gold stars and won't be changing my mind.

Fanfare: 'Gimme a C ... gimme an A ... gimme an L ... gimme an E ... gimme a Y ... what does it spell?' Ross County? This is all very American Cheerleader In Inverness, but at least the guy doesn't start off with 'Gimme an I ... gimme an N ... gimme a V ...' Otherwise we would have been there all day waiting for him to spell it out to us and for us to respond to his prompt in the name of crowd participation. I'm not sure I would've had the patience. In terms of my threshold for biting my tongue, I think I'd have let him get to maybe the second N in Inverness and I'd have just then shouted out 'Inverness Caledonian Thistle!' even if it did ruin his routine. Talking of routines, the world keepie-up champion is here and he's pretty good. He can keep it up for ages and the crowd are still hungry for more.

Music To My Ears: The Invernesians are going 'Radio Ga Ga'.

MISSION POSSIBLE

EPISODE 34

OBJECTIVE:
To go to Glebe
Park and watch
Brechin City.

SCENARIO: Brechin City are playing Ayr United in the Scottish Second Division.

DATE: Saturday, February 3, 2007. Finally. February. I thought January would never end. February's shorter. I've only got seven more games after this one anyway. I'm within touching distance. At a stretch.

LOCATION, LOCATION, LOCATION: The Ancient City of Brechin in ancient Angus. Only a few miles inland from the metropolis of Montrose. You'd think Brechin was off the radar but Brechin-born Robert Watson-Watt was a pioneer of radar!

CULTURAL NOTES: *Scotland The Braw* labels Brechin 'soporific'. I'm not entirely sure what that means. Is soporific better than terrific? You know I've just looked it up and it means sleepy. Or drugged. Brechin has its own cathedral. But let's be honest. You didn't come here to look at a cathedral. You've come here to check out the hedge.

BRECHIN CITY PROFILE

KICKED OFF: 1906. Mount Vesuvius erupts and devastates Naples. Brechin is unscathed.

TRUE COLOURS: Red and white.

BADGE OF HONOUR: A cathedral. Must be Brechin Cathedral. With a football parked in front of it. Can you park a football? Football = religion. That seems to be the message.

NAME CALLING: The City. Not the village, not the hamlet, not the town. The City!

MORTAL ENEMY: Brechin City's nearest, and least dearest, Montrose.

AREN'T WE BRILLIANT?: Brechin City have won the Forfarshire Cup four times. That's four more times than Rangers and Celtic have managed.

MISSION LOGISTICS

ALIGHT AT: The nearest train station is Montrose. But that's not a problem. From Montrose High Street, you can catch the number 30 bus to Brechin. It's an adorable adventure in the country (I sing The Wheels On The Bus song) and I am dropped off suitably close to Glebe

Park by the helpful bus driver. Which is great.

A Pint At: From the outside, The Stables doesn't look fit for a horse never mind a man with a drink problem (the problem being that I need a drink after the long journey) but once inside The Stables it proves to be not a bad option. There is a small bar and a large lounge and they do gigantic bowls of chips. They're enormous. Ginormous even.

MISSION DEBRIEFING

Field of Dreams: Glebe Park sounds like something out of The Broons. The prominent sight at Glebe Park is - of course - the hedge. This is simply a tremendous hedge. Really quite something. Admire it and stroke it, and settle yourself down in the Cemetery End with the Brechin un-dead, who are fairly awake. But watch out for stray shots. That ball will take your head clean off. I almost lost mine but for the Brechin goalkeeper warning me to be vigilant. 'You need to keep your wits about you,' he said to me during the warm-up after I had narrowly avoided decapitation and the ball thumped off the wall behind me. While you're in the Cemetery End, dodging balls, seek out the hand-prints in cement. I have never come across this at a football ground before. Hollywood comes to Brechin. I look for Humphrey Bogart's hand in this, but all I can see are some Brechin supporters who have immortalised themselves and cemented their reputations. Glebe Park's nice. Trees, distant church spires, hedge …

Super Pies Me: The Brechin pie is not the king of pies but it is pretty good. Quite pleasing in fact, and cheap. Hits the right spot.

GAME ON: Brechin City 2 Ayr United 0

BRECHIN GOALSCORERS: Russell 69, Connolly 83.

BRECHIN CITY: Nelson, R Walker, S Walker, White, Murie, Byers, Ferguson, Callaghan, Smith (King 76), Connolly, Russell.

AYR UNITED: McGeown, Pettigrew, Forrest, Robertson, Lowing, Caddis (Strain 57), Casey, Weaver, Dunn, Waddle (Wardlaw 70), Harty.

HEAD COUNT: 488

Report Card: Brechin City airbrush Ayr United out of the picture at Glebe Park and the Cemetery End celebrates. After they were tearing what's left of their hair out when they watched Stuart Callaghan miss from the penalty spot, right in front of us. But Iain Russell rattles in a home goal after the spot-kick setback and Paddy Connolly is the man to wind up a winning result with a few minutes left. Ayr's misery is compounded when Mark Casey is dismissed for violin conduct. He'd failed to pull the strings in any case.

Going For Gold: Brechin breathe life into this game after the break and for that we are all grateful. Well, apart from the irate Ayr fans, who have come a long way to see their team fall and for one of their men to be sent packing. Gold stars – six.

Fanfare: Brechin? Are you kidding me? Nada. Which is Spanish for nothing. Entiende? The Cemetery End has all the atmosphere of a graveyard. Don't come to Brechin for the party. Of course, you can chat, but keep it down, will you? This isn't a criticism by the way. It's just the way it is. Glebe Park is one of the loveliest grounds in Scotland so it is important to be lovely while you're there. Deal with yourself by dealing in decency. And decorum. Don't puke on the hedge.

Music To My Ears: 'Sit Down' by James sadly does not contain the sufficient power of suggestion to make the Cemetery End sit down. However that line about being 'touched by madness' is fitting. You would have to be a little bit touched to follow Brechin every week. You know which other tune caresses our ears? 'Axl F.' By Harold Faltermeyer! From Beverly Hills Cop.

MISSION POSSIBLE 35

OBJECTIVE:
To go to Almondvale
and watch Livingston

SCENARIO: Livingston are playing Celtic in the Scottish Cup fourth round.

DATE: Sunday, February 4, 2007. Brechin one day, Livingston the next. Monsieur, with these football matches you are really spoiling yourself.

LOCATION, LOCATION, LOCATION: Livingston is a newish new town in the Almond Valley in West Lothian. I believe that it's closer to Edinburgh than it is to Glasgow but I haven't had that verified.

CULTURAL NOTES: Well ... there is the Scottish Shale Oil Museum, at the Almond Valley Heritage Centre. And if you fancy building your own house you should visit the Scottish Self-Build Centre (I take it they built the centre themselves?). Livingston is noted for its range of shopping opportunities. As the pitch-side advertising at Almondvale says. 'Love Football. Love Shopping. Love Livingston'. But we already established that shopping is not culture. Whereas football is!

LIVINGSTON PROFILE

KICKED OFF: 1995. 'Cotton Eyed Joe' by Rednex reaches number one in the UK charts, the nation going nuts for a bit of Swedish cowboy-techno.

TRUE COLOURS: Amber and black. Or black and gold, if you prefer. I'm not that fussed to be honest.

BADGE OF HONOUR: Another poignant thistle and another lion on the rampage.

NAME CALLING: Livi. Or Livi Lions.

MORTAL ENEMY: I dunno. Bathgate?

AREN'T WE BRILLIANT?: Livingston rattled their way through all the divisions in Scotland and finished third in the Premier League in 2001. This put them in the Uefa Cup after only six years of their existence. In 2004, Livingston won the CIS Cup, beating Hibs at Hampden.

MISSION LOGISTICS

ALIGHT AT: There are two train stations in Livingston. There is Livingston North (trains from Edinburgh) and Livingston South (trains from Edinburgh and Glasgow Central). Neither station is particularly close to the ground - and you cannot exactly walk through Livingston because there is no Livingston. At least I've never found it. I decide to take the 15A bus from Glasgow Buchanan Street. It will take some time but it will drop me off outside the Almondvale Shopping Centre which is only across the road from Almondvale Stadium. The bus proves popular with the Japanese too. A group of them are off to watch their football icon, Shunsuke Nakamura, help Celtic whip Livingston. And these Japanese derive as much pleasure from the 15A as I do. They're taking pictures. Understandably. It is an intensely scenic route with perhaps the highlight being the sewage plant. There is so much picture book perfection that the excursion becomes like a funfair ride and countless roundabouts are replicating the sensation of being on the waltzers. It's such a seat-of-the-pants thrill the 15A bus. Such an urge to throw up. Livingston was actually designed by aliens once they'd got bored of drawing crop circles. My friend Richard has got lost lots of times driving in Livingston. He refuses ever to go back and swears that when you get to Livingston, or what constitutes Livingston, they switch all the roundabouts about for a laugh so as to ensure further confusion on your departure. I think there may be something in that theory. But me and the Japanese football fans can just sit back and relax - and let the bus driver worry about the many twists and turns involved in getting to Almondvale.

A Pint At: It is not my idea of the perfect pint but you will get a tremendously cheap one in the large bar in the shopping centre. The Granary is a pub nearer to the ground but it is not overly charming either. It is six-deep at the bar with Celtic fans queuing and waiting for 12.30pm to happen so that some drinks other than soft drinks can be ordered. There is a nightclub at Livingston's ground called the Livi Nite Spot but it is closed. It is early afternoon after all and not 'nite'. I'll come back another time and show off my moves.

MISSION DEBRIEFING

Field of Dreams: Almondvale Stadium is so pristine apart from all these black and gold balloons they let loose in search of a party atmosphere. I had expected Almondvale to be a sterile experience but it isn't. When it is full, as it is today with Celtic visiting, it is a good place to watch football. Perhaps when it is mostly empty, it is not so great. Really Almondvale looks like a model football ground rather than a real football ground. In its own small purpose-built way it is quite flawless-looking.

Super Pies Me: The Livingston pie is as limp as a limp biscuit. I might as well dunk it in my coffee. It won't make any difference now.

> **GAME ON:** Livingston 1-4 Celtic
>
> **LIVINGSTON GOALSCORER:** Mackay 18.
>
> **CELTIC GOALSCORERS:** O'Dea 30, Riordan 45, 59, Vennegoor of Hesselink 61.
>
> **LIVINGSTON:** Stewart, MacKay, McPake, Tweed, Golabek, Fox (Hamill 57), Mitchell, Walker, Craig (Smylie 82), Makel (Dorrans 63), Teggart.
>
> **CELTIC:** Boruc, Telfer, McManus, O'Dea, Naylor, Nakamura, Hartley, Lennon (Sno 76), Jarosik (Gravesen 68), Vennegoor of Hesselink, Riordan.
>
> **HEAD COUNT:** 7,281.

Report Card: Celtic saunter into the quarter-finals of the Scottish Cup, despite Livingston taking the early lead. Dave Mackay's dunt with his head puts the home side in front but it is not very long at all before Celtic draw level with defender Darren O' Dea blasting in an equaliser. Derek Riordan finishes from a difficult angle to put Celtic ahead and then he increases the visitors' lead with a clinical strike. Yon Avenger's clever clip from the cusp of the Livingston penalty box completes the rout.

Going For Gold: Livingston begin brightly, but Celtic soon have this tie in their pocket and, as a contest, it is over. I will give it seven gold stars.

Fanfare: 'When the lions go marching in' and 'Livi till I die' are both sung by the home supporters who are clearly up for this match until Celtic start pulling away and the Celtic fans taunt the Livingston fans with 'You only came to see the Celtic'. When Dave Mackay scores Livingston's opener the home supporters sing 'Dave, Dave, Super Dave'. The big issue with the Almondvale atmosphere, for me, and I'm sure I'm not alone on this one, is the bloody din of those dastardly drums they insist on banging throughout the match. We're in West Lothian, not Rio de Janeiro. I guess it is an attempt at a carnival atmosphere but it is bringing on the onset of drum rage. I don't mind it at half-time when you have got the band of drummers going round the pitch, but not right through the game. It's too much. Bah drumstick.

Music To My Ears: The Scissor Sisters, that staple of Scottish football ground music. How about 'The Lion Sleeps Tonight' though? Or 'Drums Don't Work' by The Verve.

EPISODE

MISSION IMPOSSIBLE **36**

OBJECTIVE:
*To go to New
Bayview and
watch East Fife.
Or so I think.*

SCENARIO: East Fife are playing Dumbarton in the Scottish Third Division. Or maybe not.

DATE: Saturday, February 10, 2007. A day etched in my memory. I shall never forget it. Despite all the therapy.

LOCATION, LOCATION, LOCATION: Methil. It is between Leven and Buckhaven if that helps. No? It is in Fife. East Fife, to narrow it down a little, without completely losing you.

CULTURAL NOTES: At Methil Heritage Centre you are free to explore the social and cultural heritage of the Levenmouth area. Don't let me stop you.

EAST FIFE PROFILE

KICKED OFF: 1903. George Orwell is born.

TRUE COLOURS: Amber and black. Or black and gold. Or yellow and the opposite of white.

BADGE OF HONOUR: A football as the centrepiece of a saltire. I asked East Fife if I could use their badge in this book. They said yes. Then they said, no, wait a minute, we have to have a board meeting. These are serious deliberations.

NAME CALLING: The Fifers. Despite the shared presence of Dunfermline, Raith Rovers and Cowdenbeath in Fife.

MORTAL ENEMY: Cowdenbeath. Whom they sing dirty songs about, without prompting.

AREN'T WE BRILLIANT?: East Fife won the Scottish Cup in 1938 and have claimed the League Cup on no less than three occasions. They must have been a good team, at some point.

MISSION LOGISTICS

ALIGHT AT: There's not a train station within many miles of Methil. So here is what I do (and I am not suggesting anyone copy me). I get on the X26 bus at Buchanan Street in Glasgow. The X26 cuts across the country, west to east, and is a much overlooked route, in my honest opinion. I don't think you can say you have lived until you have taken a trip on the X26. Glasgow … Cumbernauld … Kincardine … Cairneyhill … Dunfermline … Auchtertool … Kirkcaldy … Coaltown of Wemyss … East Wemyss … Buckhaven … Leven and this is where you get off if you know what's good for you. If you are not going to watch East Fife (and I can see no earthly reason why you wouldn't be) you can always remain on the X26, for such onward destinations as Lower Largo, Upper Largo, Key Largo, Elie and Anstruther. Apparently journey's end is St Andrews, which lacks a recognised football club but does boast a well-known golf club. Glasgow to Leven occupies two-and-a-quarter-hours of my life and the last quarter hour feels like the longest quarter hour of my life. Rain clatters the bus. The windows are steamed up. We are in the eye of a Fife storm and I can't see out the window. 'Is this Leven?' I ask a man with a dog on the bus. 'No, Buckhaven,' answers the man and the dog nods. 'Leven is where the big bus station is,' adds the man, not the dog, which has lost interest in the conversation. So I leave the bus at the big bus station and cross the Bawbee Bridge which is not named after Bawbee Ewing but is named because of the bawbee (an old Scots half-penny) being the toll for the bridge. I don't have a bawbee on me but it doesn't matter because the toll is no longer in force. I leave Leven and enter Methil. It is a monumental moment to savour. Or despair. But, maintaining a positive outlook far brighter than the foul weather, I decide to savour it and cast an admiring glance at the grey monolith that is Methil Power Station. Which matches perfectly the slate, rain-heavy sky. I fight the growing gale and push towards East Fife's ground, New Bayview, which is less idyllic than it sounds, even if it sounds like the laid-back, beach-side town in an Australian soap opera. Although, to be honest, in these conditions, I think Tahiti might look a bit rubbish. The ill-tempered tempest is trying to return me to the bus station, but I push on and get soaked to the skin as reward for my substantial efforts. I can hardly see a thing in front of me. Black horizontal rain is spiking me in the eyes. I can vaguely hear something. An announcement on the stadium Tannoy. But it makes no sense from where I'm standing and nearly falling over.

I get to the main gate of New Bayview and a man in a cagoule, his hood tied tight round his face, is waving away the cars trying to get into the car park. Abandon hope, all ye who enter here. I think I've grasped it. But in case it hasn't dawned on me, the cagoule man breaks the bad news to me. 'Game's off.' After the X26, and the great physical effort required to walk those few hundred yards from the bus station to the ground, it is one heck of a punch-line. Game's off? I pause and rearrange my thoughts. Well, I've got the return bus journey to Glasgow to look forward to. And before that I've got a couple of hours to kill in Methil. On the worst day of weather this year. Oh boy.

A Pint At: There is a bar upstairs in the main stand at New Bayview. With a party going on. The Dumbarton fans have come all this way for the match to be called off less than an hour before kick-off and they are not leaving without wading into the beer first. It suits the Dumbarton fans and it is money in the till for East Fife. I have a pint myself. You get a good view of the pitch and a new perspective on the power station. It still looks grim. But then it is a grim afternoon. Maybe on a sunny afternoon the power station is quite beautiful.

MISSION DEBRIEFING

Field of Dreams: The company First 2 Finance were the first to sponsor the First 2 Finance Bayview Stadium which was formerly called New Bayview. New Bayview replaced the old Bayview Park when the club decided to up sticks and move to Methil Docks. There is only the one stand at East Fife's ground but it is a good one. All-seated and all, with the power station looming over everything. I can't see the sea from New Bayview but the weather is atrocious.

Super Pies Me: Ah, the Elusive Pie. The East Fife pie escapes my clutches in tantalising fashion. So the game has been postponed but I have my pint in one hand and the match programme (for posterity) in my other hand. I make keen enquiries about the possibility of obtaining a pie for my personal hat-trick. Never mind the lack of a football match. If I get a pie I'll go home happy. A kind bar lady goes off in search of a pie but she returns empty-handed and with the devastating news that the butcher has just been to the ground in his van and taken all the pies away. Disaster! I learn the name of the butcher and, after I have sunk my pint quick-smart, I step back out of the ground and into the howling gale. I wander the wind-swept, rain-lashed streets of Methil, and Buckhaven, until I find the butcher shop and it is closed. It is a wasted effort. One day. One day I'll return to East Fife and taste their pie. I can't quite bring myself to say Methil No More.

GAME OFF: East Fife P-P Dumbarton

Report Card: Whit a scunner! I am unable to bring you a match report. Not my fault. I dwell for a moment on the thought of returning to New Bayview for the rescheduled fixture, whenever that is going to be, but I decide against it. I have visited in good faith. I had no idea that the match was going to be called off. There is no reason why I should feel compelled to return to Methil for the re-match. And even the pull of an untasted pie is not enough to lure me to back to East Fife just yet. Not twice in such a short period. No. Methil Once More. Not yet. I haven't seen East Fife play but maybe I can do a whole second book about them.

Going For Gold: How can you hand out gold stars for a match that never took place in the first place?

Fanfare: The Sons Of The Rock are on song. In the New Bayview bar. Determined to make the most of their day out, the Dumbarton supporters down pints and serenade their hosts with a series of songs, including 'Scared that we'd beat you, you're only scared that we'd beat you, scared that we'd beat you, you're only scared that we'd beat you.' So that's it! The postponement has nothing whatsoever to do with this woeful weather. East Fife are running scared.

Taking yet another First ScotRail train to yet another Scottish town to get to yet another Scottish football match, I read, in my Saturday newspaper, of the number of wild animal sightings that have been reported in the UK since the year 2000. It makes for interesting reading and makes me wonder what it is the British public put in their tea each morning, other than milk and sugar, and if some people perhaps should be making an appointment with an optician.

Wild animals sighted in the UK - not in zoos - since the turn of the new millennium.

6,000 big cats (they mean really big cats)
51 wallabies (remind me, how far away is Australia?)
43 snakes
13 spiders (I spotted 14 in my garden last week.)
13 racoons
10 crocodiles (!)
7 wolves (they're huskies aren't they?)
3 pandas
2 scorpions
1 penguin

I'm not sure what surprises me most. Probably the penguin. Not that I'd be blasé about clocking a crocodile in the river Clyde. As for the 6,000 big cats, well, I can improve that to 6,001, since I singularly failed to report my surprise sighting of a black jaguar in a field on the outskirts of Perth. (No, it wasn't a car.) It looked like Bagheera out of *The Jungle Book* and seemed to be eying up a neighbouring field of cows. I'm not kidding about this if that's what you're thinking. I was relieved to be a passenger in a passing vehicle on the A92 at the time. What with the UFO I once witnessed in broad daylight from a train near Stirling (and I wasn't the only rail passenger to notice) I need only catch my glimpse of Nessie now to secure an unprecedented hat-trick of wild cat, UFO, Loch Ness Monster.

When you hunt grounds, you unintentionally bump into all manner of creature. Lions and tigers and bears, oh my, and pandas and toucans and border collies. I watched so many of these animals mucking about the stadiums and parks of Scotland that I decided to select a squad of them and put them to better use.

So here it is.

THE FANTASY SCOTTISH FOOTBALL MASCOTS XI

First I had better appoint a manager. Someone with animal magnetism. Someone who boasts the ability to tame these beasts. I know! Terry Nutkins. Animal expert, animal lover (except for otters), Terry is definitely the man for the job. But even someone with Terry's powers of animal persuasion will require the aid of a trusty assistant. Someone, or something, of the animal world. Someone, or something, that can command the respect of Scottish football mascots, while keeping them on their toes and hooves.

I know! Snuffleupagus. Snuffle whit? The brown, woolly mammoth thing that's possibly imaginary and hangs about Sesame Street with his mate Big Bird.

Right. That's the managerial dream team sorted out. Terry Nutkins and Snuffleupagus. What about tactics? Well, we should probably leave the tactical side of things to Terry and Snuffleupagus, but I'm not sure they'll need tactics. How are you supposed to instil discipline in a creature as belligerent as a football mascot? Perhaps coach Nutkins can, if anyone can, but in my experience, what football mascots are inclined to do - of their own daft accord - is to roll about the pitch killing themselves laughing while the other team is read out. Other than that they like to pat children on the head at half-time and pose for pictures with their thumbs up, paws up or wings up or whatever. In the unreconstructed mind of the football mascot, a last-ditch tackle is a rugby tackle, and sometimes it's the first-ditch tackle. I've seen mascots totally lose their heads. Tynie Tiger. Happened to him at Tynecastle. Got too cocky and his head fell off. Some of those young Hearts fans were traumatised.

Anyway, let's get this shabby lot into some sort of shape. They're the pick of the bunch. We're expecting great things from them. Don't let us down lads. You're only in it to win it. Feel the pressure. Take the pain. Dish it out if you like. Once you step over that white line … give nothing less than 100%. 150% if you like. Pump you full of clichés and see what you do with them.

Teamsheet

1. Cappie the Cat (Greenock Morton): Cappielow's infamous feline sports a cap, looks the part and therefore should also be given custody of the gloves to go in goals. Cappie is the cat that got the cream and he is often mistaken for Benny the Ball from Top Cat. We might have to pay off Officer Dibble to ensure that Cappie the Cat can turn out for this Fantasy Scottish Football Mascots XI. There'll be no cat napping and no cat flapping at corner kicks.

2. Tynie Tiger (Hearts): Crap name right enough. But infinitely better than those of his less than illustrious predecessors Josh and Jemma Jambo. Tynie Tiger is a wild hep cat and commands both pace and nerve, useful commodities in this line of business. Tynie was noticed, by this scout, chasing a policeman and would seem to have that all too rare ability of being able to stand on one foot for a really long time. Then his head fell off, by accident, and children started screaming, and panicking parents rushed to place their hands over their children's eyes.

3. Dougie Doonhamer (Queen of the South): I watched this bedraggled border collie take absolute dog's abuse from the Gretna fans at Raydale Park while Queen of the South got on the receiving end of a horrible derby thrashing. But the redoubtable Dougie will never allow himself to become too doonhearted about such unpalatable mistreatment - and sure enough he was soon wagging his tail again and looking for a biscuit. Passenger most likely to poke his head out the window on the team bus.

4. Angus the Bull (Aberdeen): Heavy rocks to the squall of AC/DC. A total head-banger. Beefy headcase. Angus (da-na-na-na-na) takes no prisoners and is surprisingly proficient in the art of air guitar. You never grab this bull by the horns, or he'll gore you. Capable of stampeding the opposition into submission on his own. Does not take kindly to bullshit. Not even from the referee that time he was asked by the match official to remove his ring. Angus didn't give a toss. He just tossed the ref in the air and got on with it. It's his way of letting off steam.

5. Hammy the Hamster (Hamilton Academical): Hammy has endured his injury problems but is currently working hard at it in manager Terry Nutkins' gym - on the training wheel - and is nearing the end of the long and winding road to recovery from that horrific tackle by Kevin the Gerbil. The easiest way to motivate Hammy before the game is to pin pictures of Freddie Starr on the dressing room wall.

6. PeeTee (Partick Thistle): Not to be confused with a teepee, PeeTee, a.k.a The Firhill Flyer, looks a lot like a parrot, but technically he's a toucan. Toucans have very large and colourful bills and tend to live high in the trees of tropical rainforests in Mexico, Central, South and East America, and not forgetting the Maryhill part of Glasgow. PeeTee shows particularly nice plumage and his team-mates never have any trouble picking him out.

7. Nutz the Squirrel (Kilmarnock): Issued with the warning: This Squirrel May Contain Nutz. This psychotic rodent – I'm sorry Nutz, you're a rodent, live with it - may be cock-eyed and bushy tailed and may dance like a lunatic - he is a lunatic - but he's the sort of squirrel anybody would want on their team. Nice one squirrel! Nutz is a red squirrel, not one of those grey squirrels everybody's always banging on about, and he has got red card written all over him, but he is surely worth the risk and his brother Squirrel Regis used to play for West Brom.

8. Wullie the Warrior (Stenhousemuir): Wullie is a different kind of animal and in actual fact he is a Viking. Note the horny helmet and gigantic beard. Wullie's got a better beard than Paul Hartley in full bloom, and he's got an axe like Jack Nicholson in *The Shining*. But we won't let him grind it on the football field. There is going to be enough carnage when this team emerges from the tunnel and into the heat of battle. Yet even without his weapon, Wullie strikes the fear of death into the hearts of opponents. A lot of sides could do with a Viking on their side. They're good for pillaging, ransacking. That sort of thing.

9. Staggie (Ross County): A real dead ringer for Bullwinkle J. Moose, of Rocky and Bullwinkle fame. Staggie first caught our eye at Victoria Park in Dingwall - his natural habitat - when we caught him picking his nose. We've got the photographs to prove it. But aside from bogey harvesting we don't consider him a slouch. Those antlers should prove pretty useful at corner kicks. And when he's rutting, he's pretty much unstoppable.

10. Pandemonium (Ayr United): Pandas, they're adorable, right? Well, not this one. The Ayr United panda is the scariest-looking panda you're ever likely to see in your puff. He has the cold, dead eyes of that bloody rabbit in *Donnie Darko*. Peer into them and you'll see nothing. Nothing. I hardly slept after my night at Somerset Park. Now that may have had something to do with the deep-fried pie I mistakenly consumed, but I still reckon the panda had something to do with it. Pandemonium, with those deep-end-of-the-pool eyes, is a born penalty-box assassin. This bamboo-guzzler bamboozles opposition defences.

11. Super Saint (St Johnstone): The only cubist mascot in Scottish football. Like some freaky Picasso abomination. His face is squint, his eyes are wonky and his bloody nose is inside-out. Super Saint is no oil painting. But that mysterious cape across his shoulders is suggestive of something quite heroic and the giant S on his shirt would seem to indicate that what we have here, strutting across McDiarmid Park, is a mascot with the potential to be the super-hero of the day. As long as he gets changed in the dressing room and not in a telephone box. Not that there are many telephone boxes left these days.

Substitutes

12. Peter the Head (Peterhead): No body. No legs. Just a giant head. Peter the Head wins everything in the air. When he shouts 'mine!' you get out of the way.

14. Red Lichtie (Arbroath): Ears of the hairy-eared dwarf lemur, teeth of the hispid hare, nose of the snub-nosed monkey, tail of the sheath-tailed bat, eyes of the northern muriqui, and hooves like Mr Tumnus from Narnia. Red Lichties are rarely spotted in the wilds of Scotland, but here's one on the bench. What a freak.

15. Brian the Bridie (Forfar Athletic): Pasty-looking, but packed full of mince, onion and seasoning.

16. Livid Lion (Livingston): Prone to episodes of blind rage. Once devoured a referee in one sitting. Burped up the whistle before turning his attention to the linesman.

———————

All other Scottish football mascots were released from their contracts and into the wild.

MISSION POSSIBLE 37

OBJECTIVE:
To go to Dens Park
and watch Dundee.

SCENARIO: Dundee are playing Clyde in the Scottish First Division.

DATE: Saturday, February 17, 2007.

LOCATION, LOCATION, LOCATION: Dundee. City of Discovery. And City of Recovery after a night at Fat Sam's. Dundee is also renowned for its three Js. Jive, juice and jingoism. And three other Js. Jam, jute and journalism. Make that six Js then.

CULTURAL NOTES: 'A grim place' informs *Scotland The Braw*. Dundee's not that bad. Why not discover Captain Scott's Antarctic explorer ship *Discovery* at Discovery Point? And hang with the artwork at DCA (Dundee Contemporary Arts)?

DUNDEE PROFILE

KICKED OFF: 1893. Japan accepts the Gregorian calendar. That's big of them.

TRUE COLOURS: Dark blue, red and dark white.

BADGE OF HONOUR: The letters D, F and C interlocked. Traditional. Nothing fancy.

NAME CALLING: The Dark Blues. Or the Dees.

MORTAL ENEMY: You know that one about keeping your friends close and your enemies closer? Dundee United's ground is a couple of hundred yards away.

AREN'T WE BRILLIANT?: One Scottish Cup. Three League Cups. Once Scottish Champions. (Whisper it) Dundee are more decorated than their neighbours. The great Dundee side of the 1960s reached the semi-finals of the European Cup, where they lost out to AC Milan.

MISSION LOGISTICS

ALIGHT AT: Dundee train station. Progress through Dundee city centre and climb Hilltown. Don't forget your crampons and your toothbrush. The ascent can get pretty treacherous in winter. Great view back over towards the Firth of Tay though.

A Pint At: The Andy Penman lounge at Dens Park has a framed (and signed) photo of the Pet Shop Boys' Neil Tennant on the wall. What's that about? They won't let me in the Captain's Lounge at Dens Park. I don't know if that's the captain's decision or if I have to be a captain to get in there. I'm not a captain of industry. I'm not Captain Cook. I'm not Captain Sensible. I'm not any kind of captain. As you approach Dens Park there is a decent enough pub called The Maltman. Another possibility is the Centenary Bar, beyond the ground, on Clepington Road. This is a popular haunt of Dundee fans.

MISSION DEBRIEFING

Field of Dreams: Dens Park … what can you say about Dens Park? Well, it's no Celtic Park and it's no Central Park either. The reality lies somewhere between such extremes. Parts of Dens Park are quite overgrown. Dense foliage and the like. It is like a jungle in there. The south stand is where a lot of dedicated Dees dump themselves and when I say dump themselves, I don't mean what you're thinking. From the south stand you can see Tannadice. Which brings into sharp focus the madness of having two major football grounds sitting cheek by jowl but I won't go on about it. I like the ancient turnstiles and I feel the benefit of the long step-climb. There aren't many football grounds like Dens Park. But why do they have all four stands open? They only need two today.

Super Pehs Me: The Dundee peh is okay. I reject the opportunity to taste a 'Pizza Pod'. Had I been tempted, I might have won a trip to Venice. However, I am content to dream about winning a trip to Venice instead. It seems like a calculated gamble, the 'Pizza Pod'. I'm not entirely sure what it is.

GAME ON: Dundee 1-4 Clyde

DUNDEE GOALSCORER: Hamdaoui 83.

CLYDE GOALSCORERS: Masterton 1, Bryson 12, Arbuckle 29, Bryson 38.

DUNDEE: Roy, Shields (Higgins 46), MacKenzie, G Smith, Griffin, McDonald (Hamdaoui 71), McHale, Robertson, Swankie, Lyle, Davidson (K Smith 46).

CLYDE: Hutton, Harris, McCann, Higgins, McKeown, Masterton, Bryson (Bradley 80), Gilmour, Arbuckle (Hunter 83), Imrie, McGowan.

HEAD COUNT: 3,812

Report Card: Clyde rip Dundee to pieces with a breathtaking early show which has many distraught Dundee fans rushing for the exit. The guests set about their hosts with indecent haste. Steve Masterton's second minute free-kick misses everything but the Dundee net. The unmarked Craig Bryson quickly doubles Clyde's lead. Gary Arbuckle makes it three goals for Clyde, before the half-hour mark, with his downward header. Bryson then finds the bottom corner without the aid of a map and it is not even the interval yet. Khalid Hamdaoui manages a late second-half consolation for Dundee but it's not really a consolation is it? To fall behind at home so early, to lose another goal and another and another. 'If it's five, I'm off,' announces a Dundee fan, showing remarkable endurance. 'A'll go when the next one goes in,' says another. Goal. 'Right, am goin noo.' This is sore. 'You've got to greet,' sighs a despondent Dee. You see them all looking at each other in confusion (should I stay or should I go? This is my team, but this is terrible). What exactly is the capacity for pain when your team is getting horsed? 4-0? 5-0? 6-0? A few stomp off disconsolately after half-an-hour, but it's hardly an exodus. Most stay. And I don't know whether to admire them or shake them.

Going For Gold: A combination of ruthlessness by Clyde and incompetence from Dundee results in a whirlwind first-half. You don't often see games like this. I am giving it eight gold stars. Sorry about that Dundee but I'm looking at the bigger picture.

Fanfare: 'Please don't take my Dundee away,' is the plaintive cry, the day after the Dens Park club announce more scary financial figures. And that is before this ninety minutes fright show. Atmosphere? Well, Clyde killed it, didn't they? When the away team scores in the second minute and is three-up after half-an-hour, you are not going to hear much singing from a home support. The small band of Clyde supporters are partying however. And you can understand that. 'We are Dundee, super Dundee.' Not today you're not. 'One Gavin Swankie, there's only one Gavin Swankie.' So there is.

Music To My Ears: The Dens Park DJ wastes no time in playing 'Wasted Little DJs' by local-boys-done-good The View. On a more traditional bent, anyone who has been to Dens will surely be familiar with that very Dundonian ditty blasted proudly before kick-off. The one that goes 'Am a Dee, am a Dee, am a Dee till a deh, am a Dee, diddly-dee, diddly-dee, till a deh …'

MISSION POSSIBLE **38**

OBJECTIVE:
*To go to Tannadice
and watch Dundee
United.*

SCENARIO: Dundee United are playing Hibernian in the Scottish Premier League.

DATE: Sunday, February 18, 2007.

LOCATION, LOCATION, LOCATION: Still Dundee.

CULTURAL NOTES: According to *Scotland The Braw*, Dundee is 'less snooty than Aberdeen'. I disagree. The number of men in top hats I saw swanning about the Wellgate Shopping Centre with their noses in the air. If you want to look down on everyone, just climb to the top of Dundee Law, an extinct volcano and underground lair of an evil billionaire genius.

DUNDEE UNITED PROFILE

KICKED OFF: 1909. Birth year of Francis Bacon.

TRUE COLOURS: Tangerine dream and Tim Burton black.

BADGE OF HONOUR: Another of those rampant lions. What is it with these lions all the time? Huh? What about an indignant badger for a change?

NAME CALLING: The Terrors. Or The Arabs. The story goes that a load of sand was dumped on the pitch one winter and Tannadice resembled a desert. They brought in camels and everything.

MORTAL ENEMY: Them across the road.

AREN'T WE BRILLIANT?: Dundee United were Scottish Champions in 1983. Four years later, the club reached the Uefa Cup final, but lost it. In 1994, United won the Scottish Cup. Here's a fascinating fact. Dundee United have faced Barcelona four times in European competition, and succeeded in beating the Catalans home and away twice over.

MISSION LOGISTICS

ALIGHT AT: Dundee train station. Go the same route as you would if you were heading to D**s Park, but shield your eyes as you pass D**s Park, and unshield them again several seconds later, but not looking back, as you reach Tannadice.

A Pint At: Behind the East Stand and the allotments is the curious Troll Inn. It's full of trolls. Really. The Clep bar further up the hill on Clepington Street serves an honest pint. Not that I'm suggesting the Troll Inn deals in dishonest drinks. It's just a phrase.

MISSION DEBRIEFING

Field of Dreams: Tannadice Park. Tannadice will suffice. The cantaloupe main stand. I mean the cantilevered main stand (now the Jerry Kerr Stand) is usually where away fans sit. The home contingent tend to occupy both the East Stand and the George Fox Stand. It pleases me greatly that Tannadice still has that big black wall ad in the corner, promoting the benefits of an evening at Fat Sam's. As I said earlier, behind Tannadice are allotments. I saw that Arthur Fowler plugging away with his hoe.

Super Pehs Me: You know what? I can't remember my Dundee United peh. I must have had one. But I can't picture it and I can't taste anything of it. The Forgotten Peh ... perhaps it was unmemorable. But it couldn't have been that bad. Otherwise I would have remembered it.

GAME ON: Dundee United 0-0 Hibernian

DUNDEE UNITED: Stillie, Dillon, McCracken, Wilkie, Kalvenes, Robertson, Kerr, Robson, Samuel, Hunt (Gomis 89), Conway (Daly 78).

HIBERNIAN: Simon Brown, Hogg, Martis, Jones, Murphy (Stewart 61), Whittaker, Scott Brown, Beuzelin, Stevenson, Fletcher (Sowunmi 78), Benjelloun.

HEAD COUNT: 6,453.

Report Card: Whit a bore! The Tannadice pitch is in a sorry state. But that doesn't excuse Dundee United and Hibernian for dishing up an atrocious match. What in Heaven's name do they think they are doing? I want to sing that damning song and direct it at the pair of them, the one that goes: 'You're not very good, you're not very good, you're not very, you're not very, you're not very good.' Oh this is awful. They should be paying us to watch. And maybe travel expenses too. Guillaume Beuzelin of Hibs hits the Dundee United bar. And what else? Barry Robson is lively for United. In fact he's the only one getting any pass marks from me. So apart from that? Nothing. Another wonderful advert for the Scottish Premier League. The sponsors must be queuing up.

Going For Gold: The latest Premier League Master Class. One to consign to the dustbin of history. Rubbish. One gold star. Barry Robson can keep it. It's his.

Fanfare: I love a party with a happy atmosphere. But this isn't it. The Hibs fans are muted. The Dundee United fans are muted. Mutually muted. The United fans muster up a couple of tunes. 'Oh Barry Robson, oh Barry Robson, oh Barry Robson on the wing'. And 'Oh United. We do. Oh United. We do. Oh United. We do. Oh United we love you'. How nice.

Music To My Ears: The Tannadice DJ wastes no time in playing 'Wasted Little DJs' by local-boys-done-good The View. Wait a minute. We've had that one already. I heard it at Dens Park yesterday. Nice to see two city rivals holding the same viewpoint. They both like The View. 'Same Jeans'. Same songs.

MISSION POSSIBLE

OBJECTIVE:
To go to Stair
Park and watch
Stranraer.

SCENARIO: Stranraer are playing Morton in the Scottish Second Division.

DATE: Saturday, February 24, 2007.

LOCATION, LOCATION, LOCATION: Stranraer is in the Dumfries and Galloway region in the south-west of Scotland. It is one of the most far-flung football destinations in Scottish football. A bit like Dingwall. But at the other end.

CULTURAL NOTES: There are the remains of Castle of St John. And Stranraer Museum has the largest plough and all manner of farming equipment. Tongs, snedders, sowers, grubbers, scythes, shovels, cutters. 'No one could say that Stranraer was beautiful,' says *Scotland The Braw*, putting the boot in once more and dragging another Scottish town through the mud.

STRANRAER PROFILE

KICKED OFF: 1870. Stranraer are the third-oldest club in Scotland. 1870 is the year Charles Dickens died after suffering a stroke.

TRUE COLOURS: Blue and white. In classic Italian fashion. Stranraer have been known to employ the *cattenaccio* approach when the going gets tough.

BADGE OF HONOUR: A ship. Of course you can catch the ferry to Ireland from Stranraer.

NAME CALLING: The Blues. Not the most imaginative of sobriquets. An alternative is the Clayholers which just sounds filthy.

MORTAL ENEMY: Queen of the South. Although Dumfries is seventy-six miles distant, so you can't really class it as a local rivalry.

AREN'T WE BRILLIANT?: Stranraer's Scottish Cup best is quarter-finalists (in season 2002/03). Their League Cup best is quarter-finalists (in season 1968/69). The Clayholers (ha-ha) won the Challenge Cup (in season 1996/97) and have been Scottish Second Division champions twice (in season 1993/94 and season 1997/98). The club also won the Brewers Cup in 2005 which involved beating a bunch of pub teams.

MISSION LOGISTICS

ALIGHT AT: It's more than two hours from Glasgow Central to Stranraer train station which is near the Stranraer ferry terminal. It's about a fifteen-minute walk to Stair Park. You enter through the wrought iron gates of a park and past a skateboard park and a playground and a bandstand and it is all very Trumpton apart from the skateboard park.

A Pint At: The Stranraer FC Social Club is not at the ground. It is actually in the town centre, but it is a cracking place for a pint and you are made to feel very welcome. There is a £1 admission fee (you can pay £6 for the year if you are planning to come back) and you can buy Stranraer FC merchandise there. Not too far from the social club is the Arkhouse Inn, which has a tight door policy. 'No Tinkers, Drifters or Tattie Hoakers.' They also offer the following advice, before you step over the threshold: 'Gentlemen advised to carry firearms'. Blimey.

MISSION DEBRIEFING

Field of Dreams: Stair Park is as pretty a football ground as you will find in Scotland. It is up there with Forthbank in Stirling and Glebe Park in Brechin. You can see the sea and behind one set of goals there are lots of trees and bushes. In fact you can't see the wood for the trees. The Coo Shed is the popular spot (now how many Scottish clubs have Coo Sheds or Cow Sheds? Loads) and has wooden slats for seats but a lot of the supporters just stand anyway. The main stand opposite is all seated and the Town End is terracing with a roof, but there aren't many fans in there. Maybe six. The pitch looks bumpy to say the least and clearly they should call Bill Murray in to deal with the gopher that's been tearing up the six-yard box. I reckon you could take a shot and it would be stopped not by the goalie but by the mound of dirt. I could sit (or stand) at Stair Park all day and stare at it. Lovely. Super rural.

Super Pies Me: The £1 Stranraer pie is simply excellent. I would have been tempted to have another one but I am saving myself for a fish supper from the Central Café in town.

GAME ON: Stranraer 2-1 Morton

STRANRAER GOALSCORERS: Moore 82, Janczyk 88.

MORTON GOALSCORER: Templeman 2.

STRANRAER: Black, McKinstry, Dillon, Crilly (Mullen 70), Walker, Sharp, McPhee, Mitchell, Moore, Hamilton, McAlpine (Janczyk 62).

MORTON: Mathers, Weatherson, Macgregor, Harding, Greacen, McLaughlin, Millar, Stevenson (Finlayson 66), Templeman, McGowan (Linn 80), McAlistair.

HEAD COUNT: 597

Report Card: Stranraer gob-smack league leaders Morton with two goals in the final eight minutes for a mind-expanding victory. All the drama is at Stair Park. A Chris Templeman header gives Morton the early lead. He should be good at headers since he's at least 8 ft 3 in. I like it when he puts his hands up when his goalkeeper is taking a goal kick. It's okay, Chris, he can see you. One of the Stranraer fans keeps calling him Hen Broon. Hen's not a bad man to have on your team but he will be on the losing side today. Morton manage to pass up a series of chances, which they will rue, because Michael Mullen sparks the fightback from Stranraer, scaring Morton with a low fired shot in the closing spell before his fellow substitute Neil Janczyk despatches an expert finish to give Stranraer all the glory. The Stranraer fans go crazy, and quite right too.

Going For Gold: A stupendous fight-back from Stranraer against the odds. Nine gold stars.

Mike Check: The trouble at Stranraer is that we can hear the MC but we are not supposed to. The home team are hanging on dearly to their 2-1 lead over top side Morton and the game is deep in injury time. The referee will be sounding his whistle, anytime soon, but the crowd can't bear the waiting. 'C'mon ref blow the whistle min.' It sounds like a man stuck in a barrel. I look around me. There is no barrel and no-one about me would appear to be responsible for such a strange manner of shouting. 'Hurry up min ref, c'mon.' It's getting much louder now, an anxious, dislocated voice, reverberating around the ground. 'Ref time up min c'mon.' Where on earth is it coming from? Maybe it's coming directly from Heaven. Maybe God is a Stranraer supporter and he is staring down on Stair Park and commanding the ref to finish this match. 'For Christ's sake ref, finish it.' No. That can't be God. He wouldn't use his Son's name in vain like that. I hope it's not a voice inside my head. But other fans are looking around. They're hearing it too. And a couple of them are laughing. Because this voice of desperation and exhortation is being transmitted through the speakers. The man on the mike at Stair Park, or someone sitting next to him, is shouting without realising that the microphone is switched on and that his haranguing of the referee is audible to all of us, including the referee and the players, and some of them look a little perplexed. But hold on. What if the microphone has been turned on deliberately? Surely this is illegal to be harassing the match official in such an amplified manner. 'Hey ref min, blow the bloody whistle.' Nah, it can't be intentional. Can it? Eventually the referee signals time up - and Stranraer celebrate. And a rather public torment is over.

Fanfare: 'Come on Blues.' Oh, come on.

MISSION POSSIBLE 40

OBJECTIVE:
To go to Links
Park and watch
Montrose.

SCENARIO: Montrose are playing Arbroath in the Scottish Third Division. No less than an Angus derby. I have brought Brian along again. He enjoyed Peterhead so much he wants more. He had better bloody not win the 50/50 half-time draw here as well though. Or I will be calling a stewards' enquiry.

DATE: Saturday, March 3, 2007.

LOCATION, LOCATION, LOCATION: 'Here's the basin, there's Montrose, shut your een and haud your nose.' Montrose has a basin, which is an enclosed estuary that attracts migrating birds. If you want to blend in with the locals pronounce it Mintrose. Mintrose is twinned with Luzardes in France. I'd imagine you can't tell the two apart.

CULTURAL NOTES: Watch the birdies at Montrose Basin Wildlife Centre. Some birds use the basin as a stop-off point between Siberia and Africa.

MONTROSE PROFILE

KICKED OFF: 1879. Albert Einstein was born.

TRUE COLOURS: Royal blue and white.

BADGE OF HONOUR: A ship's steering wheel. To steer Montrose through stormy seas.

NAME CALLING: The Gable Endies. The town's merchants built their houses gable-end to the street. There are a few examples of this on the High Street if you're at all interested.

MORTAL ENEMY: Where there's smoke, there's Arbroath.

AREN'T WE BRILLIANT?: The Gable Endies ended up reaching the League Cup semi-finals in season 1975/76. They won the Second Division title in 1984/85. And they have won the Forfarshire Cup no less than ten times!

MISSION LOGISTICS

ALIGHT AT: Montrose railway station (step away from the basin). Except that Brian and I are forced to take the replacement bus service from Aberdeen because they are carrying out some work on the railway lines. Inconvenience us? How dare they. When we reach Montrose an hour later we cross the High Street and keep walking but are careful crossing the park because of the warning sign: 'Emerging crocus bulbs'.

A Pint At: Ash Bar close to the train station has a fine selection of beers on tap and, even more impressively, 'Elephant Stone' on the stereo. The Golf Inn very near to Links Park is a more traditional drinking house, keeping it real with Pale Ale, Heavy and Export. If you are peckish, they will rustle you up a mince roll for a bargain 80p.

MISSION DEBRIEFING

Field of Dreams: Links Park Stadium is more of a park than a stadium but I guess they are hedging their bets by using both. Links Park is a curious affair and feels pretty exposed, today at least. It's very windy with lots of gulls flapping about. We are next to the North Sea after all. There is a colourful main stand but a lot of the home fans gather under the roof of the Wellington Street End which is the end where you enter the ground. Standing room only. The Beach End is given over to Arbroath as it is derby day. Some home fans lean on the wall in front of the pie shed and just watch the match raging from there. One thing Brian notices that I fail to notice are the square goalposts. You don't get too many of those these days.

Super Pies Me: The Montrose pie is as unpalatable as the match itself. It is also very greasy.

> **GAME ON:** Montrose 0-1 Arbroath
>
> **ARBROATH GOALSCORER:** Reilly 8.
>
> **MONTROSE:** Bell, Cumming, Stirling, Stephen, McLeod, Donachie, Henslee, Gibson, Rodgers (Baird 63), Michie (Reid 76), Docherty (Davidson 46).
>
> **ARBROATH:** Peat, Rennie, McCulloch, Raeside, Bishop, Dobbins, Black, Martin (Savage 78), Brazil, Sellars, Reilly (Webster 63).
>
> **HEAD COUNT:** 1,211 (including a few head-cases, but derby day brings them out and brings out the worst in them).

Report Card: Arbroath celebrate a slim but deserved win over local rivals Montrose who pose as much threat as a pacifist with his hands tied behind his back in the boxing ring. The Smokies, sorry visitors, strike early with Andy Riley chasing the ball and lifting it over the Montrose keeper. Willie Martin prangs the post but a goal is enough for Arbroath, and Montrose's Keith Gibson is sent off in the last minute following a flareup with Kevin Webster - but not Kevin Webster off *Coronation Street*.

Going For Gold: Some of the verbal jousting at this derby is massively entertaining and some of it is totally over the top. As a football match it is as ugly as the Elephant Man with hay fever. Three gold stars.

Fanfare: The Montrose fans are armed and ready with a selection of sea shanties which are designed to rubbish Arbroath and all that it stands for. 'Sing when you're fishing, you only sing when you're fishing' is just them warming up. We soon get a medley of songs liberally sprinkled with the word Smokie, which, of course, refers to Arbroath and their ancient practice of smoking fish. 'You can stick your fucking smokies up your arse' is direct and to the point and the suggestion is too depraved to contemplate any further. So then it's 'Glory, glory, what a hell of a way to die, to die a Smokie bastard'. Blimey. The next onslaught is 'We hate Arbroath, Smokie bastards, and we chase them everywhere'. When the Arbroath physio takes the field to treat an injured Arbroath player a young girl scowls at the physio and shouts: 'Oi! Codhead!' Then, when a former Montrose player dares to make an appearance as an Arbroath substitute, one displeased Montrose fan yells: 'Smokie Judas!' An absolutely priceless combination of words that surely has never been uttered before in the English - or indeed any other - language. There is a brief respite from the Smokie bashing and other fish-related insults when the Montrose supporters decide to sing about themselves for a change. 'Hello, hello, we are the Links Park Dynamo'. But a new nadir is reached when a young Montrose boy, he can be no more than ten surely, cries out (to the tune of 'If You're Happy and You Know It') 'If you're gay and you know it you're a poof …' I don't know what to say about that. The police, trying to keep the calm amid this colourful derby background, then get it in the neck from the Montrose fans who strike up a chorus of 'Tayside polis, wank, wank, wank' just as two of Tayside's finest walk past the Wellington Street End where some of the Montrose fans look seriously wellied. The travelling Arbroath support get their own back after the game as they toast their latest derby victory with a clever reworking of the classic 'We Hate Jimmy Hill' song. They point at the downbeat Montrose fans and sing 'We thought you were shite, we were right, we were right'. Montrose versus Arbroath. Ye cannae whack it. Although the football itself is rendered almost irrelevant.

MISSION POSSIBLE 41

(The Penultimate Thrill)

OBJECTIVE:
To go to Shielfield Park and watch Berwick Rangers.

SCENARIO: Berwick Rangers are playing Queen's Park in the Scottish Third Division and I have three travelling companions for this one. Neville is back again along with my friend Helen and Kenny who once kept goal for Berwick Rangers! This is bound to bring back some happy memories for him.

DATE: Saturday, March 10, 2007.

LOCATION, LOCATION, LOCATION: England. How's that allowed?

CULTURAL NOTES: At the outbreak of the Crimean War, Britain declared war on Russia, in the name of Britain, Ireland and Berwick-upon-Tweed. But when it came to signing the Paris Peace Treaty, Berwick was omitted from the details and remained technically at war with Russia for 110 years. Until a Soviet official visited Berwick in 1966 to make peace.

BERWICK RANGERS PROFILE

KICKED OFF: 1881. The year Hungarian composer Bela Bartok was born.

TRUE COLOURS: Black and gold.

BADGE OF HONOUR: A bear chained to a tree. And two lions not chained to a tree. One lion rampant, the other English. Quite a busy badge then.

NAME CALLING: Berwick Rangers boast a few epithets. The Wee Gers. The Borderers. The Dream Team (dream on, more like).

MORTAL ENEMY: Berwick Rangers versus Stranraer often gets billed as the Borders derby. Despite the two towns being 160 or so miles apart. A few years ago at Shielfield Park, a Stranraer fan complained of being pelted with celery, despite celery being a rich source of vitamin C.

AREN'T WE BRILLIANT?: In January 1967, Berwick Rangers pulled off the greatest cup shock in the history of humanity when they beat Glasgow Rangers 1-0 at Shielfield Park. Then, in 2001, the Wee Rangers hosted the big Rangers once more in the Scottish Cup, forcing a draw and a replay at Ibrox (which the big Rangers won).

MISSION LOGISTICS

ALIGHT AT: Berwick-upon-Tweed train station. It's a very pleasant rail journey down the east coast. The first segment for me though, from Glasgow Queen Street to Edinburgh Waverley, is a nightmare. An hour-long ticket queue and a packed train. Rugby fans. Heading for Murrayfield. In fleeces, kilts and Timberland boots, discussing holiday cottages in Islay and sipping lattes in a revolting manner. And not one of them, once we are on the train, cracks open a can of lager. I mean, what's that all about? You're going to the match, right? Okay, it's a rugby match, but you're on the train with your friends and what is it you do? You throw caution to the wind and order more coffee from the trolley service, lamenting the fact that no *lattes* are available on the train. Then you all pile off at Haymarket with your picnic baskets and step the gaily to the oval ball jamboree. Rugby fans, I mean honestly. At least the remainder of my journey passes in peace. I get to Berwick, march down Castlegate (you must march) under the town wall arch and cross the Royal Tweed Bridge, leaving Berwick behind and bidding good day to Tweedmouth. I advance under the viaduct and I'm there. A long walk, but a rewardingly scenic one. Neville, Helen and Kenny are here. They have come by car and I think they are looking forward to it. As am I.

A Pint At: I defy you to show me somewhere more suitable than the Black & Gold social club. The Black & Gold social club is beside the main stand at Shielfield Park, and you will be made most welcome. Unless you happen to go on about Berwick being English and all that business. Don't. They don't like it. This is a Scottish Football League club. Albeit one based in England.

MISSION DEBRIEFING

Field of Dreams: Shielfield Park is oval-shaped. Like Hampden, but not really. Berwick Rangers share their dusty domain with the Berwick Bandits whose business is speedway. Football and speedway don't mix. It's dangerous. So Rangers and Bandits play and race at different times. When the wind blows at Shielfield and you are not wearing sunglasses, shield your eyes from the sand, if you have not already been shielding your eyes from the football. But duck for cover in the Ducket enclosure, where you will find most of the banter and most of the sand. You get a good view of the giant shiny silver maltings. There is a little wooden shed with the painted sign 'Tea Bar' but the shutters are down. And there are kids having a game of football behind the Ducket. The action is currently better than what is on the pitch.

Super Pies Me: After my awful Ayr United experience, I can't be tempted by the Berwick Rangers pie. It has that unmistakable deep-fried sheen to it. Either that or they have painted it that colour and I have never heard of anyone painting a pie. Neville plunges for the Berwick pie. Brave man. He says it tastes okay, but afterwards he's remarkably quiet. I deliberate over whether to get fish and chips or a nutritious chip roll, but I end up deciding on nothing. Maybe because I have shunned the menu, I turn round and trip over a hot dog someone dropped. How can you trip over a hot dog? I don't know, but I did.

GAME ON: Berwick Rangers 0-2 Queen's Park

QUEEN'S PARK GOALSCORERS: Trouten 68, Ferry 78.

BERWICK RANGERS: O'Connor, Notman, McGroarty, Fraser, McNicoll, G Greenhill (Lucas 81), D Greenhill (Noble 39), Thomson, Wood, Diack (Haynes 78), Manson.

QUEEN'S PARK: Crawford, Paton, Dunlop, Canning, Agostini, Trouten, Kettlewell, Cairney (Carroll 65), Ronald (Quinn 89), Weatherston (Dunn 87), Ferry.

HEAD COUNT: 704.

Report Card: Queen's Park collect their seventh win in eight games to narrow the gap on league leaders Berwick. The Spiders start to spin their magic when Alan Trouten rides two tackles and a Grand National winner to leave the Berwick keeper fishing the ball out of his net. Later, when the bungling Berwick defence fails to clear, up pops Mark Ferry to ferry in the second Spiders goal, leaving Berwick's hopes hanging by a thread, and they never recover from that. A black day to be a Berwick Rangers fan and some black moods in the Ducket. Meanwhile we seem to have entered another Ice Age.

Going For Gold: Rotten weather and a rotten game of football. Three gold stars. Slightly tarnished.

Fanfare: 'You are my dream team, my only dream team, you make me happy, when skies are grey.' Proof if proof were needed that the Berwick Rangers supporters have rejected reality in favour of fantasy. The Ducket is a lively spot. 'Away the lads, away the lads' reminds you where exactly in the world you are. The Berwick fans are separated from the Queen's Park fans by a mesh fence. So they can shout at each other and see each other without being able to pat each other nicely on the head or whatever it is they'd like to do to each other. 'Come on you Goooolllllds ... Come on you Gooooollllllds.' Nope, it's not working. This game is out of sight. 'Get this shite over with,' growls one Berwick fan.

EPISODE

MISSION POSSIBLE 42

(The Final Frontier)

OBJECTIVE:
To go to Gayfield
and watch Arbroath.

SCENARIO: Arbroath are playing East Stirlingshire in the Scottish Third Division.

DATE: Saturday, March 17, 2007. D-day. Done day. The end of the road.

LOCATION, LOCATION, LOCATION: Arbroath is on the Angus coast, not far north of Dundee. There is something fishy going on in Arbroath. They tie up haddocks in pairs and smoke them! It's a filthy habit.

CULTURAL NOTES: The Declaration of Arbroath was signed in Arbroath Abbey on 6 April, 1320. 'For, so long as a hundred remain alive, we will never in any degree be subject to the dominion of the English. And we will never get beaten by Montrose.'

ARBROATH PROFILE

KICKED OFF: 1878. Cleopatra's Needle arrives in London … sorry I've lost the thread again.

TRUE COLOURS: They paint the toun maroon when Arbroath win. But it looks, from here, as if the colours have run in the wash and the Arbroath players are sporting pink numbers on their shirts! Which is not very manly, really.

BADGE OF HONOUR: A portcullis! How about that? There's one at Arbroath Abbey too.

NAME CALLING: The Red Lichties. Maybe less to do with whorehouses than lighthouses. A red light used to highlight Arbroath harbour to boats in the North Sea. I'm quite sceptical about this explanation and would not rule out hookers playing some part in it. Because if we are talking boats, we're talking sailors.

MORTAL ENEMY: Montrose. The feeling is mutual.

AREN'T WE BRILLIANT?: Arbroath hold the world record for the biggest-ever win in football. 36-0 they beat Bon Accord, with some other Arbroath 'goals' chalked off by the referee. This was way back in September 1885. Bizarrely, Dundee Harp beat Aberdeen Rovers 35-0 on the same day.

MISSION LOGISTICS

ALICHT AT: Arbroath train station is about fifteen minutes' walk from Gayfield. Downwind. Wind against: you are talking half-an-hour although I may be talking bollocks here. The train journey to Arbroath proves pretty hairy. I am part of the anxious majority as a self-proclaimed Ned terrorises the carriage. 'I'm a Ned wi' a laptop!' Mr Ned announces, between liberal drags of Smirnoff Ice. 'I don't start fights … I finish them!' Crikey. Mr Ned next treats us to a selection of tunes from his laptop. His taste is eclectic, to say the least. We get The Proclaimers, a bit of Johnny Cash and an awful lot of that dance music with chipmunks on vocals that Neds are fond of. When Mr Ned tires of those chipmunks (of course we shout for more) he starts pacing up and down the carriage in search of a bottle opener. Which, I suppose, is better than him pacing up and down the carriage with a corkscrew.

A Pint At: The Portcullis is an award-winning sports bar and base camp for the 36-0 Club (the Arbroath fan club). You can see Arbroath Abbey from The Portcullis, but you cannot see Gayfield, because it is miles away. Opposite Gayfield is the legendary Tuttie's Neuk which is well worth a pint of your time. If you want more of a salty sea dog experience, you can choose from the Fisherman's Inn, the Ship Inn and Smuggler's Tavern.

MISSION DEBRIEFING

Field of Dreams: Gayfield Park. Used to be a refuse dump. Currently crumbling into the North Sea, if you believe these whipped-up tales of fish being storm-tossed on to the pitch and a player being knocked over by a wave while trying to take a corner kick. Gayfield is a fine hunting ground. The fans switch ends at half-time and risk being blown over the wall into the water. If you don't like the wind, you can always shelter in Pleasureland next door. It is an indoor amusement park. With Waltzers! Bumper cars! And Ramboland! Gayfield is the closest stadium to the sea in European football, so I hear. The Pleash End is behind the goals terracing that backs on to Pleasureland.

Super Pies Me: The Arbroath pie is anti-climactic. Why don't they sell smokie pies at Gayfield? You can pick one up from one of the fishmongers at 'the fit o the toon'.

GAME ON: Arbroath A East Stirlingshire A
Swept away!

Report Card: It is blowing a gale at Gayfield. No waves crash-landing on the pitch from the swollen North Sea but the Angus air is turbulent all right. This here is a mighty wind. Hurricane-like, if you like. And the oddest thing is that Arbroath and East Stirlingshire are trying to play football. The key word there is 'trying' because they can't. It is so windy the gulls are flying backwards. One corner flag is bent nearly horizontal by the buffeting. Out of the corner of my eye, I am sure that I see a cow pass up into the clouds. You know the film *Twister*? Triple it. Maybe it is like this every time Arbroath play a home game. I wouldn't know because this is my first visit and I can't wait to come back. I recommend everyone catch a match contested in a squall at some point in their lives. This is brilliant! Of course the regulars seem to be taking it in their stride, as they struggle to remain on their feet, teetering on the brink of falling over. 'It's a wee bit windy,' notes one Arbroath fan. 'Breezy,' offers another, who won't buy windy. 'There's nae wind a ta,' scoffs a third who just has to be kidding himself. One of the three regrets aloud not bringing a hat and the other two laugh at him. A hat? Imagine that. This is football in another dimension. The ball is a balloon. It is all over the place as 20 men chase after it. None of them are having much luck. The team formations have gone to pot. More than is normal at this level. It is like watching primary school football. Players all bunched up, in one corner of the pitch. Here is an illustration of how windy it is. Arbroath win a direct free-kick and two players are required to take it. While one prepares to take the free-kick the other crouches down and places a finger on the ball to prevent it from blowing away. His finger is withdrawn seconds before impact so that it isn't staved or kicked clean off. Timing is everything. For the spectator, the best thing about watching Arbroath and East Stirlingshire trying to play football is the East Stirlingshire goalie. The worst thing about Arbroath and East Stirlingshire trying to play football is being the East Stirlingshire goalie.

The Arbroath keeper is coping okay considering the circumstances. Perhaps he is accustomed to keeping goal during a perfect storm. In stark contrast, the East Stirlingshire goalie is struggling. He is having a terribly torrid time of it, and the couple of hundred Arbroath fans behind him aren't helping. They put the boot in big time and revel in the goalie's strife. They howl with laughter as he tries (in vain) to tame the balloon. You'd think a goal kick would be the least of a goalkeeper's worries but you would be wrong. He plants the ball on the edge of the six-yard box and retreats a few paces - while the ball rolls ten yards to the right. Flustered - and why wouldn't he be? - the East Stirlingshire goalie chases after the ball to retrieve it and puts it back where it was. He makes a tentative retreat in preparation for a second attempt at a goal kick, but the ball is off again on its wind-propelled journey. This slapstick routine is repeated three times with the home fans hooting sarcastically and the referee giving the poor goalie a hurry-up-will-you look. When it is hardly the goalie's fault. From somewhere (the beach?) a bucket of sand is handed to the harassed goalie. It should help. Otherwise we will be here all day. The goalie goes back to the edge of the six-yard box, ball in one hand, bucket of sand in the other. He makes a nice little molehill out of the sand and presses the ball down on top. 'Build us a sandcastle!' shouts one Arbroath fan. The goalie ignores this request, and gears up once again for the goal kick that should have occurred several minutes ago. Mercifully he succeeds. Sort of. The ball shoots high in the sky. Less like a balloon and more like a kite. It pauses in mid-air for a moment and then it starts spiralling backwards towards the penalty box. The goalie is forced to defend his own goal kick. Somehow he succeeds and the next goal kick he nearly concedes for a corner. Such a crazy state of affairs, except that it's so much fun to watch. It is almost as if the gods are having a game of blow football using Gayfield as the table. There had been an indication of what was to come during the warm-up when I watched an East Stirlingshire player boot the ball vertically upwards. It may have been that he wanted to see if the ball would come back to him. It didn't. It bounced over a team-mate, over the crossbar, over the crowd and the roof of the stand and clean out of the ground. It brought fresh meaning to the old football maxim about keeping the ball on the ground. During the match, several balls go similarly AWOL because they are not kept on the ground. Arbroath endure the first-half playing into the eye of the storm, but there is no discernible advantage for East Stirlingshire. When one of their men tries a short pass, the ball speeds thirty yards beyond the intended recipient. Are they playing shite? Is the harsh weather exacerbating the ugliness of the game? Or are they playing brilliantly, but the weather is making them look shite? I start to wonder if Cristiano Ronaldo would cope in these conditions. Would he perform in his usual manner, with the ball seemingly attached to his boots, or would he display the touch of an elephant and be firing frequent balls into the sea? After seventy-five minutes of Arbroath and East Stirlingshire trying to play each other at football, and neither side looking as if they will score before the cow comes down from the sky, the referee blows his whistle to signal an end to this absurdity. Match abandoned. The game should never have blasted off but I am so glad that it did. I would not have missed it for the world. This is a surreal end to my odyssey. To have Gayfield as the finishing post, except that the match does not finish, bringing my ground hunting to an abrupt end. End of the road but no final whistle. Perhaps the perfect ending is no ending. Unless I come back for the replay. Bugger that. The lines of Arbroath fans and ten or so East Stirlingshire fans shuffle out of the ground. Some supporters are muttering about the abandonment. Others are laughing at the lunacy of the seventy-five minutes of football we have been treated to. It is time to call it quits. It is time for that last and final pint in Tuttie's Neuk before I head home.

Going For Gold: I never thought it would end like this. I am blown away by it. Nine gold stars, what the heck! It has been a huge amount of fun, Galefield.

Fanfare: I don't catch much of the chanting, what with the wind blowing in my ears. The Arbroath fans try a chorus of 'We are Arbroath, super Arbroath, no-one likes us, we don't care, we love Montrose, handsome bastards, and we chase them everywhere.' Then there is the one Arbroath fan who goes it alone with 'Ooh ah, ooh to be, ooh to be a Red Lichtie!' Brilliant.

Music To My Ears: 'Blowin' In The Wind'? 'Catch The Wind'? 'Wind Beneath My Wings'? 'When Smokies Sing'? Nah, none of those are aired. But 'Yellow Submarine' fits in with an aquatic theme.

Mission Accomplished!

I'm grounded.

POST-MATCH ANALYSIS

Miles Travelled: 4,768.

Train trips: 33.

Bus trips: 5.

Train-bus trips: 4.

Pies Scoffed: 34 (another three rejected, one sold out, one elusive, one forgettable, two 'potential' pies superseded by bridies).

Pints Necked: I have no idea. But there were many more pints than pies.

Matches Witnessed: 41 (including one abandoned, not including one postponed).

Total Cost of Match Tickets: £647. The real price of a Scottish football season ticket.

Goals Scored: 125 (that's three goals per game).

Red cards: 7 (4 in the Second Division).

Own goals: 5.

Streakers: 0.

TRUE COLOURS
Blue or navy teams: 14.
Black and white teams: 9.
Red teams: 5.
Black and gold teams: 4.
Maroon teams: 3.
Green teams: 2.
Yellow and red teams: 2.

Red and blue team: 1.

Tangerine team: 1.

Amber and claret team: 1.

Largest Crowd: 54,620 at Celtic Park for Celtic v Kilmarnock.

Smallest Crowd: 228 at Cliftonhill for Albion Rovers v Stenhousemuir.

Biggest Win: East Stirlingshire (5-0 over Stenhousemuir), Elgin City (5-0 over East Stirlingshire), Gretna (5-0 over Queen of the South), Rangers (5-0 over Dundee United).

Biggest Defeat: See Biggest Win.

Most Goals In A Game: 6 (Partick Thistle 1-5 St. Johnstone, Stirling Albion 3-3 Stranraer, Morton 4-2 Peterhead, Queen of the South 3-3 Dundee).

Goalless Draws: 3 (Ross County 0-0 Dundee, St Johnstone 0-0 Ayr United, Dundee United 0-0 Hibernian).

Hat-Tricks: 4 (Richie Foran for Motherwell, Jason Scotland for St Johnstone, Marc McKenzie for East Stirlingshire, Martin Johnston for Elgin City).

Teams With 100 per cent Records: Celtic, Rangers, St Mirren, Gretna, Hamilton Academical, Airdrie United, Raith Rovers, Brechin City, Dumbarton.

Best Goal Difference: Celtic, Rangers (+7).

Worst Goal Difference: Dundee United (-9).

Goal Magnets: Queen of the South (their two fixtures delivered 11 goals).

Score Draw Experts: Stirling Albion (3-3 with Stranraer, 2-2 with Cowdenbeath).

Match-Throwers: Peterhead (take the lead in two games and lose them both, nothing untoward, but careless).

Familiar Sight: Stenhousemuir (three times in the space of a month).

Out Of Sight: East Fife (haven't seen them kick a ball yet, I'm blaming the weather).

Goals Scored In The Final Ten Minutes: 26.

Most Common Result: 2-0 (on 8 occasions).

Next Most Common Result: 2-1 (on 7 occasions).

Home Wins: 19.

Away Wins: 13.

Draws: 8.

Match That Never Got Started: East Fife v Dumbarton (strong winds).

Match That Never Quite Finished: Arbroath v East Stirlingshire (hurricane).

THE SCOTTISH FOOTBALL PIE CHART

I am breaking down the pies in my stomach and into some kind of pecking order. Now you might say 'Look they are pies for God's sake.' But there are degrees of pies and there are standards and without standards we are nothing.

So without further ado …

… drum roll …

… sausage roll …

… The Scottish Football Pie Chart …

1. Dunfermline Athletic steak bridie (okay, so it's not a pie, live with it).
2. St Johnstone pie.
3. Kilmarnock pie.
4. Peterhead pie.
5. Forfar bridie.
6. Stirling Albion pie.
7. Raith Rovers pie.
8. Brechin City pie.
9. Cowdenbeath pie.
10. Airdrie United pie.

Not forgetting (how could I?) the Rogue Pie Gallery Of Shame …

1. Ayr United pie (shudder).
2. Dumbarton pie (what Dumbarton pie?).

3. Gretna pie.
4. Montrose pie.
5. Hearts pie.

(Plus the St Mirren pie, if what I think I saw was what I think it was I saw.)

HANG THE DJ

Listen up! Here, for your ears, is a carelessly chosen play-list … Hunting Grounds Official Soundtrack (unavailable in all good record shops).

Now, Do You Call That Music? (Volume One)

'Back In Black', AC/DC.
'A-Team Theme', Mike Post and Pete Carpenter.
'Town Called Malice', The Jam.
'Sit Down', James.
'Axel F', Harold Faltermeyer.
'I Think We're Alone Now', Tiffany.
'Heaven Is A Place On Earth', Belinda Carlisle.
'Nothing's Gonna Stop Us Now', Starship.
'Live Is Life', Opus.
'Heroes', David Bowie.
'Sunshine on Leith', The Proclaimers.

A special limited edition of *Now, Do You Call That Music? (Volume One)* is available for Hearts fans. It contains a magic rubber so that the final track can be erased.

HUNTING GROUNDS MISCELLANY

Sing When You're Winning (Scottish Football Karaoke).

Practise these and you too can gloat like a Scottish football fan.

'And it's all gone quiet over there'.

'Always look on the bright side of life'.
('You all live on the shite side of Fife' being an alternate version of the above.)
'SPL, you're having a laugh'.
'Division One, you're having a laugh'.

'Division Two, you're having a laugh'.

'Division Three, you're having a laugh'.

'Champions League, you're having a laugh'.

'We're top o' the league and you're no.'

'Can we play you every week?' ('No, seriously'.)

'What a shitey home support'.

'Shall we sing a song for you?'

'You're no singing any more'.

'You'll never get promotion'.

'Who are ya? Who are ya?'

'Stand up, if you hate [INSERT APPROPRIATE TEAM]'.

'Sit down, if you hate [INSERT APPROPRIATE TEAM]'.

TRAIN OF THOUGHT

How about a train test for all the trainspotters?

Alight at the following train stations for which Scottish football clubs?

Airbles.

Coatdyke.

Croy.

Drumgelloch.

(Answers: 1. Motherwell 2. Albion Rovers 3. Clyde 4. Airdrie United.)

Finally, the moment you have all been wailing for (I hear you) …

THE FIRST SCOTTISH FOOTBALL ACADEMY AWARDS (THE OXTERS!)

And the Nominees for Best Game are …

Stirling Albion 3 Stranraer 3, East Stirlingshire 5 Stenhousemuir 0, Elgin City 5 East Stirlingshire 0, Morton 4 Peterhead 2, Arbroath A East Stirlingshire A.

And the Scottish Football Academy Award goes to …

East Stirlingshire 5 Stenhousemuir 0.

And the Nominees for Best Ground are …

Celtic Park, Forthbank, Glebe Park, Ibrox Stadium, Stair Park.

And the Scottish Football Academy Award goes to ...

Glebe Park.

And the Nominees for Best Crowd are ...

Ayr United, Dumbarton, East Stirlingshire, Hibernian, Queen of the South.

And the Scottish Football Academy Award goes to ...

Hibernian.

And the Nominees for Best Social Club are ...

Elgin City, Peterhead, Queen of the South, Queen's Park, Stenhousemuir.

And the Scottish Football Academy Award goes to ...

Stenhousemuir.

And the Nominees for Best Pre-Match (Or Post-Match) Pub are ...

Diggers (Athletic Arms) in Edinburgh, The New Goth in Cowdenbeath, Tuttie's Neuk in Arbroath, White Horse in Elgin, Big Owen's Bar, Coatbridge.

And the Scottish Football Academy Award goes to ...

Diggers (Athletic Arms) in Edinburgh.

RUNDOWN OF REMAINING SCOTTISH FOOTBALL ACADEMY AWARDS

Best Special Effects: Gayfield, Arbroath.

Best Waste Of Time: Methil.

Best Hedge: Glebe Park, Brechin.

Best Rock: Dumbarton Rock.

Best View: Recreation Park, Alloa.

Best Supporting Wife: Mrs Sutherland.

BONUS MISSION

OBJECTIVE: To go to Galabank and watch Annan Athletic.

SCENARIO: Annan Athletic are playing Montrose in the Scottish Third Division. Annan weren't part of the Scottish Football League set-up when I traipsed round 42 grounds in season 2006-07. They are now, so here I go.

DATE: Saturday, March 24, 2012.

LOCATION, LOCATION, LOCATION: Surely Annan is the town with the least variety of letters in its name? Unless there's a place called Rrrrrrr somewhere. Anyway, Annan is the principle town of Annandale and Eskdale and is the third largest town in Dumfries & Galloway which is the third largest region in Scotland which is... I've stopped.

CULTURAL NOTES: On his retreat from Derby, Bonnie Prince Charlie stayed in an Annan inn. Robert Burns was a frequent visitor to the town in his day. And the distinguished Victorian artist William Ewart Lockhart, painter to Queen Victoria, was brought up in Annan.

ANNAN PROFILE

KICKED OFF: 1942. Instant coffee is introduced, replacing delayed coffee.

TRUE COLOURS: Black and gold. Much like Alloa Athletic, East Fife and Berwick Rangers.

BADGE OF HONOUR: Two thistles flanking a hand that is either carrying aloft a flaming torch or a steaming poke of chips.

NAME CALLING: Black and Golds. Or Galabankies.

MORTAL ENEMY: Well there was Gretna, I guess.

AREN'T WE BRILLIANT?: Annan are four-times Premier League winners – East of Scotland Premier League, that is. They've also competed in the Carlisle and District League and the South of Scotland League. Annan applied to join the Scottish Football League in 2000 but lost out to Elgin City and Peterhead. They were finally voted in in 2008, following the demise of Gretna.

MISSION LOGISTICS

ALIGHT AT: My fraught journey to Annan on a Glasgow Central to Newcastle train begins with a queue for the use of the onboard toilet. I'm at the head of said queue with half-a-dozen drunk and desperate Motherwell supporters behind me. I attempt to lighten the mood by saying I won't be long. No response, save for one teenage Motherwell fan looking like he wants to hit me. I refrain from any further chit-chat. The tension on the train eases once the inebriated Motherwell fans get off at Kilmarnock. From there on in, it's just me, several other lone travellers and a family a few rows down. 'Far's the butteries?' the woman asks her husband at one point. They are most definitely from my neck of the woods. There don't appear to be any Montrose fans on the train and frankly I'm not surprised. Montrose to Annan is one heck of a journey. It's a glorious spring day though and, with the windows open, we're getting farmyard scents from all angles. All aboard The Manure Express. Once I get to Annan I ask the first person I see for directions to the ground. The man is wearing a Rangers top and is walking his dog. It soon becomes clear that everyone in Annan has a dog. If they don't have a dog, they have two dogs. I cross the High Street, as instructed, and soon I'm on the edge of town, passing a stunning-looking football pitch surrounded by an athletics track. It's not Annan's pitch but it looks cracking anyway. I fancy rounding up 21 others for a kickabout. Moments later, I reach Galabank. It's taken me about 20 minutes from the train station.

A Pint At: The pub at the ground, just by the main entrance. I take my pint of Tennent's and sit over by the window from where I have a decent view of the pitch. I could just sit here for the next hour-and-a-half. It's Chelsea–Spurs on the telly, but I turn to the match programme I've bought. It contains a piece about Annan native Cammy Bell whose recent goalkeeping heroics against Celtic helped Kilmarnock to League Cup glory. '*Bell Gives Celtic Hell*' reads the headline. There's also a feature on Tomas Brolin, the Swede who starred for his country at the 1994 World Cup then flopped at Leeds. The title of the feature is '*Was He Really That Bad?*' After the match, I fit in a pint at the Bluebell Inn, before my train. It's an old coaching inn at the bottom of the High

Street with a choice of real ales, wood-panelled walls and Burns poems everywhere you look – including one about pawning your troosers and shoes for guid ale. I'll keep my trousers on and pay cash, thanks.

MISSION DEBRIEFING

Field of Dreams: 'On this lovely spring day, may we welcome you to Galabank' says the man on the mike and I'm full of the joys of spring and thrilled to be here. Galabank enjoys a very open aspect with trees and open countryside beyond the compact main stand with its black and gold seats. The dugouts are on the opposite side of the pitch where there is open terracing. You can stand behind the goals at the pub end and watch the game. The other end has just a wall behind the goals. But it's all very agreeable, this modest arena with licence to roam and watch the game from various angles.

Super Pies Me: The pie shop is beside a hospitality tent, inside which I can see tablecloths, teacups and cake stands crammed with sandwiches for the VIPs. In terms of crust and filling, the Annan pie passes muster. I'd go as far as to say I'd have another one. But I resist temptation as I'm somewhat out of practice with pies.

> **GAME ON:** Annan Athletic 1-2 Montrose
>
> **ANNAN ATHLETIC GOALSCORER:** Muirhead 27 pen.
>
> **MONTROSE GOALSCORERS:** Wood 5, Winter 43 pen.
>
> **ANNAN ATHLETIC:** Mitchell, Muirhead, Watson, Swinglehurst (MacBeth 46), McGowan, McKenna, Steele, Jardine, Sloan, Winters (Gilfillan 58), O'Connor (McKechnie 80).
>
> **MONTROSE:** Andrews, McNalley, Cambell, Lunan, Cameron, Young, Crawford, Winter, Johnston, Boyle, Wood (McPhee 30).
>
> **HEAD COUNT:** 418.

Report Card: Annan are hoping to make the promotion play-offs but it's Montrose who take the lead after five minutes, Gary Wood scoring with – of all things – an overhead kick. The hosts fight back and there are claims for an Annan penalty. 'He wiz haudin him back ref!' shouts a man in a bunnet. Then Annan have the ball in the net, Peter Watson with the header. But it won't count. The ball had gone out of play before the cross. 'And the goalscorer for Annan after 24 minutes... oh.' The man on the mike has just realised it's been chalked off. Annan draw level though midway through the first-half. Sean O' Connor is bundled off the ball in the box by Jamie Winter and the penalty is awarded. Aaron Muirhead sends Montrose keeper Michael Andrews the wrong way and the man on the mike has another go. 'Well, I'm sure I've got this one right... the goalscorer after 27 minutes is... Aaron Muirhead!' The battle continues and an Annan man makes for the byline to cross but slices horribly for a goalkick to Montrose. 'Aw, it bobbled, man,' he says. I'm giving him the benefit of the doubt. Then, after 43 minutes, Montrose win a penalty, Martin Boyle hauled down by Annan keeper Alex Mitchell who receives a yellow card for his efforts. Winter makes amends for conceding the earlier spot-kick by converting this one, firing it straight down the middle. Not a great deal happens in the second-half. Too many hopeful punts and a couple of stray balls ending up in people's gardens. 'Aw, what's he doing?' groans a boy as an Annan player fails to control the ball. Montrose are taking their time to the extent that some angry home fans think they're taking the piss. Men start drifting off to the pub. 'Mine's a pint of 70,' says one to his pal. The final whistle brings victory to Montrose and a blow for Annan's promotion play-off hopes, but I'm not that fussed since it helps Elgin's chances.

Going For Gold: I genuinely enjoyed my afternoon at Galabank, even though the game itself didn't amount to much. Yes, there were a few goals, including a couple of penalties, but the football was thin on the ground, mainly because of the time it spent in the air. Five gold stars.

Fanfare: Hmm. There's the faint cry of 'One Jamie Winter' from the tiny band of Montrose fans after Jamie Winter scores from the spot. And the Annan fans are good at clapping, if that counts.

Music To My Ears: Pulp's 'Common People' is playing as I enter the ground. The Annan players run out to the tune of the A-Team. They're allowed that. They begin with A.

METHIL ONCE MORE

'Have fun in Methil,' says my wife as she and the kids get off the train at Linlithgow. They're off to see the palace. Whereas I'm bound for Bayview, five years after my previous attempt to see East Fife ended in failure, the match called off shortly before kick-off thanks to cataclysmic weather conditions. Never saw the game, never tasted the pie. Now I'm aiming to put all that right.

The weather looks infinitely kinder as I alight at Haymarket to catch my connecting train to Kirkcaldy. Last time round, I bussed it from Glasgow to Bayview. I've decided to freshen things up, make things more interesting. If a Journey To The Centre Of The Earth (i.e. Methil) can be deemed interesting.

I reach Kirkcaldy and walk the few hundred yards from the train station to the bus station where I board the No. 8 service to Leven. I opt for the top deck where it's just me and one other bloke who's muttering to himself. I'm wondering if I should go and sit downstairs when he stops muttering and starts singing – I think – 'Nothing's Gonna Stop Us Now' by Starship. I decide to stick around for the show. Eventually he stops singing and starts muttering again. We pass through Buckhaven and I marvel at the existence of a hairdresser's called Curl Up and Dye.

From Leven bus station, all it takes is a walk over the Bawbee Bridge and I'm in Methil. The first thing I notice is that the power station has gone. It's been demolished. The second thing I notice is that I can see East Fife's ground. Partly because the power station has gone, but also because it's not raining horizontal like it was last time. I'm feeling pretty confident I'll see a football match today.

Back in 2007, I had a pint in the upstairs lounge of the main stand as I tried to come to terms with the game being cancelled and having to wait two hours till my next bus. The upstairs lounge is still welcoming visitors in 2012, but there's also the downstairs option of Sid's Bar, which I plump for. I ask the barman who Sid is. Turns out he's the chairman.

Suitably refreshed, I take my seat in the main stand which is filling up fast. Today's opponents are Stenhousemuir. It just had to be Stenhousemuir. On my original Scottish football safari, I ended up catching Stenhousemuir three times in the space of a month. It was simply the way the fixtures fell.

Now the power station's gone, you can see the rooftops of Leven from Bayview, and the bright blue flumes of the leisure centre. Gulls flap over the North Sea and I notice a stretch of golden sand in the distance. Bayview indeed. It's not warm though. An easterly wind cuts through the main stand and it's hard not to shiver on this spring afternoon.

The teams take to the pitch for this Scottish Second Division fixture. Finally I get to see East Fife in the flesh! I wonder how the family's getting on at Linlithgow Palace. Historical attractions are all well and good, but this surely is the main attraction. I had tried to sell East Fife v Stenhousemuir to my wife as a fun family outing, but oddly she'd found something else for her and the children to do.

A chant of 'East Fife! East Fife!' builds from the back of the main stand and it's not long before the hosts take the lead. Ryan Wallace drills the ball past the Stenhousemuir keeper from the edge of the penalty area to give East Fife the dream start. The big cheer that greets the goal is shortly followed by another cheer when a flustered Stenhousemuir defender fresh airs whilst trying to clear the ball.

Long before the interval, the home fans start drifting towards the exit. Not because they've had their fill of East Fife leading Stenhousemuir, but because they're needing fed.

The East Fife pie had escaped my clutches last time, what with the game being called off, so I'm not taking any chances. I join the queue and when I get to the counter there are only a handful left. I pay my £1.30, add broon sauce to my pie and wolf it down. Only when I've finished do I realise it's the best pie I've ever scoffed at a Scottish football ground.

I'd gone for a steak pie rather than a Scotch pie. My approach to pies is to go for whatever kind of pie I feel like on the day – and today had felt like a steak pie day. It's no scientific test, but I rate the East Fife pie better than the Kilmarnock pie which is often held up as the gold standard of Scottish football pies. The East Fife pie, with its soft golden crust and tender chunks of meat, is not overly salty and there isn't too much gravy either. In terms of a taste experience, I also place the East Fife pie ahead of the Dunfermline steak bridie which is saying something since it had been a revelation. After all this time, I encounter the perfect Scottish football pie. It's a fairly emotional moment.

The second-half gets underway and the well-fed East Fife supporters are getting all worked up. Stenhousemuir are piling on the pressure and forcing some frantic rear-guard action from East Fife, with one home defender heading off the line. The biggest threat is Kenny Deuchar who nods wide of the post when he perhaps should have scored. The anxiety of the home fans increases. 'One-nil's no' enough,' says a father to his son. 'We need anither ane.'

East Fife goalie Ally Brown makes a fantastic finger-tip save from a curling free-kick. Then a Deuchar glancing header hits the inside of the post, the ball spinning across the goalmouth and Brown scrambling to save with a leg.

It's hard to see East Fife holding out forever and they don't. Stenhousemuir are awarded a penalty when Scott Durie is judged to have handled in the box and Brown Ferguson makes no mistake from the spot.

Minutes from time, East Fife defender David White is sent off for a second bookable offence. The home fans feel their player has been treated harshly and react furiously. With cries of 'cheat' still ringing round the ground, there's a flare-up by the touchline with players pushing and shoving each other. There's even time for a couple of flying tackles before the final whistle sounds.

Rage on the pitch, outrage in the stand. And two teams battling for the promotion play-offs have to settle for a point each. I head off to catch my bus, chuffed to have finally seen East Fife in action and to have feasted on the finest pie Scottish football has to offer. It might even be enough to tempt me back to Bayview sometime in the future.

GAME ON: East Fife 1-1 Stenhousemuir

EAST FIFE GOALSCORER: Wallace 8.

STENHOUSEMUIR GOALSCORER: Ferguson 81 pen.

EAST FIFE: Brown, Durie, McCormack, White, Cook (Ovenstone 22), Linn, Smith, Janczyk (Muir 77), Sloan, Wallace, Dalziel (Hislop 71).

STENHOUSEMUIR: Brown, Nicky Devlin, Mike Devlin, Thomson, McKinlay, Anderson, Ferguson, Miller, Rodgers, Deuchar (Murray 77), Kean.

HEAD COUNT: 742.